WHY PUBLIC SPACE MATTERS

WHY PUBLIC SPACE MATTERS

SETHA LOW

OXFORD
UNIVERSITY PRESS

OXFORD
UNIVERSITY PRESS

Oxford University Press is a department of the University of Oxford. It furthers
the University's objective of excellence in research, scholarship, and education
by publishing worldwide. Oxford is a registered trade mark of Oxford University
Press in the UK and certain other countries.

Published in the United States of America by Oxford University Press
198 Madison Avenue, New York, NY 10016, United States of America.

CIP data is on file at the Library of Congress

ISBN 978–0–19–754373–3

DOI: 10.1093/oso/9780197543733.001.0001

1 3 5 7 9 8 6 4 2

Printed by Lakeside Book Company, United States of America

For Gavin, Skye, and Max
who showed me the importance of public spaces for play, recreation, and
creativity, and for all of us who need spaces to grow, learn, and explore

Contents

Illustrations

Table

Maps

Figures

Acknowledgments

This book grew out of a long journey to learn about and collect evidence on how public space contributes to socially just, equitable, and sustainable cities. Along the way many people and organizations funded, supported, and encouraged this endeavor. Many of the projects and ideas discussed have found their way into the scholarly literature, but here, I am responding to the call for action from UN Habitat, the New Urban Agenda, and colleagues around the world who are asking for research-based guidelines and a methodology to uncover inequalities and exclusionary practices. Javier Otero Peña encouraged the initial involvement with UN Habitat to find others committed to improving public space design and planning. Colleagues such as Michael Mehaffy of International Making Cities Livable; Laura Petrella, Jose Chong, and Cecilia Andersson of the Global Public Space Programme; Tigran Haas and Peter Elmlund of the Center for the Future of Places; Kristie Daniel of HealthBridge; Lance Brown of the Consortium for Sustainable Urbanization; Katherine Kline of the GAP on Aging; and Luisa Bravo of CitySpaceArchitecture have collaborated on this project to provide public space for all.

Conversations with Julian Agyeman, Jeff Hou, Matilde Cordoba, Suzanne Scheld, Dana Taplin, Jeff Maskovsky, Julian Brash, Ursula Rao, Shirley Strum, and John Jackson influenced many of the ideas presented. Monthly seminars of the Public Space Research Group (PSRG) co-organized with the Barcelona Lab for Urban Environmental Justice and Sustainability and Isabelle Anguelovski provided thoughtful discussions about these issues. Closer to home, graduate students (and now professors) Manissa Maharawal, Zoltan

Gluck, Claire Panetta, Chris Baum, and Pengfei Li, and the current members of the Public Space Research Group—Javier Otero Peña, Evie Klein, Erin Lilli, Troy Simpson, Shokran Rahiminezhad, and Reilly Wilson—contributed to my thinking. I am grateful to have had a lively scholarly community to accompany me on my intellectual travels. Many of you will recognize yourself and your work here, and I hope you are pleased with the results. Thank you for everything that you have contributed.

The Center for the Future of Places (CFP) directed by Tigran Haas at KTH in Stockholm and Peter Elmlund of the Ax:son Johnson Foundation invited me to present my ideas in 2014 at the second CFP conference in Buenos Aires. That was the beginning of several projects funded by the CFP that led to the creation of Tierra Publica, a public space database; the development of the Toolkit for the Ethnographic Study of Space (TESS); and funding to complete the research for this book. It was the comradery of my public space database co-creators, Vikas Mehta, David Brain, Peter Elmlund, and Michael Mehaffy, that sustained a focus on trying to figure out and communicate to a wider public why public space is so important. This book could not have been written without their financial and intellectual support.

The database project in New York was headed by Erin Lilli and Troy Simpson who took on conceptualizing the categories, defining the terms, and reviewing the literature in the fields of environmental psychology, anthropology, geography, and urban studies. They both contributed to the writing and testing of the TESS and moved the project forward. I want to particularly thank Erin, who has been my research assistant for the past three years. Erin was a co-presenter of the TESS at the World Urban Forum 10 in Abu Dhabi. Her insights into the chapters, the graphics, and general tone of the book were always valuable. During COVID-19 when I was often immersed in research or writing she kept the PSRG on track, as well as located books and articles in moments of desperation.

During the writing phase of this project, Joan Spivak, Javier Otero Peña, Shirley Strum, Susan Gooberman, Anna Harwin, Dana Taplin, Charles Price, Suzanne Scheld, Melissa Checker, Rodolfo Hernández,

Babette Audant, Chiara Martinuzzi, Mark Ojai, Andrew Newan, and Joel Lefkowitz came to the rescue by reading chapters and offering suggestions and constructive criticism. Melissa Checker suggested a developmental editor and found someone who was perfect. Andrew Newman, Mariano Perelman, Merrit Corrigan, Elisandro Garza, Greg Smithsimon, Susan Gooberman, Rodolfo Corchado, Bengi Sullu, Dana Taplin, and Suzanne Scheld not only read but carefully reviewed the sections that referenced their work to be sure that I got it right. Erin Lilli and Aurash Khawarzad conceptualized and created the graphics and Tompkins Square Park maps, while Greg Smithsimon, Mariano Perelman, Dana Taplin, Claire Panetta, Elisandro Garza, Andrew Newman, Joel Lefkowitz, and Merle Lefkowitz supplied photographs of the public space sites. I am indebted to these friends and colleagues for their intellectual, emotional, and substantive help.

While co-teaching landscape architecture and urban planning studios with Laurie Olin and the late Robert Hanna at the University of Pennsylvania, I learned that site surveys, circulation plans, social activity programs, and schematic designs are crucial components of imagining and creating public space. In planning and design studios and on design consulting projects they encouraged the use of ethnographic methods to produce better understandings of the role of the social and cultural as well as the architectural in creating places of opportunity rather than inequality. My colleagues at Pratt Institute, Ron Shiffman and David Burney, highlighted the importance of ethnographic understandings in the creation of a Place-Making program and gave me the opportunity to co-teach a Social Justice, Democracy, and Public Space semester that stimulated many of the ideas presented. I want to thank these dedicated colleagues for providing the opportunity to explore how ethnographic methods can make a difference in the analysis and design of public space and cities.

The ethnographic case studies presented in this book depended on the funding and teamwork of many people. I particularly would like to thank Erik Kulleseid, currently the commissioner of the Office of Parks, Recreation, and Historic Preservation for New York State, who funded the research at Lake Welch, Jones Beach, and Walkway Over the Hudson when he was head of the Alliance for New York State Parks. His enthusiasm was infectious, and we learned from his experience and commitment. I would also like to thank the National Park Service and especially Diana Pardue at the Statue of Liberty National Museum, Doris Fanelli at Independence National Historical Park, Richard Wells at Ellis Island, William Garrett at Jacob Riis Park, the late Muriel Crespi (PhD, past director of the National Park Service Applied Anthropology Program located in Washington D.C.), and Rebecca Joseph and Chuck Smythe (past East Coast regional directors of the ethnography program) for their support. Mitchell Silver, the New York City Department of Parks and Recreation commissioner from 2014–2022, inspired the research at Tompkins Square Park with his vision of "Parks Without Borders." I would also like to thank the Graduate Center of the City University of New York and the Center for Human Environments for their assistance. Without Jared Becker's expertise as an administrator, these research projects would have been impossible to manage.

Numerous foundations and granting agencies provided the financial support for ethnographic fieldwork. The writing of this book was funded by a series of generous fellowships from the Center for the Future of Places directed by Tigran Haas at KTH in Stockholm with funding from Peter Elmlund of the Ax:son Johnson Foundation. The research on the history and ethnography of the plaza in San José, Costa Rica, was funded by a research grant from the Wenner-Gren Foundation for Anthropological Research, a National Endowment for the Humanities Fellowship, a Fulbright Research Fellowship, and a John Simon Guggenheim Memorial Foundation Fellowship. The gated community research was funded by the Wenner-Gren Foundation for Anthropological Research and the Research Foundation of the City University of New York. The Moore Street Market study was part of a project undertaken by the Project for Public Spaces in New York City. And the Russell Sage Foundation funded the study of Battery Park City community change post 9/11. I would like to thank the many foundations that made these projects possible and the Graduate Center of the City University of New York for providing sabbatical and research leaves so that I could complete the fieldwork and write up findings.

A long list of graduate students at the Graduate Center of CUNY collected the data for the National Park Service and New York State projects most of whom are now professors or working in foundations. They include Suzanne Scheld, Dana Taplin, Tracy Fisher, Larissa Honey, Charles Price, Bea Vidacs, Marilyn Diggs-Thompson, Ana Aparicio, Raymond Codrington, Carlotta Pasquali, Carmen Vidal, Kate Brower, Gabrielle Bendiner-Viani, Yvonne Hung, and Nancy Schwartz. Many of the ethnographic projects were undertaken by research teams that were part of the Public Space Research Group. The Battery Park City project included Mike Lamb and Dana Taplin, who I continue to work with. The gated community co-researchers— Elena Danaila, Andrew Kirby, Lynmari Benitez, and Mariana Diaz-Wionczek—were graduate students at the time and collected many of the New York City interviews. The Moore Street Market project included Babette Audant, Rodolfo Corchado, and Bree Kressler and the Project for Public Spaces. The Tompkins Square Park study was part of my Ethnography of Space and Place course and Merrit Corrigan, Bengi Sullu, Anthony Ramos, and Elisandro Garza contributed their fieldnotes, maps, interviews, and many insights. I am grateful to these young scholars who made the research process fun and compelling. Their ideas, enthusiasm, and hard work kept projects going even when faced with adversity and setbacks. I could not have completed this work without them, and it would not have been as meaningful or fulfilling without them.

My editor David McBride was encouraging throughout the writing and publication process, finding excellent reviewers who made the manuscript better. His own careful reading caught many errors and clarified important points. I am delighted to work with David again so many years after publishing *Behind the Gates: Life, Security, and the Pursuit of Happiness* and grateful to be back working with him and Oxford University Press. I would like to thank him along with him effective and gracious editorial assistant Sarah Ebel. Also working for OUP, I would like to thank my production manager, Jeremy Toynbee, who was careful and considerate while moving the manuscript along. Anupama Gopinath saved the day during the production process, calming my fears and finding a few extra days to complete the copyediting process.

My developmental editor Tana Wojczuk encouraged taking chances by adding a bit of myself to the text and constantly asked "what are the stakes here?" She transformed the academic tone and cadence into something more readable for a general audience. Her editing and rethinking of the order and importance of ideas—putting them up front instead of hidden in a conclusion, transformed the manuscript into the book that you are now reading. I am appreciative of her time and attention.

Family support counted in many ways. My sister, Anna, and my niece, Alexandra, listened to the ongoing saga of my writing progress and finally pitched in at the end to help with some of the memoir pieces. Their encouragement and belief in my work were essential to keeping me going. My sister and niece were the basis of a book I wrote twenty years ago about living in a gated community, but this book addresses issues confronted by my grandchildren Gavin, Skye, and Max. They highlighted the importance of play, playgrounds, and open spaces for creativity and child development, and they supported this work by understanding that at times I could not be available for a game or meal. Thank you so much for your generosity.

And finally, I would like to thank my partner—Joel Lefkowitz—for his love and support throughout the long research and writing process. He was essential to its being finished, reading draft after draft, editing and encouraging me to keep going. Joel is an academic but also a professional photographer who accompanied me to the field taking many of the photographs. His faith in the importance of this book and his willingness to do everything from cooking dinner to scanning, faxing, and finding lost sources to allow it to be completed was crucial. I am grateful for his humor, good sense, and care.

I

Why Does Public Space Matter?

I often ask people what their favorite place is in their city or town. What are the places they particularly like and think about as having a special meaning or memory? The answer inevitably is a public space, sometimes a large park to walk, play, or picnic in and other times a local square or plaza with shaded paths and comfortable seating. Benches outside a café or on the sidewalk are commemorated with the names of those who spent time sitting with friends and neighbors. In residential neighborhoods, steps in front of an apartment building or library offer gathering places. Open schoolyards and church grounds are mentioned as favored to hold informal markets, clothing swaps, voter registration drives, and bake sales to benefit local organizations.

Many times, the response is accompanied by a smile and reminiscence about a day at the beach, historic monument, or art museum, or an afternoon spent strolling a scenic walkway or bicycling along a nature trail. Young people look for streets and paved areas of parks that provide exhilarating skateboarding or basketball courts and soccer fields where pick-up games happen. Children enjoy lively playgrounds, while caretakers select locations with high visibility and protection from ongoing traffic. Teenagers prefer places they "own" and just "hang" to watch others away from prying eyes. The favorite spots of rough sleepers are out-of-the-way edges or deep-forested centers of parks and the interstices of buildings and roads. Tourists point to open areas with tables and chairs to sit and watch the ongoing action even with honking cars or densely packed walkways. Some people love busy avenues and marketplaces full of energy to participate in the buzz of urban life, while others prefer quiet alleyways, solitary meadows, and tree-lined boulevards.

Public spaces—sidewalks, streets, playgrounds, plazas, squares, parks, beaches, libraries, art museums, historic monuments, and more—are some of the most beloved, enjoyed, and cared-about places. They are not just part of the physical fabric of the built environment, but vital for people to socialize, learn, and play, and they form an infrastructure of inclusion and exclusion. The network of streets and sidewalks, punctuated by plazas and public institutions, structure the circulation of people, commercial goods, and natural resources. A smoothly running transportation system provides city-wide mobility while waterways and drainage ditches contribute to environmental sustainability. Some scholars argue that public spaces provide the most important aspects of the social infrastructure for the promotion of democracy and equality.[1]

★ ★ ★

Recent events remind us that public space matters because it is where social interaction, community building, and political dissent take place. During the initial lockdown to reduce the spread of COVID-19, residents longed to walk and socialize outside. A few months later, Black Lives Matter marchers filled city streets to protest racial injustice and police violence against people of color. The social dislocation and emotional loss caused by closing public spaces and the significance of gaining access to streets for democratic practices and political action reveal the centrality of public space in everyday life.

Initially COVID-19 regulations and fear of contagion closed public spaces, creating a stark landscape with streets and parks devoid of people. While directives varied from state to state and country to country, the only way to stop the increasing number of cases was to stay home and limit contact with others. Cities closed public spaces, cordoned off streets, restricted commerce to essential services, and reorganized urban spaces in restrictive, yet in some cases innovative, ways.

The demands of sheltering-in-place generated a sense of isolation and loneliness. Many people experienced a shrinking sense of the world that exposed their dependence on one another for well-being and happiness through social connections. Like residents of gated communities who worry when outside their walls,[2] constant warnings to social distance when in public induced a generalized fearfulness. The daily separation of us and them, or "people like us" and "others," increased spatial segregation and social prejudice.

The loss of "third spaces," such as churches, cafes, gyms, bars, and corner stores, reduced the sense of being part of a local community. Families with children and youth suffered from the closure of playgrounds and playing fields, while older adults missed sidewalk benches, enclosed malls, and places to gather with enough space to feel safe. The depression and anxiety of physical distancing and not seeing people during lockdown reflected how much a feeling of belonging is based on face-to-face interaction in familiar places.

Just two and a half months into the pandemic the landscape changed, and streets were packed with demonstrators contesting racial injustice. People hugged and chanted together, forging social bonds through political commitment. Hundreds of thousands protested the murder of George Floyd and expressed their outrage and solidarity in the United States and around the globe.[3] The number of violent deaths of Black Americans at the hands of white police officers whose responsibility is to protect public space for all not only reflected—but reproduced—the embedded racism of American society.

The response of the US government and local police was punitive and swift, with President Trump calling on the National Guard and military personnel to impose curfews, clear the streets, and fence off Lafayette Square in front of the White House. The SWAT-trained police force in Los Angeles barricaded streets with their shields and then used tear gas and pepper spray on the remaining demonstrators. While

Figure 1.1 Black Lives Matter Demonstration Fills City Streets

camouflaged police with combat-ready gear pushed back protesters in most cities, others took a knee in respect.

At the same time, activists and city officials reclaimed public space in ingenious ways. Working with artists and the Department of Public Works in Washington D.C., Mayor Muriel Bowser painted a mural with 50-foot-high brilliant yellow letters reading "Black Lives Matter" on the stretch of Sixteenth Street in front of Lafayette Square. She renamed the area occupied by marchers "Black Lives Matter Plaza."[4] The chain-link fence surrounding the renamed plaza and the White House was a vibrant wall of colorful banners, handmade signs and collage, and a makeshift art installation about police violence instead of a forbidding obstacle.[5]

Public spaces remain the preeminent locations of bringing political issues to the forefront because of their accessibility, openness, and symbolic significance. The Black Lives Matter (BLM) protests reiterate that public space is essential for democracy and collective well-being, a resource that in national crises becomes the stage and the substance of struggle, negotiation, and ultimately healing.

★ ★ ★

Democracy does not require perfect equality, but it does require that citizens share a common life. What matters is that people of different backgrounds and social position encounter one another, and bump up against one another, in the course of everyday life. For this is how we learn to negotiate and abide our difference, and how we come to care for the common good.[6]

Public spaces enable people to encounter those they would not normally come across and transform "others" into individuals who are recognized and engaged in social interaction and political activities. Even fleeting moments of visibility or communication produce liberalizing qualities like a broader worldview and better problem solving. Contact with other people increases flexibility of thinking and results in a more vibrant and democratic public culture that recognizes difference and enhances people's sense of place, belonging, and inclusion.

Columnist Frank Bruni writes that dogs can fix a broken democracy because dog walkers are forced out of their homes and into contact with strangers.[7] Whether dog walking on streets, in parks, or in doggie playgrounds can reverse a reluctance to engage in public space, he is correct that leaving his apartment with his dog results in conversations and encounters with all kinds of people. There is a vibrant sociality of people with dogs in most parks, on sidewalks, and on beaches that form the basis of a diverse community. Not all of us, however, have dogs, but there are other leisure activities that promote contact. Community gardens, playgrounds, ball fields, street fairs, parades, cultural festivals, and public library programs, as well as the plethora of activities that public spaces facilitate are potential sites for interracial, interethnic, and intergenerational interaction.[8]

Living with difference is a skill that can be learned through public spaces that offer unpredictable situations and opportunities. It is not that dissimilarities dissolve, but that groups become comfortable through everyday frictions and adjustments that are the essence of being urban.[9] The politics of encounter in urban spaces creates a critical zone in which social protest can unfold through the coalescing of diverse groups and voices.[10] The nature of this encounter is not reducible to direct interaction, but part of the structure of feeling constituted by "co-presence" that brings people together with more relaxed social boundaries and claims of relationship.[11] Each incident points to some underlying process that enables groups to accommodate one another in ways that do not occur elsewhere.

Take for example how I learned what was acceptable behavior in the Parque Central in San José, Costa Rica.[12] When I first appeared with my notebook and clipboard, everyone—from the older men who read their papers, the policemen who patrolled the sidewalk, the shoeshine men and lottery ticket sellers who worked—watched my every move. I was uncomfortable in this space dominated by men, trying to fit in, but continued to write notes and annotate field maps. Finally, two police officers in uniforms walked up and looked over my shoulder: "*What are you doing here, gringa?*" the younger officer asked me. I showed them my map and colored pencil notations while they continued to ask questions. Once satisfied they walked away, and I sighed with relief. Talking to other users I discovered they thought I was a CIA agent (the police), a tax collector (the informal workers), or a journalist reporting a sordid story (the pensioners). On another morning when I started to sit on a different bench from my usual perch, a lottery ticket saleswoman, Maria, waved me away: "*That bench belongs Pacito—don't sit there*," she cried. "*He will arrive soon and needs his place.*" These tacit understandings of the "correct" way to behave revealed aspects of Parque Central's public culture and how it was reinforced through actions and directions.

Public culture develops as strangers watch and converse acquiring new ways of being and acting. Through the negotiation of the rules of common life, people adjust to each other's presence and reduce their sense of anxiety.[13] This alteration is also shaped by the structural constraints and power dynamics of the local situation that produce a kind of force field within which social negotiations take place. Public culture-making is often invisible and covert and only made manifest through the breaking of fragile norms and reactions to transgressions.

In this sense, public culture is always "becoming"[14] and never fixed, but located in a particular scene and temporality.

A park atmosphere of mutual affinity for a place also creates opportunities for social encounters and promotes an "indifference to difference" that encourages an openness to others.[15] Anna Barker and her colleagues who study Victorian parks in Leeds, England, identify "affective atmospheres" as central to conviviality and feeling connected.[16] They propose that an affective atmosphere is formed through informal norms and formal legal orderings that shape park interactions by regulating behavior and civility.

An affective atmosphere is not limited to experience and perception by an individual or group but is an attribute of the place.[17] It does not require an event or social movement to exist, though events can trigger an atmosphere, whether positive (e.g., Woodstock, V.E. Day) or negative (9/11, the shooting of Martin Luther King). An atmosphere can be located, circulated, and transmitted spatially as well as through other mediums such as poetry, music, tweets, images, and movies, as well as the built and natural environment.

Affective atmosphere plays an important role in unscripted social interaction. Consider the mood in the parking lot and streets surrounding Yankee Stadium in the Bronx after the home team wins. Strangers laugh together, pat each other on the back, and give "highfives" and fist bumps to anyone walking by, while those in cars flash their lights and honk their horns. But on nights when the Yankees lose, people leave silently, physically pulled into themselves or sadly shaking their heads. Park atmospheres vary from anxiety after a park mugging to elation watching children slide down a snowy hill or play on the first warm day of spring.

A positive affective atmosphere contributes to conviviality and social interaction, but without a supportive and egalitarian public culture, it is not likely to create a socially just public space. Historical, political, economic, and cultural contexts frame individuals' and groups' perceptions and interpretations. Contact and interaction in a society where racism, sexism, ablism, homophobia, xenophobia, and other

Figure 1.2 Greening Changes Lincoln Center into a Playful Space, New York City (Photograph by Merle Lefkowitz)

kinds of prejudice dominate daily life limit the possibility of developing a public culture that can sustain difference. Indeed, Frederick Law Olmsted, the famed designer of Central and Prospect Parks in New York, suggested that tolerance and fluid identities require mediating spatial structures and socially integrative programming. He coined the term "communitiveness" to convey his faith that people could be made to care about each other through the arrangement of public space.[18]

Contact, public culture, and affective atmosphere work in a synergistic fashion, amplifying or dampening each other depending on the specific public space and context. Contact and face-to-face interaction are foundational since it is through these encounters that public space takes on a social life. Public culture emerges out of these ongoing social interactions and their framing through everyday negotiation and contestation. The affective atmosphere—whether produced by an event, physical setting, media discourse, sensory experience, or political climate—changes the nature of the contact by activating the space in such a way that social interaction is more or less likely to occur and be sustained. The affective atmosphere and degree and quality of contact are reciprocal and intimately related. For readers interested in a deeper analysis of the scholarly arguments and development of these concepts, the Appendix fleshes out what is only painted in broad strokes here.

★ ★ ★

Most significantly, public space contributes to the flourishing of individuals, communities, cities, and societies. It goes beyond the usual standards of what urban planners and designers mean by well-designed space, considering what it is to be human and an agent in one's own life. Using this psychological attribute as a guide offers an emancipatory approach to the design and planning of the built environment and social infrastructure.

Flourishing refers to essential components for human life from a positive psychology perspective. The best-known proponent, Martin Seligman, argues that we need to focus on what encourages well-being and happiness rather than on measures of poor mental health.[19] Seligman and Mihalyi Csikszentmikhalyi define positive psychology as "the scientific study of positive human functioning and flourishing on multiple levels that include the biological, personal, relational, institutional, cultural, and global dimensions of life."[20] Based on their research findings, flourishing is made up of a constellation of factors composed of encouraging positive emotions, engagement through activities, relationships with other people, meaning and purpose, and accomplishments (PERMA).

John Kinyon, Ike Lasater, and Julie Stiles offer additional ways to characterize optimumal human functioning based on three sets of universal human needs and values: 1) well-being, 2) connection, and 3) self-expression.[21] Their model includes sustenance/health, safety/security, and beauty/peace/play as part of well-being; love/caring,

empathy/understanding, and community/belonging as components of the need for connection; and autonomy/freedom, authen-
ticity, and meaning/contribution as elements of self-expression. Tyler
VanderWeele adds physical factors such as environment to this list and
considers the role of character and virtue.[22]

Social justice, which at the individual level is a sense of inclusion
and fairness, and at the community and societal level refers to representation and recognition of difference, is missing from these criteria.
Justice attributes broaden Seligman's PERMA and Kinyon, Lasater,
and Stiles' human needs and values model to include rights-based
and liberating factors that enhance human life. Positive psychological
theories offer a useful framework for thinking about the importance of public space for individual flourishing and community outcomes when combined with attention to issues of equity, equality, and
inclusion.

Thirty-five years of ethnographic fieldwork on plazas, walkways,
parks, and beaches provide the evidence that public space contributes
to flourishing in at least six domains:

1) social justice and democratic practices
2) health and well-being
3) play and recreation
4) informal economy and social capital
5) environmental and ecological sustainability
6) cultural identity and place attachment

These domains are broken down into specific topics that were
studied empirically. Social justice and democratic practices comprise
social inclusion, belonging, representation, recognition of difference,
and care as well as contestation and resistance. Health and well-being
encompass physical health, mental health, safety and accessibility, a
sense of security, and resilience. Play and recreation include the socialization of children, sports and team building, relaxation, retreat
and religion in everyday life, and creativity. The informal economy
and social capital incorporate flexible workplaces, innovative forms

of work, integration of immigrants, and building social networks. Environmental and ecological sustainability cover community gardens and urban agriculture, ecological planning and design, ecosystems services, and environmental justice. Cultural identity and place attachment integrate cultural symbols and monuments, artistic expressions such as music and dance, collective memory, and cultural continuity. These domains and topics organize this book.

★ ★ ★

Even though public spaces contribute to a flourishing society, they are threatened by temporary closure by contagious disease, permanent erasure by rapacious urban development, or avoidance because of fearfulness and anxiety. While public space is a beneficial material resource and improves the economic success of neighborhoods, its value to residents is ordinarily not measurable in financial terms or by capitalist logics. It is always at risk of conversion from its use value for locals to its exchange and commercial value depending on the historical–political context, economic supply and demand, and type of ownership or governance strategy. Incidences of racial profiling and prejudice, assaults on women, attacks on LGBTQ individuals, gun violence, and other crimes continue to plague public spaces and can make them dangerous and fearful places. Without financial and political investments, intervention programs, event planning, and community-based participation and support, positive benefits are easily eclipsed, and public spaces abandoned. This growing vulnerability contrasts with the breadth of its contributions.

How do cities decide where to invest for greater social justice and equality when there are so many demands on national, state, and municipal budgets? Where does public space fit among demands for affordable housing, equitable education, low-cost public transportation, and mediation of climate change? Public space is only one component of creating a just city, but crucial because of its capacity to foster an emotionally open atmosphere and networks of relationships that address other forms of inequity as well. Yet public spaces remain underfunded, poorly managed, constrained by exclusionary policies and corporate development, and overlooked in urban planning and design.

There is a regrettable incongruity between the significance of public space and its low status as an urban priority. One reason for this discrepancy is that residents often take public space for granted and only appreciate it when it is gone. Perceptions of crime and physical danger have a negative impact and encourage people to stay away. Even policy- and decision-makers are often unsure what is meant by public space and unaware of its crucial role in building an equitable and just city.

This book aims to realign urban priorities and demonstrate the importance of public space for socially just cities. I first presented the ethnographic research on threats to public space in 2016 at a UN Habitat Public Space conference in Barcelona, Spain. Researchers and practitioners met to produce a list of findings and recommendations in preparation for the UN Habitat III meeting in Quito, Ecuador, to be held later that year. With colleagues from the Center for the Future of Places and UN Habitat Global Public Space Programme, we added evidence-based public space principles to an early draft of the New Urban Agenda (NUA). The NUA establishes the policy objectives and planning goals for promoting sustainable and equitable cities, especially for those countries experiencing rapid urbanization in the Global South. The draft was discussed and modified at the meeting in Quito and ultimately passed by the United Nations Assembly in December 2016. Working with colleagues to ensure that the human right to public space would appear in the language of the NUA, and elaborating how this right could be substantiated, measured, and implemented, resulted in the writing of this book.

The following chapters lay out the evidence and tools used.

Chapter 2 answers the question "what is public space" from a personal, cultural, and urban design point of view. It begins with a broad definition that includes neighborhood parks, plazas, and libraries, but extends to the street system, social infrastructures, and environmental linkages. It concludes with a rethinking of the definition of public space, one based on multiple characteristics unique to each venue.

Chapter 3 explores social justice and belonging through an ethnographic study of Jones Beach on Long Island, New York. Visitor behavior and interviews portray how the components of social justice—inclusion, representation, recognition of difference, an ethic of care, and contestation and resistance—are experienced and valued. The chapter concludes with a discussion of the Public Space and Social Justice Evaluation Framework and how it can be used to identify and design just public space.

Chapter 4 tells the story of the rebuilding of a derelict railroad bridge between Poughkeepsie and Highland (in New York State's Hudson Valley) to create a linear park. The ethnography of Walkway Over the Hudson Historical Park reveals the potential of a resident-initiated intervention to transform the health, well-being, and resilience of a small city. The over one-mile-long expanse crossing the Hudson River encourages physical exercise and mental health by offering an accessible, safe, and scenic place to be with others.

Chapter 5 focuses on the role of public space in children's play, youth team building, and creative development. The ethnography of Lake Welch in New York reflects how a natural environment encourages children's exploration and adventure while simultaneously providing relaxation and retreat for the entire family. Lake Welch highlights the importance of cultural context in the socialization of children and offers a place where the entire family can be together outside of their small apartments and the busy streets of NYC.

Chapter 6 examines the central role that public space plays in the lives of informal workers throughout the world. Ethnographic case studies from Latin America, Asia, Europe, and North America depict how sidewalks, streets, and markets offer workplaces for vendors, trash pickers, nannies, and many others. When viewed from an informal economy perspective, public space offers flexible workplaces, innovative forms of work, integration of immigrants into the local economy, and social capital that can lead to better jobs and supportive relationships.

Chapter 7 considers the role of environmental sustainability and the greening of public space by tracing the history and impact of these interventions. Community gardens, urban agriculture, and sustainable parks contribute to ecological sustainability by building stronger communities, supporting social reproduction, and promoting environmental justice. Human ecological planning and ecosystem services assessments offer strategies for enhancing sustainability through scientific methods that identify the best ecological practices and indicators for public space design.

Chapter 8 identifies place attachment and cultural identity as significant aspects of public space use. Culture-related activities such as music, dance, festivals, and celebrations reinforce cultural values, beliefs, and meanings. The removal of monuments and symbolic icons of an oppressive and violent past—and the struggle over these decisions—are essential to recognizing and respecting all people's cultural histories and collective memories. Symbolic and material aspects of public space also play a crucial role in a community's response to a crisis or disaster. The examination of the symbolism of the Statue of Liberty and the post-9/11 use of public space at Battery Park City deepen our understanding of how cultural expressions, identities, and continuity are essential to the meaning of public space.

Chapter 9 investigates the contraction and expansion of public space in New York City during the COVID-19 pandemic. A personal and archival account of the transformation of public spaces from March 22, 2020, through December 1, 2021, reveals the loneliness and depression of sheltering in place as well as the euphoria of resuming social interaction even while wearing masks and physically distancing. New forms of public space use—including the democratization of the arts and culture in local parks and streets, and the closing of streets and parking spaces to enable a vibrant restaurant scene of sidewalk cafes and restaurants—reflect the importance of public space during the crisis. Lessons from the impact of public space openings and closings reiterate many of the findings of the previous chapters.

Chapter 10 suggests ways to improve and protect public space in the future, and how to undertake grassroots research and utilize local knowledge to protect and promote neighborhood public space. Tompkins Square in Manhattan offers a case study of how to study the conflicts of neighborhood residents, regular park users, and other visitors that lead to a rejection of the NYC Parks Without Borders Program.

The **Appendix** provides a scholarly review of the foundational concepts of contact, public culture, and affective atmosphere and how they interact to produce "publicness" in public space.

★ ★ ★

Why Ethnography? A Note on Methodology

I often am asked what it is like to "do ethnography," and how it is different from other kinds of research. Observing, talking, mapping, and taking fieldnotes is a form of multitasking that when done right captures the experience of a place with a freshness and immersion that other methods fail to achieve. Rather than producing just an overview of what is going on or descriptions such as the number of people who were there, and the time people spend in each activity or place, it focuses on why people are doing what they are doing from their own point of view.

Ethnographers are interested in the experiential, relational, and meaning-based aspects of human behavior. It is the difference between knowing how many people walk across Walkway Across the Hudson each day as discussed in Chapter 4, and why the individual users find the experience so appealing or meaningful that they do it every day. There are excellent statistical analyses of the relationship of public space to health-enhancing activity, but when examining public spaces' contribution to well-being or resilience, then an ethnographic perspective is more revealing.

One question that often comes up when using ethnographic methods is how you know when you have learned something. Instead of it being a statistical concept, ethnographic studies rely on the people who are undertaking the research, and the way that they portray what they see and hear with considerable detail about the experience to communicate effectively. No one set of fieldnotes, or maps, or interviews, or even a survey is adequate to be considered a finding. But the integration of multiple kinds of data over time will show patterns of behavior, thoughts, conflicts, and interests.

A critical aspect of ethnographic practice is the centrality of the researcher's perspective and subjective experience. The ethnographer is the instrument—in a scientific sense—of data collection and analysis. Questions about the degree of "objectivity" of ethnographic research need to be answered in terms of the researcher's "positionality"—their physical and social characteristics that locate them within local power dynamics.[23] These identity markers influence how the researcher perceives and understands the field site, and more importantly, how people respond to them and whether the researcher can establish adequate rapport to form a relationship or complete an interview. The researcher's subjective experience—how they respond to places, people, situations, and feelings—forms the foundation of participant observation that relies on an ability to reflect and empathize with the people and places being studied. "Reflexivity," the ability to examine one's own feelings, reactions, and motives, and how these influence the research process, is essential for ethnographic fieldwork, especially in public spaces where one's public and personal personas are on display.

That's why I included snippets of my life and field experiences throughout. The fieldwork includes projects completed from 1978 through the present, and my subjective experience has changed as I have over time. As a young, white, unmarried, cisgender woman, public space users responded to me in very different ways than they do now. My marital and parental status, age, physical abilities, language fluency, and cultural competence changed over the years and influenced what I could see and learn. On the other hand, my social class, heteronormativity, and racial identity remained, creating potential blind spots that I have tried to offset by working with teams of researchers from diverse cultural, national, and racial backgrounds. Care was taken to represent people and communities in the ways they identified themselves and only included when relevant to the discussion.

The political circumstances and societal concerns of today--racial injustice, climate change, socioeconomic inequality, social exclusion, and belonging—were always important, but have reached a point that attention is crucial to sustain the planet and maintain any semblance of a collective society. In response to current imperatives, I have focused on these problems rather than others. Today's issues are very complex, and it is hoped that those highlighted can provide a window onto other interrelated issues such as gender violence, the consequences of unregulated gun control, and the many forms of intersectional vulnerability experienced by women of color, trans youth, differently abled older adults, and children with special needs.

The following ethnographies of plazas, parks, beaches, sidewalks, and markets in North America, Latin America, Asia, Europe, and Africa present how public spaces contribute to flourishing and clarify the roles of contact, public culture, and affective atmosphere in each context. These close-up, multi-layered inquiries demonstrate how public spaces provide for the socialization of children and improve physical and mental well-being by encouraging walking and sports as well as exposure to natural landscapes. Sidewalks and plazas offer business opportunities through markets and informal selling and locations for festivals and celebrations that allow people to belong and transmit cultural practices. Parks, urban gardens, and waterways create sustainable greenways for water retention and wildlife, and during disasters, public spaces are centers for coming together and offering support. Public space outcomes such as social justice, well-being, creativity, social capital, cultural identity, and ecological sustainability are only some of the ways that public space improves individual lives and society as a whole.

2

What Is Public Space?

The first time I ask the question "what is public space" is in 1985. I am descending from a skywalk to reach Harborplace, a Rouse-designed urban redevelopment project that revived the historic Inner Harbor of Baltimore, Maryland. The skywalk is puzzling—open to the public but connecting only the surrounding offices and hotels to the Inner Harbor area—it rarely has anyone using it. As I step onto the sidewalk across the street from the 1980 reconstruction of a market hall filled with restaurants, food stalls, shopping, and tourist activities, a young African American girl wearing a white school blouse and black skirt stops and points across the street.

"Is it ok to go there?" she asks. "Does it cost money?"

I am surprised and offer my hand to help her safely cross the street. I reassure her that she can visit even if she doesn't have anything to spend and is welcome to enjoy the sights and walk around.

But then I begin to see it from her point of view. Her mother may have warned her not to go where she did not know anyone. How does she know she is welcome? She can't see anyone who looks like her. Families carrying cameras and shopping bags are not from nearby Federal Hill, a neighborhood that in 1985 is not yet gentrified. No children are playing by themselves; those who are visible are accompanied by parents or caretakers.

At the time, I thought parks were simply left over from the construction of the city and part of "nature" rather than intentionally designed. But through living in different cities over the years, public space's ability to transform neighborhoods into welcoming, healthy, and socially cohesive places became more apparent. Incidents such as the encounter at Harborplace illuminated why public space could not be taken for granted and needed to be made open to all.

While living in a Baltimore rowhouse our neighbors suggested we remove our backyard fences to create one large garden with a barbeque, table, and chairs. We spent most nights having dinner together and designed a collective landscape with a patio, flowers, and shrubs. Just blocks away the same rowhouses were abandoned with their yards cemented over and surrounded with barbed wire and metal siding.

What is this young girl seeing and feeling as she looks across the street? Is her reaction more attuned to the implicit racism of contemporary public space developments than mine? In many ways she is right—Harborplace was built and governed by a public-private partnership with the goal of bringing more investment and people with money into the heart of the city. It is meant to be a place for consumption, and consumption costs money. There are security guards at the entrances and even the outside spaces have "ambassadors" and police to help, and control, visitors. Maybe it is not a public space intended for her to play, much less visit.

★ ★ ★

The Latin American plaza is a core metaphor and physical space of encounter, essential to the social, cultural, and political life of the city. Working on my doctoral fieldwork in San José, Costa Rica, I frequently crossed Parque Central, a verdant oasis, to reach San Juan de Dios, the largest public hospital. Walking under leafy shade trees, sitting on the damp stone benches, and listening to the conversational murmurs and shouts of bus drivers and ambulatory vendors, I imagined the interior lives of people meeting, talking to friends, selling flowers and lottery tickets, or just watching passers-by.

A photographer dressed in a white shirt and suit jacket flirted with a young woman posing for a picture to give to her *novio* (boyfriend). He smiled and I waved hello, shaking my head. The sweet smell of caramelizing peanuts wafted by: *cinco colones* bought a small bag, and, crunching my treat, I joined the noon crowd. A small group encircled a preacher in a blue role carrying a staff; he called out for those who believe in God to raise their hands. Nearby a shoeshine man looked on commenting to his customer about a healing ritual that took place earlier in the day. Pensioners reading *La Nación* argued about politics,

Figure 2.1 Parque Central in San José, Costa Rica

while mothers carrying children and heavy shopping bags stopped for a few moments to catch their breath. A day in Parque Central was a microcosm of everyday sociality and cultural activities awash in color and a cacophony of sounds.

Los Angeles, where I grew up, is a car-dependent suburban city with vast areas of undeveloped land, long streets, and freeways that run east to west—from downtown to the ocean. The downtown *placita* on Olvera Street, where I played Mary in the Christmas *Las Posadas* as a child, is a touristic reminder of Southern California's Spanish origins—not a vibrant social center like Parque Central. Los Angeles is made up of mostly unplanned neighborhood centers that accommodate low-density, sprawling housing developments interspersed with industrial areas and commercial malls. The beach, the main public space, is legally accessible to everyone, but limited public transportation and guarded wealthy homes and private beach clubs restrict public access.

Leaving Costa Rica to become a faculty member in the Department of Landscape Architecture and Regional Planning at the University of Pennsylvania introduced me to another kind of public space. Philadelphia is a densely settled, compact city with apartments and townhouses around a street grid with purposely planned public squares. Designed by William Penn in 1683 to be a "greene town" with a clear hierarchy of streets, large house lots for gardens are organized into four quadrants with additional greenspace in the form of small parks. Philadelphia offers an urban model of intersecting streets and squares forming a system that, unlike Los Angeles, encourages pedestrian socializing as well as the circulation of people and vehicles and a more equitable distribution of public space.

Philadelphia's squares also provide clues to racial issues that public spaces face. One of Penn's five original squares, Washington Square was the first African American meeting and burying ground in colonial America. Washington Square's history, however, was not initially recognized by nearby Independence National Historical Park (INHP) and not marked or interpreted as an African American sacred site. Further, the lack of representation of the free Black laborers who constructed Independence Hall and African American culture resulted in local African American residents avoiding the park, unaware of its significance.[1] The neglect of signifying Washington Square and Black contributions is a form of historical erasure, one of the contemporary racist elements of urban planning and an obstacle to social inclusion.

Another square in William Penn's original plan, Rittenhouse Square, is located amid luxury condominiums, upscale restaurants and shops, and expensive townhouses. Popular with tourists and locals, gentrification creates an unwelcome environment for some. African American young men are asked to leave by police citing loitering laws, and older homeless and tired individuals are deterred by benches with central arm rests—a version of hostile architecture—that make it difficult to lie down. This is the neighborhood in which two African American men were arrested in the local Starbuck's while simply waiting for a friend.[2] Like historical erasure, racial profiling and physical deterrents like those in Rittenhouse Square restrict who is welcome to use the space.

Utilizing the potential of public space to improve rather than threaten historical connections and neighborhood cohesion was the focus of the Farnham Park studio taught with colleagues Robert Hanna and Laurie Olin.[3] Originally constructed in 1905, the eighty-acre strolling park contains scenic lakes, a rustic stone bridge, carriage roads and winding paths, a gazebo for gatherings, sport fields for baseball and football, sunny meadows, and dense forests. Initiated by the Women's Parks Association as a public amenity for the Parkside neighborhood in Camden, New Jersey, Farnham Park was the centerpiece of a private development made up of single-family and row houses on tree-lined streets. Maps and old photographs depict middle-class families promenading along lush walkways or riding in carriages along picturesque roads.

With the incursion of schools, churches, and a large housing project, and exacerbated by the downturn of Camden's economy in the 1970s, the park began to decline. Many of its original features deteriorated, and ongoing conflicts with teenagers over the use of the playgrounds and playing fields flared. The carriage paths took on new prominence as a prime location to cruise and wash cars. The dumping of trash and the occasional dead body deep in the remaining forest added to the park's notoriety.

The studio began with graduate students mapping, observing, and participating in local activities, as well as interviewing park users and neighbors. Students accompanied residents to their favorite places and learned about the problems they encountered. A local history was reconstructed from news reports, oral histories, and archival documents, and interviews with the Boys and Girls Clubs of America, the local elementary and middle schools, and a Senior Center added an institutional perspective.

Using the collected data as a guide, design priorities and schematic plans reflected the various stakeholders' requirements and preferences. Working with "constituency groups" (e.g., homeowners, school children, teenagers, families, car owners, seniors, school administrators, and others) faculty, students, and local participants were brought together to address conflicts in their values, needs, and desires to consider renovation alternatives.

Elementary school children wanted more playgrounds. They could not use those that existed because the high school students dominated the swings. The teenagers, when asked about the swing area, complained they had no place to go. High school students and young adults requested more basketball courts farther away from the playground. Local school administrators wanted more access to the playgrounds because of their limited schoolyard areas, but also needed sports fields. The residents who lived along the streets facing the park hoped for more greenery to buffer the noise and visual impact of active play. Many of these constituency needs were accommodated by rethinking the adjacencies of activities and facilitating new ones. Constructing basketball courts away from the playground, expanding the number and kinds of play equipment, adding sports fields, and placing shrubs and trees along the perimeter of the park solved many of the identified problems.

But there were conflicts that design solutions could not solve. Residents wanted to limit park access from the housing projects and objected to young adults hanging out and purportedly vandalizing the forested areas. Families wanted picnic tables and barbeque grills because the original ones were ripped out long ago, but municipal administrators refused to supply more because they feared they would disappear. The car washers wanted the interior roads open, while the municipal transportation and sanitation departments proposed blocking roads to limit dumping. Resolving these disagreements was difficult because the various constituencies had little face-to-face contact and did not know one another. Instead of trying to design away these issues, we proposed community activities and family-focused programming as part of a collaborative plan. Such events offered residents opportunities to talk and potentially develop a greater sense of belonging, tolerance, and trust.

Conflicts over the exclusivity of public space formed the center-piece of ethnographic fieldwork in gated communities located in New York City and Long Island, Mexico City, and San Antonio, Texas. Gated community residents tend to be socioeconomically homoge-neous and perceive the world outside their private development as full of dangerous "others." Mothers worry constantly about their children being kidnapped because *"just anyone could snatch a child off the street if we were not living inside a gated community."* There are guards, walls, and electronic barriers as well as surveillance systems that monitor resi-dents and visitors to reinforce their sense of safety. Yet residents remain anxious about *"workers who are here today and gone tomorrow coming in and out without anyone checking."*[4]

Their secured enclaves are idealized as "old-fashioned" neighbor-hoods with security maintained through social segregation. Residents talk about their interior walkways, streets, and parks as "public space" in the sense that everyone in the gated community uses them, but they are constantly on the lookout for those who do not belong. Any person who looks "out of place" is stopped and questioned.

The tragic outcome of this often-racist practice was dramatically illustrated when George Zimmerman, a neighborhood-watch co-ordinator, fatally shot Trayvon Martin, a seventeen-year-old African American, while he was visiting relatives in a gated community in Sanford, Florida.[5] In this neighborhood context "public space" was restricted to the homeowners, renters, and their guests—and in this case, not even to their guests. As the gated community research found, who is deemed part of the public depends on ownership and govern-ance structure, and it plays a major role in determining its inclusivity, diversity, and accessibility.

The Concept of Public Space

Strange as it may seem, there is no one accepted definition of public space. Architects, planners, designers, and social scientists focus on different features—design professionals emphasize spatial form and environment/behavior interactions, while social scientists draw attention to social relations, spatial appropriations, and political practices. The reason for the ambiguity is there are multiple dimensions or facets that characterize public spaces. Some characteristics have to do with historical development, some to do with their physical attributes, or the way they are financed, or governed, or how accessible or restrictive they are.

Public space is often characterized by what it "does" or "accommodates" rather than in prescriptive terms. Sverre Bjerkeset and Jonny Aspen observed hundreds of hours of activities and behaviors in Oslo, Norway, and created a classification system. Their typology includes recreation, transportation, selling and buying, civic participation, culture and entertainment, teaching and learning, and public aid, as well as the production, management, construction, and renovation of the built environment. These distinctions are fluid, combining and interconnecting to form generic patterns of use.[6]

Spaces can be made "public" by people, meanings, and practices and can manifest different degrees of publicness at various times. Stephen Carr, Mark Francis, Leanne Rivlin, and Andrew Stone[7] point out that some evolve naturally—that is, without a specific plan or design as people adopt them for their own use. A playing field in a vacant lot or a community garden where a building has been torn down are inspiring examples. Even "left-over" or "accidental" spaces under a bridge, on the side of a large building or next to a highway become public spaces when used by people for playing, sleeping, or spending the day. An abandoned pier appropriated by LGBTQ youth in the Chelsea neighborhood of Manhattan had a ripple effect and was ultimately reconstructed for their use, although it is now gentrified to such a degree that it is heavily policed and scrutinized.[8]

The public/private distinction is also quite muddled since the private sector is most often responsible for construction and maintenance.[9] To keep public spaces "public" Matthew Carmona offers a charter of user rights—to roam freely, rest and relax, demonstrate peacefully, trade or perform, take photographs, and collect for charities. But he also lists the responsibilities of users—not to litter and to respect the rights of others—and of the owners and managers to treat all in an equitable and inclusive manner while keeping the spaces safe, clean, open, and well maintained.

I propose defining public space by incorporating all these aspects into six dimensions. Each dimension can be scored along various scales—small to large, rural to urban, closed to open, few to many, public to private, and by other descriptors. The idea is that any public space can be defined by some combination of basic characteristics:

1. **physical aspects** (e.g., size, shape, location, amenities)
2. **ownership** (e.g., public, public-private partnership, limited partnership, private)
3. **governance or management authority and funding** (e.g., business improvement district, homeowners' association, common interest development, governmental agency, conservancy, nonprofit organization)
4. **control and influence** (e.g., nature of governance, policing, surveillance)
   rules and regulations (e.g., strict versus lenient)
   access (e.g., open versus closed, free versus paid, temporary versus all-day)
5. **symbolic/historical meaning** (e.g., representation, historical markers, recognition)
6. **political activity** (e.g., allowed versus prohibited)

This framework enables researchers, designers, planners, community members, and public space activists to delve into the similarities and dissimilarities of public spaces, furnishing a template for comparison. It addresses the "what is public space" question by positing that there are many kinds, not one ideal type. Any analysis should begin with identifying the details of the specific place—geographically, materially, historically, socially, and politically.

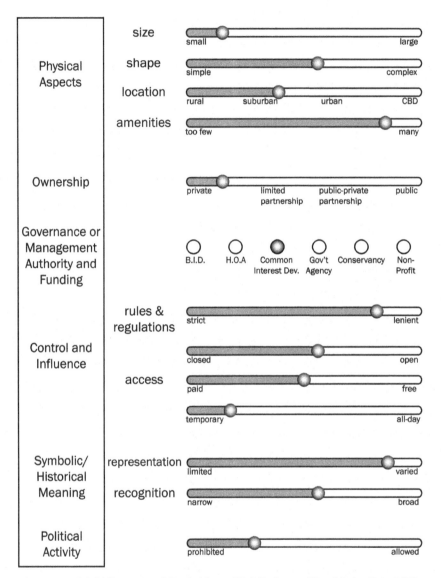

Figure 2.2 Multidimensional Definition of Public Space (Graphic by Erin Lilli)

For example, large public parks like Golden Gate Park in San Francisco, Bois de Boulogne in Paris, or City Park in Nairobi afford a kind of publicness quite distinct from a neighborhood playground or *placita* (small neighborhood plaza). What might be less obvious is how ownership by an urban developer or management by a private/

public authority such as Hudson Yards in Manhattan, Harborplace in Baltimore, or Westgate Mall in Nairobi restricts publicness and the cultural and political activities that are permissible. Public spaces in the center of the city, that are freely accessed and open to host political activities and cultural festivals, have a more positive impact on perceived social justice and sense of inclusiveness than privately owned and managed public space surrounded by high-rise towers and shopping malls.

Consider the array of public spaces in a neighborhood including sidewalks, streets, playgrounds, parks, small plazas in a housing complex, or squares in front of a community center or civic complex. Using the dimensions of public space, rank each in terms of size and location (large/small, urban/rural), ownership (somewhere between public and private), governing authority (public to private such as city parks department and police versus corporations and private security guards), control (open to closed, free to paid), history and symbolic meaning (varied to limited representation, broad to narrow recognition of difference), and political activities (allowed to prohibited).

What you discover is that streets and sidewalks are the most public—have the most publicness—since they are owned by the city, maintained by a local transportation department, controlled by community police, and accommodate parades and political demonstrations. Playgrounds are more restricted with fences, extensive rules and regulations, and caretaker surveillance to protect children who play there. While playgrounds are normally publicly owned, many have private parents' groups who pay for upkeep and manage the grounds, which limits their publicness.

If a neighborhood is recently developed, there are likely to be privately owned public spaces designed as part of a housing complex or shopping area with restrictions on political meetings, loitering, and skateboarding. Thinking about the distinctions of who owns or manages the space as well as describing its physical properties provides a way to understand why some are experienced as encouraging social interaction while others feel exclusionary becoming places that people avoid.

Central Park—a large, geographically central, symbolically significant space in Manhattan—is a Frederick Law Olmsted- and Calvert Vaux-designed historical site owned by the city of New York. Since 1998, the Central Park Conservancy (CPC), a nonprofit organization made up of wealthy, mostly white, nearby residents, has managed the park. The CPC raises 85 percent of the annual operating budget and is responsible for its basic care-making decisions and implementing changes that reflect the funders' aesthetic and maintenance standards. Even though it is a well-endowed park, when asked to share a portion of their allotted tax dollars with neighborhood parks that lack an economic base, the CPC refused.

Political activity is often prohibited in Central Park, and permission is required for any gatherings. Yet at the same time, the park hosts the arts through free theater, dance, and music performances. While the park is accessible with entrances that punctuate its low stone walls, it is surveilled and policed with strictly enforced rules and regulations.

Central Park's aesthetic control, private funding, professional decision-making, strict surveillance, and restrictions on political activity create a particular kind of environment where not everyone feels at home. There have been a series of racially inflected incidents that suggest it functions as white public space.[10] Young Black male researchers report that police officers trail behind them when they are photographing or mapping social behavior, and they find it difficult, if not impossible, to interview in this setting.

Although most surveillance by police and other users is gender-, age-, and race-based, targeting young men of color and some immigrant groups, members of the LGBTQ community are also harassed. Havens such as the Rambles of Central Park and the "piers" where bisexual and transgendered youth hang out have become increasingly monitored and controlled.[11] Pier 45 at the end of Christopher Street was a mecca for gay men in the 1960s and 1970s, and a second home for bisexual and transsexual youth in the 1980s and 1990s. In

2001 it was closed, redeveloped, and reopened in 2003 as part of the family-friendly, event-programmed, heavily policed, and surveillance-camera-monitored Hudson River Park.[12] Even as societal norms and state laws recognized the LGBTQ community by the 2000s, queer spaces—including queer public spaces—contracted due to other social and economic forces.[13]

A multidimensional definition does not assume that there is one kind of public space and instead reveals how specific social, political, and physical conditions impact "publicness." In New York City almost all squares and parks including Battery Park, Herald Square, Prospect Park, and Bryant Park were open to a broad public with a variety of users and activities when the Public Space Research Group (PSRG)—a group of faculty and graduate students at the Graduate Center of the City University of New York focused on improving public spaces—formed in 1990. They were also rundown, dangerous, and in disrepair. By 1995 each had acquired financial support and governance through the addition of a private conservancy (Prospect Park Alliance in 1987 and Battery Park Conservancy in 1994), or a public-private partnership and business improvement district (Grand Central Partnership in 1980 and 34th Street Partnership in 1989). These spaces were successfully "cleaned up" through private initiatives by these conservancies and partnerships, but also transformed in terms of the degree of social control, form of management, and elite aesthetics that changed the sense of belonging and accessibility for many of the original occupants.

New York City, of course, is a harbinger of privately owned public spaces (POPS) created by a 1961 law that permits developers additional floor space and building height in exchange for public pocket-parks, mid-block gardens, and corporate plazas. This innovative zoning based on the research and advocacy of William Hollingshead White demonstrated how small spaces enhance the sociality of the city.[14] New public/private arrangements and corporate-sponsored POPS arose from this decisive change in public space planning. But a study by Gerald Kayden found that a majority of New York City's

550 privately owned public spaces were not well used and had features that deterred people from entering or staying.[15] Jeremy Nemeth studied 163 spaces produced through New York City's incentive zoning program and determined that the resulting POPS had deleterious effects on citizenship and representation because of their limited approach to their political, social, and democratic functions.[16]

One example of the impact of private ownership and regulation is the "smart" public space of Hudson Yards in Manhattan, where visitors

Figure 2.3 The Vessel at Hudson Yards, New York City

were required to register and sign an agreement before entering the *Vessel*, Thomas Heatherwick's towering sculpture.[17] This agreement gave Hudson Yards the rights to "photos, audio recording, or video footage depicting or relating to Vessel" for "any purpose whatsoever in any and all media (in either case, now known or developed later)."[18] Less is known about the purpose of two tiny cameras on each side of thirty kiosks that dotted the landscape with sensors to track atmospheric levels. When asked about this breach of privacy norms, the Related Hudson Yards president, Jay Cross, answered: "From our point of view, the data is our data for the purposes of allowing us to make Hudson Yards function better."[19] Yet the evidence suggests that the data are used for marketing rather than social improvements. The *Vessel* is currently closed due to four suicides by teenagers at the site. For the moment it functions as an Instagram photograph attraction rather than a center for gathering data on park users.

A Brief Prehistory of Public Space

Public space has always been part of human settlement patterns. Recent archaeological excavations demonstrate that the less well-known prehistory of public space stretches back 12,000 years. While the recorded history of public space is familiar due to extensive writings by Greek philosophers, European colonists, urban planners, and architectural historians, much of its prehistory has yet to be discovered.[20]

Human settlements have always had some type of open or empty space, whether near the house for dumping trash, washing children, and corralling animals; neighborhood-level for daily interaction, religious ceremonies, and children's play; and civic centers for collective activities such as markets, festivals, and council meetings.[21] Archaeologists working in Africa, Latin America, and Southeast Asia write about the universality of empty space going so far as to argue that the provision of empty space was a "safety valve" for human well-being and consensus especially in dense populations.[22] The ubiquity of open space in ancient settlements with built structures facing onto a common area were used for many of the same purposes as today.

One of the world's oldest circles of limestone monoliths is Göbekli Tepe located in the hills of Turkey discovered by Klaus Schmidt in 1995. Built by hunter-gatherers for ritual or domestic use over 11,000 years ago, the site challenges archaeologists who thought that agriculture provided the time and food surplus needed to build monuments and develop a rich vocabulary of symbolism.[23] Rather, this monumental architecture organized in circular form enclosing open spaces predates early agricultural settlements and villages, showing that sociocultural change came first and agriculture later.[24]

Stonehenge, a Neolithic site in south England constructed 3,800 years ago, is composed of large monoliths delimiting an open space still used as a ritual site.[25] It is located within a complex landscape of other monuments, smaller arrangements of monoliths, and permanent farming settlements with avenues and pathways that connect them.[26] Virtually abandoned in 2500 BCE, rebuilt in the Early Bronze Age (2100 BCE), and the center of conflict between the church and local peasants in the twelfth century CE, it became a contested terrain. A religious order was housed nearby and an Anglo-Saxon church built to erase the vestigial paganism during the medieval period. Today Stonehenge is owned and protected by the National Trust as a symbol of nationhood. It retains its magical Druid aura, attracting New Age religious worshipers and tourists from around the world.[27]

Archaeologists make distinctions between open and public spaces based on their performative qualities as sites of everyday life or places for the integration of the community. Spaces of domestic and private activities relate to the socioeconomic functioning of the house such as washing, cooking, and working. Larger spaces, such as plazas and ball courts, support political negotiations and religious ceremonies.[28]

The excavations of Songo Mnara, a fourteenth to sixteenth century CE Swahili town and island off the Tanzanian coast, suggest that

Figure 2.4 Stonehenge, England

the central open spaces were public.[29] The Songo Mnara town plan includes multiple housing blocks and cemeteries and great amounts of space devoid of architecture within an enclosing wall.[30] Using a range of scientific techniques, Jeffrey Fleisher found that open areas near houses were employed in drying fish, making crafts, and cooking food, and regularly kept clean by sweeping. A more centrally located space near the cemetery was used to commemorate the dead and was an active town center crisscrossed with pathways. Early African towns had a hierarchy of open spaces from private domestic to public ceremonial spaces configured in various ways.[31]

In Mesoamerica the Main Plaza at Monte Albán, an ancient Zapotec city in today's Mexico, founded in 500 BCE, was reconfigured many times as a ceremonial and administration center, and then abandoned in 800 CE.[32] Multiple excavations and interpretations of its architecture, distribution patterns, and cultural biography trace its continuous modification beginning with its construction and use as a stage for public ceremonies until its collapse. The ruins survived as a religious site for ritual offerings and burials.[33] Even during the Spanish invasion and subsequent suppression of indigenous beliefs, the Main Plaza preserved its importance and sacred character.

The scale of civic public spaces in early Mesoamerican cities was immense by European standards. In 1300 CE, Teotihuacán had 100,000 people living in a twenty-square-kilometer city laid out in a grid plan with a large ceremonial plaza at its center. Tenochtitlan had over 250,000 inhabitants by 1500 CE with many public institutions including an elaborate network of public spaces, markets, and elite ritual centers.[34] Hernán Cortés's letters described great Aztec cities built on urban planning principles with vibrant central spaces that were not found in Europe at that time.[35] The archaeological evidence of indigenous ingenuity and architectural skill in the building of Mexico City corrects the historiography of this period and reassesses the impact of the "Spanish conquest" on the urban environment.[36]

But even much smaller lowland Amazon and Mayan settlements were characterized by permanent communities organized around plazas that functioned as centers of politics and ritual practices.[37] Each chief had his own demarcated space where competitions among ruling chiefs were held. Some of these spaces were ball courts, surrounded by structures and stone markers, and date back much earlier to 1000–1100 CE, long before the Spanish American plaza was established.

During my 2018 visit to the Taino ball courts at Parque Ceremonial Caguana in Puerto Rico, I am struck by how these open spaces surrounded by stone markers resemble larger-scale monumental Aztec and Mayan plazas. I imagine Taino chiefs in their regalia discussing politics and conducting religious ceremonies sitting on the rough-cut grass.

The Latin American plaza evolved from these Aztec, Mayan, and Taino spaces. When laying out colonial cities, the Spanish engineers built directly on top of indigenous plazas, a process called superposition.[38] Thus, the plaza is not European or Spanish, but syncretic, based on these indigenous precursors.

The contemporary Zocálo in Mexico City remains a contested terrain of architectural and political representation with the Aztec Templo Mayor and the Spanish colonial cathedral competing for space in the city's symbolic center. The archaeological restoration of the Templo Mayor destabilized the surrounding colonial structures resulting in a political battle over which landscape—the Spanish colonial or the Aztec—would be protected. Colonial and Aztec struggles of the past become part of the present through these fragments of prehistory in a civic public space. The plaza retains spatial, architectural, and symbolic elements from diverse cultural traditions with the tensions and meanings of conquest and resistance encoded in its built form and spatial location.

Reflecting on the prehistory of public space and exploring its earliest precursors highlights how important these places are and have been for everyday activities and relationships as well as for governance and community identity. Ideas about public spaces as well as their

Figure 2.5 Visiting Parque Ceremonial Caguana, Puerto Rico (Photograph by Joel Lefkowitz)

urban design, architectural forms, and categories of use were transmitted through contact, colonialization, and modernization in count-
less ways, finding fertile soil in many locations and cultures. There is
much that can be learned from the way that societies build, adapt, and
reuse public space not just in the present moment, but by studying the
prehistory and deeper meanings of its origins.

3

What If Jones Beach Was Not Public?

Social Justice and Belonging on Long Island, New York

The relationship between public space and democracy has a long history in Western thought dating back to the earliest discussions of political questions.[1] The agora in ancient Athens as a place of assembly for those empowered to speak has become metaphor for this relationship notwithstanding its gender, race, and class exclusionary practices. The association of public space and social justice has a shorter history based on claims to be visible and heard and demands to be recognized and politically represented. Public parks and plazas reflect this association and often contain the reformist strategies of progressive city planners and designers.[2] Contemporary histories and research studies emphasize the role that public space plays in struggles for social justice and how they have become iconic of protest and resistance.[3]

Robert Moses, the Long Island State Park commissioner, urban planner, and builder of hundreds of miles of parkland and highway including Jones Beach, had a restricted view of a deserving public. While he imagined public facilities designed in a manner that everyone would appreciate, his "public" consisted of middle-class families with automobiles who would use the generous parking lots and walk-through flower gardens to enjoy the day. His biographer Robert Caro[4] comments that "Moses did not want poor people, particularly poor people of color to use Jones Beach, so they had legislation passed forbidding the use of buses on parkways."[5] But Moses knew that legislation could be changed, so he ordered his engineers to build the Southern State Parkway's bridges extra-low, to prevent public buses from accessing the beach.[6]

Whether this is an urban myth or an intentional intervention by Moses, we will never know; however, the irony is that today Jones Beach is a place of diversity where people of feel included and recognized. Moses did not foresee the post–World War II boom that lifted working-class wages so that by 1955, 87 percent of families had some type of motor vehicle, and by 1980, 88 percent of families owned cars. New public transportation routes from the Long Island Rail Road to Jones Beach soon bypassed the Southern State Parkway and its restrictive infrastructure.

At Jones Beach, access, cultural representation, recognition of differences, and an ethic of care create a socially just public space. It illustrates how social contact can develop into a public culture of acceptance and tolerance by finding one's own place and a sense of belonging and sharing with others. The sunshine; expansive vistas; sparkling water; breaking waves; soft, sandy beaches; and co-mingling of people of coalesce into a joyful and respectful atmosphere enhancing the visitors' experience. This story offers a framework for understanding the behaviors, activities, and underlying principles that produce this outcome. It suggests ways that a social justice framework can be used to understand the impact of public space on democratic practices.

★ ★ ★

Growing up in Los Angeles the beach is never far away. A bus ride along Santa Monica Boulevard and a long walk down the steep escarpment brings you to the Pacific Coast Highway and a crescent of white sand beaches with crashing waves. Beaches are free except for parking, an expansive public space and natural resource. Every weekend and during summer vacations my friends and I sit on terrycloth beach towels, slathered with baby oil, and like Sandra Dee in the "Gidget" movies watch surfers riding the waves. When I move to Philadelphia, the open skies and white sand of the Jersey Shore are reminiscent of the pleasure of those days.

My first visit to Jones Beach on Long Island is with a cousin who lives in Roslyn Heights, Nassau County. The scale and beauty of the beach with thousands picnicking, strolling, sunbathing, or playing in the waves immediately attracts me to this magical place. Returning years later, on a harsh winter day braced against the wind and blowing sand, I join other intrepid visitors bundled up and walking while sipping coffee. Joel reminisces about going to a rock concert during college and being impressed with the grand architecture of the bath houses and theater. When the Public Space Research Group is asked to take on a cultural user study of Jones Beach, I am interested in learning more.

Jones Beach is one of New York's most popular state parks. Located on a barrier island off the southern shore of Nassau County, the park's picturesque bays and white dunes make it seem remote and pristine, even though between six and eight million people visit each year. Three state parkways as well as train and bus connections provide easy access for visitors coming from New York City only thirty miles away. A well-developed highway system allows for others to arrive from Suffolk County farther east on Long Island, New York, and even New Jersey. Jones Beach seems like a place where nature is largely left on its own, but the park is thoroughly integrated into the metropolitan area. It is a primary recreational destination and public space that plays a central role in the summer lives of visitors and locals.

The park is a vast expanse of 15.68 square miles with 6.5 miles of sand beach facing the Atlantic Ocean. It contains 2 miles of boardwalk, several bay beaches, and acres of open lands with salt marshes, natural pools, and dunes dotted by beach grass and bayberry shrubs. Diamondback terrapins, ospreys, and the endangered piping plover inhabit the park, as well as cottontail rabbits, white-tailed deer, bluefish, and striped sea bass among other wildlife, and of course, the ubiquitous seagulls.

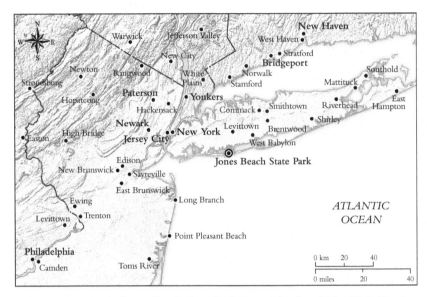

Map 3.1 Location of Jones Beach State Park, Long Island, and New York Region

Suzanne Scheld, Dana Taplin, and I meet Sue Giuliani, the park manager, on a thaw spring day. The sky is overcast and gray, though some visitors walk the boardwalk, and a few sitting on the beach wait for the sun to burn off the morning fog. Sue summarizes her concerns: *We don't have much interaction with the nearby towns or regular community people, so it is hard to get locals involved. Worse, there are budget cuts. We've lost a lot of staff and had to close the East Bathhouse, but we have been able to keep the West Bathhouse open. It's hard to sand, varnish, and paint the wood railings along the boardwalk every year.*

She wants to encourage staff and visitors to take on more responsibility to care for the park. But to improve park services and decide where to put their limited resources, she needs to know more about who visits, what they do, and what aspects of their experience are culturally and personally meaningful. We suggest a quantitative user survey and an ethnographic study to answer these questions and begin the project the summer of 2012.[7]

★ ★ ★

Figure 3.1 West Bathhouse at Jones Beach, Long Island (Photograph by Claire Panetta)

Entering the park from the Wantagh Parkway, Dana points out the historic 231-foot brick and limestone water tower built in 1930 and restored in 2008. Dana is an environmental psychologist, history expert, and urban planner fascinated by the historic preservation of public landscapes. Intrigued by the complicated history and conflictual politics of Jones Beach, he dug into local archives and microfiche newspaper clippings to learn if the past contributes to present challenges. As we walk the park for the first time, he explains that "*the tower is the main landmark and symbol of the park because it's so tall that it's visible from miles away.*" It marks the entrance to the winding walkways that bring you from the open parking fields through tunnels and colorful gardens into the park's central mall.

In the 1920s Moses consolidated existing wetlands, dredging sand from the bottom of the ocean, and stabilizing it with beach grass to form sand dunes to protect the beach. The extensive project continued

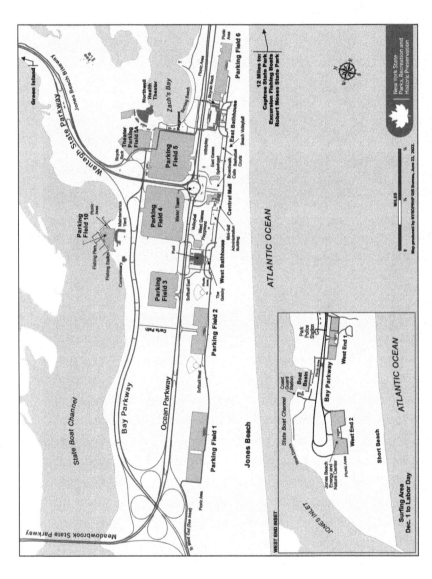

Map 3.2 Jones Beach State Park Core Area (New York State Parks, Recreation, and Historic Preservation)

throughout the mid-1920s and opened in 1929. "*Look at the architec-tural details he used to create a modern middle-class destination,*" Dana adds. "*Moses wanted Jones Beach to be a model of what a public recreational en-vironment could be.*"

As we pass the stately but worn-looking East Bathhouse still closed in 2012, Dana recounts how Moses constructed two large swim-ming and diving pools, ornate bathhouses with changing rooms and showers, a large amphitheater, a grand dining hall, and archery field. He even built an Indian Village that was popular from 1930 to 1950 with a Lakota tipi and indigenous storytellers for children. Whereas the area had been swampy and empty in the 1920s, by the 1930s the parking lots, beach, and boardwalk at Jones Beach were often filled with visitors from the city and other parts of Long Island.

The park expanded in the post-World War II era to include more facilities and enjoyed high visitation until the 1980s. Visitation and budgets declined, and many of the facilities popular in its heyday were closed or lost to high tides, storms, and hurricanes. Others were remodeled such as the original amphitheater and the Jones Beach Theater renamed the Nikon Theater and restored as a state-of-the-art performance center. Some concessions were renovated, but the res-taurant, The Boardwalk, burned down, and the vacant lot awaited de-velopment. Friendly's Ice Cream shop, occupying half of the original main dining room at the West Bathhouse, was the hot spot during the summer, but was closed by the end of our study.

"*I think the part of the design that is most impressive is its striking art-deco and nautical style,*" Dana comments as we walk past the West Bathhouse. "*The art-deco details reflect technology and engineering, romanticizing modern inventions such as airplanes and ocean liners. It was meant to project Moses's image as the master engineer of the city and a modern trend setter.*" The buildings and tunnels constructed by his young architect, Herbert Magoon, feature smooth curves, angles, and streamlined shapes. Moses designed the boardwalk to look like the deck of an ocean liner, com-plete with ship funnels that double as trash receptacles. A ship anchor and mast with nautical flags still adorn the central mall. Dana laughs

Figure 3.2 Boardwalk and Railing at Jones Beach, Long Island (Photograph by Claire Panetta)

as he recounts that the park staff no longer must wear outfits that resemble the uniforms of captains and sailors that were popular in the 1930s, but nautical symbols are still visible although not prominently displayed.

While Jones Beach has a growing national image through the celebrity of the national air show—attracting nearly a half-million people in 2015—it has been difficult to create a local support organization because of the park's location. Limited funds for modernizing and antiquated technology challenge park managers to find ways to publicize events and activities. But there is an active Jones Beach Club on Facebook with 5,898 members in 2018 (and 22,300 in 2022) who post photographs and comments about their recent visits and memories. This club adds to the sense of community especially among regulars.[8]

★ ★ ★

Different kinds of groups—couples, families, individuals—of various ages, abilities, and cultures wander down the boardwalk. Young adults are heading to the beach while older people are leaving. A pair of men speaking Mandarin cross my path as they wheel a large BBQ toward the concession area. An African American man comes by in a high-tech-looking wheelchair with a crew of men behind him. He runs training sessions for this group of veterans who frequent the beach. A few others are exercising too—among them a trio of young girls speaking Spanish running slowly, breathless as they try to speak. People are chatting at the picnic tables in many different languages—a few of which I can't identify, but it doesn't seem noisy or crowded.[9]

Two years of ethnographic research at Jones Beach reveals a complex story of how diverse individuals and groups of users construct a place where most feel accepted and cared about. It is a testimony to how public space contributes to a sense of belonging not just to Long Island locals and beach regulars, but to people who describe themselves as "city folks," including first-generation immigrants and second-generation Americans from the largest urban center in the United States.

Based on our user survey, many groups benefit from its recreational and educational resources.[10] There is even distribution of gender identities in most sections of the park, although Zach's Bay is more popular with women and children, and men outnumber women in the more secluded eastern beaches. Nearly half of the respondents come with their families and relatives, while another quarter come with friends. The majority come several times a month, while others visit several times a week. Only a few are visiting for the first time.

Most visitors relax on the beach or swim in the ocean, though some prefer to hang out on the boardwalk. Others use the mini-golf course, swimming pool, or basketball courts. Some families avoid the ocean, spending their time at locations such as Zach's Bay, where it is easier to supervise small children in the calm water and enjoy the playground with slides and swings. Or they drive to the boat basin to meet up with friends who arrive aboard their boats and set folding tables, portable chairs, hibachi grills, radios, and umbrellas on the dock. A few spend their time in Field 10, where avid fishermen cast lines off the pier, and where nature lovers search for crabs in the tidal pools.

Figure 3.3 The Beach at Jones Beach, Long Island (Photograph by Claire Panetta)

Over two-thirds of the people we spoke to have been coming to Jones Beach for over ten years. They recall family events and parenting experiences such as birthdays and other celebrations or talk about "good times," socializing, meeting friends, and celebrating holidays such as the Fourth of July. A woman from El Salvador who has been visiting for over twenty years observes, *"You're out on the beach with strangers, but once the fireworks start, everyone becomes friends."*

Visitors recall ordinary moments such as playing in the sand, being surprised to see a grandparent do a handstand in the ocean, or just being with family evoking emotional resonance. As a young woman from Roslyn Heights put it, *"Jones Beach has special meaning to me because it makes me think of my childhood, just going with my family as a child and swimming, all of us being together. It makes me feel like a little kid again."*

Jones Beach is a familiar place, part of a summer routine, and some claim it as their own. A retired female doctor who has been going to

Figure 3.4 Swimming Pool at Jones Beach, Long Island (Photograph by Claire Panetta)

the beach for years says: "*I like this park because you can have your own spot. What's not to like about the beach? It's nice. It's quiet. It's our beach, even though it gets taken over on the weekends. I think of Jones Beach as my 'Hideaway Beach.'*"

Most visitors perceive the park as a place where everyone gets along and say that park visitors are open and tolerant and that they do not have conflicts with one another. Yet a few admit there are differences that can result in confrontations. A sixty-five-year-old woman who we interviewed in Spanish at Zach's Bay explains, "*The children all interact with one another here. They share things, their sand toys. It is very good. In the other parts of the park, it is not the same. There is not as much interaction with others. People don't share.*"

Most visitors feel quite strongly that the park should remain public. They consider natural environments part of the public realm accessible to everyone. A long-term visitor to Field 6 exclaims, "*I think everything about this park should be public.*" Pointing to the ocean, he says, "*Look at this! This doesn't belong to anybody.*" A woman interviewed in Arabic while picnicking at the pier in Field 10 says, "*People are now more aware of the environment, even more than before. This should remain public because everyone has their right to nature. If you make it private you exclude groups, and this is a summer resource for all people to enjoy.*"

A fear of losing access to beaches due to privatization or residential restrictions is an issue for some. A middle-aged man sitting on the boardwalk contrasted Jones Beach with Connecticut beaches: "*They have big fights over the beaches in Connecticut because they are town beaches. A lot of people live close to the beach but cannot go to it.*" A resident of Westchester County, New York, explains she drives an hour and a half to arrive at Jones Beach when she lives only ten minutes from a town beach where she is not permitted to go.

A young man from Suffolk County feels locked out of beaches on the eastern end of Long Island due to town restrictions.[11] He drives to Jones Beach from eastern Long Island to a beach whose beauty is on par with the Hamptons. Similarly, a young man from Jamaica, Queens, worries, "*If the beach is privatized, then maybe we can't go . . . if I didn't live in a beach zone, maybe I wouldn't be able to go to the beach at all.*" A regular beachgoer from nearby Seaford, Long Island, adds, "*Forget about privatization—stay out of my backyard! This is the only beach that we have. If it is privatized, then only the highfalutin will have it.*"

★ ★ ★

Social inclusion, representation, recognition of differences, an ethic of care, and the ability to safely express conflict and contestation are important factors in the transformation of this middle-class landscape into a place where most people feel welcome. Talking to visitors, hanging out at the beach, sitting on the boardwalk, playing catch at Zach's Bay, or fishing at the pier, I start to appreciate how a public culture of social equality and mutual understanding evolves. People go out of their way to explain how their daily social interactions and interpersonal communications contribute to their place-making and community-building experiences.

For example, social inclusion and sense of belonging develop in different ways. Some create a "home away from home" by bringing portable cookout equipment, chairs, blankets, pillows, games, and a tent for families and friends to spend the day. Three women from Flushing, Queens, replicate their kitchens by heating up home-cooked food in aluminum trays on a nearby barbeque while they sit around a picnic table playing mah-jongg with bright green tiles. They chat and laugh in Mandarin. When we ask why everyone was laughing, one of them points to a bucket brimming over with crabs that they had collected.[12] Their spouses, in contrast, had not caught much of anything and the women were enjoying having turned the tables on their husbands.

A middle-aged man who grew up in El Salvador articulates his sense of belonging even as a newcomer to the United States: "*The first time I visited the park with my wife I finally felt like I belonged to this country. We played in the ocean with hundreds of other folks. Somehow this made me feel special. That is a special memory for me. Now walking the boardwalk with my wife is a special tradition.*"

A thirty-eight-year-old resident of Baychester in the Bronx reiterates this sentiment by observing, "*At Jones Beach there is a friendly crowd. People are out with family and friends. It's a diverse place. I feel welcome here. Just look at this place. This is America!*" His equation of diversity with America is reiterated by many including newcomers and longtime visitors as well as tourists and Long Island residents.

Thus, an important way that this public space encourages social inclusion is by providing a place for individuals and their friends and family to relax and be "at home," and at the same time enabling newcomers to feel that they too belong as part of a diverse America.

Jones Beach implicitly communicates who is welcome and invited to participate through activities, rules and regulations, signage, and physical design. Visitors are particularly sensitive to who is visible, the quality of social interactions, and how they are treated by others. They consider whether the activities are appropriate for their personal or family needs, whether the rules are too restrictive or lenient, and whether they can expect to feel comfortable. Special requirements and a "design for all" environment that accommodates children, seniors, and those with disabilities or special needs is critical to attracting and supporting many users. The smooth boardwalk and ramps for wheelchair access attract differently-abled veterans' groups, while older adults appreciate the frequent benches along the walkways.

An older couple perceive a change in the population of visitors over the past forty years. They remember when it was mostly "elites" who came to the park. "*They were extremely harsh with the rules also—you could get a ticket for spitting. This changed with public transportation, and it is now a place anybody can come.*" The wife contrasts Jones Beach with private beaches where only residents are allowed and finds the people here to be very friendly. "*There is a camaraderie among people here . . . people help each other.*" She feels welcome because she sees people like herself and feels "*everybody is watched over . . . everything is under control and quiet.*"

Representation and safety also draw LGBTQ visitors to the far eastern beaches where fewer people, nude sunbathing, and same-gender couples create a tranquil environment. While ticketing for nudity is remarked upon by one interviewee, it is infrequent, and the beach has a long history of welcoming the LGBTQ community. Maintaining a safe space with enough privacy and respect for its mostly male users requires a different kind of public culture with specific norms of behavior and forms of social interaction that are contested even within the group itself.

Even on a busy day, I counted eighty-five men and only two women. One man offered his history of the beach as being "born out of necessity forty years ago, but only on Mondays. For a long time, it was only on Mondays . . . Do you know why? Because Monday is the day that hair salons across the city are closed. We can thank gay male hairdressers for creating this space. Can you imagine what kind of courage it took to do that?"

Even on a crowded day in the middle of summer the distance between beach users is striking in comparison to other areas of Jones Beach, where people think nothing of setting down blankets and beach chairs just a few feet from each other.

As one interviewee told me, "People here respect the 50-foot rule," giving each other more space for privacy.

Many of the men at Jones Beach want to maintain their separateness and safety. They talk about the continuing "territorial invasion" that infringes on their need for solitude, personal safety, sexual and romantic freedom, and a quiet place to experience nature. This stretch of beach is considered by some users to be a mecca of visibility and inclusion, yet many appreciate Jones Beach as a haven where, for a brief time, they can shield themselves from the demands of heteronormativity and its accompanying sanctions.

When asked about how the beach might be improved, someone in every group suggested adding trash cans, bathrooms, or lifeguards. One man said, "I deserve to swim safely too. The rest of the beach has lifeguards for the people who want to swim. Should I risk drowning because I'm gay?" Another added. "Why should I have to carry my trash two miles to the car?" And a third older man complained: "Just today I went to pee over by the dunes . . . But why should I have to . . . The other people have bathrooms. I think we should too."

But some users worried that these additions would impact the solitude, privacy, and safety they value: "Bring lifeguards and bathrooms here and see what happens. This sacred place that we love will stop being ours. Do you really think that all those people, all those families with kids . . . won't start showing up? This place is special because we don't have those crowds."[13]

Other "regulars" establish activity-based groups at specific locations. The pier attracts those interested in fishing and creates such a strong community that many maintain their relationships throughout the year, cooking and socializing at each others' homes. Older adults who sit at tables along the boardwalk singing encourage others to join in while those playing cards or chess appeal to those who want to play or just *kibbitz*. Couples and families speaking Spanish while grilling *empanadas* and other Latin American specialties invite passersby to join the festivities, offering food and drink to people who stop. Subtle forms of welcome through similarity of interests encourage strangers to interact with one another.

The perception that a person or group is represented in the public space—whether based on interests, activities, kinship, language, age, or any other kind of similarity—is critical to visitors feeling welcome and comfortable. The design of the environment—playgrounds for children, chess tables and comfortable benches for older adults, and

level walkways from the parking lots and smooth surfaces that extend out onto the beach for people in wheelchairs or caretakers with
baby strollers signal representation through features that accommodate their needs. Historical markers and signs honor and represent a
diversity of people with different pasts such as the Lakota Village. But
the most important aspect of representation is that there are people
who look familiar, act in familiar ways, or share similar interests, backgrounds, or activities. This is one of the often unrecognized contributions of a public space like Jones Beach, where there are so many
kinds of people, environments to experience, and things to do that
most people find a place for themselves and thus feel represented and
welcome.

It is not just that people are represented, but that they feel recognized and respected regardless of their values and preferences. This
kind of recognition is expressed by a twenty-eight-year-old man originally from Kingston, Jamaica, who opines that "*everyone should have
a chance to come to this beach. There are a lot of families here, it's pretty lively
and everyone gets along. That's what New Yorkers are—tolerant and they recognize that we are all different.*"

A group of young men who had recently moved from Southeast
Asia to Valley Stream in Nassau County agree that there is respect for
everyone at the park. One member of the group observes that "*there
are more 'brown' people playing ball and hanging out. It's getting more animated . . . People do not look at you just because of your color.*"

A fifty-two-year-old woman from Honduras sitting under a tent
for shade surrounded by her large family tells us that she thinks that
"*public space is a place where everyone is included*" and insists that recognition includes "*color and race*" and not just class and age differences. On
the other hand, a local woman from a nearby Long Island town says
she is concerned about the "*takeover of the park by city folk.*" But most
interviewees feel comfortable partly because people tend to respect
one another.

Families have been coming to Jones Beach for generations and become involved in caring for the environment as well as each other.

When I ask about the meaning of the park, they mention "*people helping each other.*" Over time some are emotionally as well as socially attached to specific areas. As an older woman from Long Island explains, "*We don't go to other places because when we go to a place that we like, we just keep going there. We say, 'this is my area to take care of.'*" She adds that once she arrives at "her" area she does not want to leave so if she forgets things like matches or charcoal, she borrows from other people.

One young man explains, "*When you are walking in the park you feel you're walking in something great and want to take care of it.*" People talk about picking up trash left by others; aiding families with small children with their strollers; lending each other firewood, matches, newspaper, and even suntan lotion; and signing up to work on park projects such as planting dune grass, and repairing and cleaning the bathroom areas. Of course, not everyone is involved in such intimate caring for the park and others, but those who do promote an ambiance of goodwill and stewardship that permeates the place.

And yet even though social justice qualities attract people and promote contact and communication, it does not mean that everything is 100 percent harmonious. Struggling constructively over differences—whether about rights, politics, or appropriate behavior—is also crucial. If it is not possible to handle conflict and provide a forum for disagreement, then other aspects of social justice and democratic practice erode over time, and places are vulnerable to becoming extremely homogeneous or even abandoned.

One way conflict is handled is through maintaining boundaries of other visitors' private space. As a woman from Port Washington suggests, "*You need to respect others' personal space, and sometimes there is a conflict about it.*" A man who did not want the obligation of being "on" and "fitting in" walks to the far end of the beach to relax: "*I always come here to get away from people. The further east you go, the more peace you have . . . Nobody bothers you if you don't want to be bothered.*"

Conflicts emerge on environmental issues, especially after major storms such as Hurricane Sandy, around decisions to replenish the sand by dredging or to build hard barriers to fortify the beach. Large-scale protests were mounted against the building of an offshore wind farm in 2019 and for increasing salaries for the lifeguards in 2010. There are highly vocal conflicts between "bird people" and "cat people" over how to deal with the increasing number of feral cats and disagreements over the use of jet skis, loud music, and bathrooms.

While not a central site for demonstrations and social action, many visitors see themselves as activists. They bring their own garbage bags and spend time picking up trash strewn across the beach. One "trash activist" considers it a community protest when they pile their bags together for the park staff to pick up. The pile symbolizes their efforts to protect the natural environment and their dislike of those who do not pick up on their own.

Jones Beach still retains traces of an aspirational middle-class past through its aesthetic motifs of mass modernity, technology, transportation symbolism, and grand architectural iconography. Nevertheless, the current environment has been re-scripted as a place for everyone, where people help each other and enjoy being together, sharing, when necessary, with a minimum of conflict and irritation. That is not to say that there is no conflict or contestation—indeed, a critical part of the condition of social justice is the ability to contest unjust situations and circumstances. But the tensions of cooperation and conflict, privacy and sociality, friendship and avoidance are accommodated and protected.

★ ★ ★

Jones Beach plays an important role in representing and recognizing visitors as "citizens," regardless of their immigration or legal status. It offers them the opportunity to feel they are a part of an imagined "America" or "New York" where their voice and presence matter. This sense of belonging is a critical component of democracy and public space, a cornerstone of its foundation.

Democratic societies are those that allow for the potential of politics and resolution of dissent and inequality.[14] Public space is often the material location of these political activities and "public" only when people have the right to engage in protest, conflict, and contestation.[15] Often it is the visibility of a problem that motivates a public to action, and without places where problems can be seen and expressed, politics can become impoverished.[16] Historically they have been the physical sites of democratic performance where the right to assembly is guaranteed or demanded and where the physical occupation of space takes on political meaning.[17]

Urban civic spaces such as Tahrir Square, Cairo; Tiananmen Square, Beijing; Wenceslas Square, Prague; Azadi Square, Tehran; Place de la Bastille, Paris; Plaza de las Tres Culturas, Mexico City; Decembrists' Square, St. Petersburg; Trafalgar Square, London; Syntagma Square, Athens and Red Square, Moscow, have been centers of revolution and protest around the globe. Over the past few years there have been protests in Liberation Square in Baghdad, Iraq, over high unemployment, poor basic services, and state corruption. In Hong Kong, students fought for a more democratic government on the streets and in the university. On Plaza Murillo in La Paz, Bolivian citizens united to remove President Morales, who unfairly claimed the last election, while workers demanded fair wages and lower transportation fares in Santiago, Chile, on the Plaza des Armas. Not all pro-democracy protests have occurred in public spaces though; the Occupy Wall Street Movement took over privately owned Zuccotti Park in Manhattan, rendering it "public" during its occupation.

The relationship of civic public space and democratic practices stems from a long history of the association of politics with ceremonial centers—whether marked by religious institutions such as a cathedral or indigenous temple on a plaza, a military installation on a plaza de armas or parade grounds, a courthouse or town hall on a civic square, or a marketplace on the main square. Even with growing concern over the shrinking of collective action and a reciprocal expansion of the personal sphere, protests and demonstrations continue to take place in the symbolic heart of the city.[18]

A Social Justice and Public Space
Evaluation Framework

Because social justice is crucial to a flourishing society, it is important
to know how to evaluate it in existing public spaces. It is difficult
to enhance a social condition—or any phenomenon—without first
defining and assessing it. Public space advocates at UN Habitat employ
"equity indicators" that are measured at the city scale.[19] Ethnographic
research though suggests that it is equally if not more important to
consider people's perceptions and experiences of justice to promote
belonging, and inclusion.

Several urban design models evaluate the publicness and quality
of a public space.[20] These models measure the type of ownership,
degree of control and freedom, inclusiveness, comfort, engagement,
and safety that figure into the overall success of downtown areas. An
evaluation of California state parks finds that good access and distribution of parks including culturally appropriate programming and
facilities as well as removing psychological, cultural, and economic
barriers such as fees, restrictive signage, poor park maintenance, and
safety encourages park use.[21] These studies and models resonate with
the findings from Jones Beach.

Other scholars argue that a "just city" should be the criterion for
allocating urban space and propose a planning theory based on distributive justice to produce a better city for all citizens within a capitalist economy.[22] To achieve social justice ends would require 1) the
redistribution of space and services to address inequalities of wealth,
2) recognition of identities that are systematically devalued, and 3)
opportunities for people to break free of fixed identities through encounters with diverse people and practices.[23] The idea of providing
"spatial justice" in a city has an even broader meaning that includes
freedom, liberty, equality, democracy, and civil rights.[24]

Asking people what is important and meaningful to their experience of social justice captures other aspects of its complexity. Listening

to visitors talk about Jones Beach certainly includes elements of distributive justice, that is, whether there is enough room for everyone and their activities. But they express concern about much more.

Organizational justice concepts capture the breadth of experiences and outcomes observed in public space. Developed to appraise businesses and corporations, they predict the quality of social relations and a sense of fairness in the workplace.[25] A meta-analysis of 413 organizational justice studies found that four kinds of justice—distributional, procedural, interactional, and informational—are crucial to promoting trust, helping behavior, courtesy, and positive affect within complex social organizations and public institutions.[26] The types of justice are defined as:

1) **distributive justice or fairness** as it pertains to the equity of outcomes
2) **procedural justice or fairness** as it pertains to decision-making processes
3) **interactional justice** as it pertains to the quality of interpersonal and intergroup interactions
4) **informational justice** as it pertains to the adequacy of explanations given in terms of timeliness, specificity, and truthfulness

From the ethnography of Jones Beach and other parks and plazas, there is evidence that two additional kinds of justice, **representational** and an **ethic of care**, are also significant. Integrating these different kinds of justice into a unified framework offers a normative stance on what constitutes a "good" public space that can be employed at both a site-specific and a city-wide scale.

A researcher, designer, community member, or activist can draw upon these justice principles to design, plan, evaluate, and/or improve a public space. Each identifies a relevant and quantifiable indicator of equity and inclusion. Distributive justice is determined through ease of access, physically and financially. Procedural justice is dependent on the processing of justice claims and operationalized as the degree to which people can influence the use of the park in substantial ways. People's experience of welcome and social inclusion or exclusion is an indicator of interactional justice, although indicators of the quality of social interaction experienced also can provide a robust assessment. Informational justice can be gauged by the signage and whether there is adequate information about the location of activities and/or the rules and procedures for park use in multiple languages and communication modalities. Representational justice can be assessed in many ways, including whether people recognize themselves in the interests portrayed, available activities, or histories that exist within the specific public space. Questions about whether people feel encouraged to care for others or the environment can be used to assess whether an ethic of care exists.

This social justice framework provided evaluative criteria for the design of a large multi-functional park in Panama City. The planning process focused on how different design choices, programming strategies, signage types, and landscaping and management decisions might impact people's sense of inclusion. The six kinds of justice structured a set of questions discussed among community members, local leaders, students, designers and urban planners, and social workers from the surrounding neighborhoods. The questions guided a week-long process of community participation that enabled stakeholders to decide whether the proposed park plan would promote social justice on issues that were important to them and their future. Instead of relying on general proscriptions unrelated to community needs and desires, it helped to articulate what might work for everyone in this northern suburb.

Public space activists are already implementing aspects of the framework. The University City District in Philadelphia developed a "just spaces" tool employing mobile technology and a software application to evaluate and improve public spaces.[27] Urban planners, landscape architects, and policymakers in cities across the United States applied three of the dimensions (distributional, procedural, and interactional justice) to enhance environmental justice outcomes with positive

Figure 3.5 Social Justice and Public Space Evaluation Framework (Graphic by Erin Lilli)

results.[28] Utilizing the framework to resolve the ongoing conflicts in Tompkins Square Park suggests ways to improve social relations and reduce fearfulness as discussed in Chapter 10.

Jones Beach exemplifies the positive ways that public space makes a difference in everyday democratic practices. Visitors accommodate each other's needs, welcome strangers, and share activities, while respecting others' privacy and need for personal space. At this New York State site, publicness is legally mandated, and management committed to making it a place for all. The staff do their best to accommodate difference even with limited resources.

There are beaches, however, that instead of being open to a wide public are organized to serve the needs of only town residents. They are limited by expensive parking passes ($500 in 2022 for East Hampton

Village), police surveillance, and rigid rules of conduct as well as constant surveillance by other users to enforce a village- or town-only mentality. While public in the sense of being owned by the township and governed by an elected board, the regulations are exclusionary, as Jones Beach visitors pointed out. There are de facto private beach clubs that prohibit non-member use through gated parking areas and security guards, like Gurney's Inn, a resort on the ocean at the tip of Long Island that bans access to the beach to anyone but their guests.

Other forms of restrictions, specifically in East Hampton, include the transformation of an eighty-year-old LGBTQ beach where nude sunbathing and same-sex couple romance safely occurred, into a heteronormative family-friendly place that inhibits these activities. Local fishermen who traditionally drove their trucks onto Napeague beach to catch striped bass and "blues" find the vehicle entrance blocked because beachfront condominium owners won legal control of beach access to stop this practice. A popular public pond used for crabbing and clamming was closed when wealthy neighbors decided to lower the water level because it caused flooding in their basements.[29]

By comparison, Jones Beach is an ideal public beach, one to be emulated and protected. All public spaces have the potential to contribute to social justice and a sense of belonging, but cannot fulfill their promise especially when designed or governed solely for a limited and exclusive public.

4

Rebuilding a Bridge and a Community

Health and Resilience at Walkway Over the Hudson, Poughkeepsie, New York

❝ *Look at the light and river reflecting the yellow and red trees and robin's-egg-blue sky,"* exclaims Suzanne as our commuter train takes a turn along the Hudson Valley. *"It reminds me of nineteenth-century landscape paintings. The river bordered by hills ablaze with fall foliage and small farms dotting the green and brown pasture."*

My colleague Suzanne Scheld arrived from Southern California to participate in a collaborative study of Walkway Over the Hudson State Historic Park, a new addition to the New York State Parks and Recreation system. The Open State Institute, a state-park advocacy group,[1] wanted to learn if this linear public space built in 2009 is successful and why.[2] An anthropologist at the California State University at Northridge, Suzanne specializes in the study of beaches and public markets in Dakar, Senegal, and on community-based museums in the San Fernando Valley.

"I think we might find it's less idyllic than you're imagining," I reply. *"Poughkeepsie and Highland suffer from a lack of investment since many old factories closed and the reduction in the workforce at the IBM campus in 2008.*[3]

Looking out the scratched Metro-North train window, the Hudson River winds its way through a popular farming and recreation area. We head 75 miles north of New York City to spend a few weeks doing fieldwork in Poughkeepsie, home of elite Vassar College. Featuring both town-and-gown tensions and a large IBM plant, Poughkeepsie is known for its high violent crime rate, deteriorating industrial base, unemployment, and failed attempts at urban renewal.[4] The small city of 32,736 has a diverse population, a median income of $29,389 for families, $31,956 for single males, and $25,711 for single females. Twenty-two percent of the residents live below the poverty line, and socioeconomic disparities lead to occasional flare-ups.[5]

"*Can public space actually make a difference here, where there are such serious economic problems to deal with?*" I ask looking at Suzanne. "*Is it really possible that one park can change the health and well-being of an entire community?*" "*We'll find out soon,*" Suzanne replies as we arrive at the station.

Descending from the train, we enter the restored brick and iron-work station and walk out to the street. A man brushes Suzanne so hard she quickly moves out of the way of the crowd that melts into the twilight. Except for the flurry of commuters walking to parked cars and a college student jogging by, the street is quiet with few stores still open and no restaurants in sight.

"*I feel so at home and even nostalgic when I see these historic buildings,*" Suzanne comments. "*It reminds me of other New York towns built at the turn of the last century when the New York Central Railroad provided transportation up, down and across the Hudson. It reminds me of the towns where I grew up on Long Island.*"

I, on the other hand, am struck by the silence, sense of decline, and lack of activity in the downtown, expecting to find places to have dinner and shops to explore. There are so few taxis I worry that we will have trouble getting to where we booked a room for the night. But we want to see Walkway and then stroll around to get a feel for the place.

At first, we do not see it though it is hard to miss. Rising 212 feet above the Hudson, it is 1.28 miles long, making it the longest elevated footbridge in the world. The reconstructed bridge that originally opened in 1889 as the Poughkeepsie-Highland Railroad Bridge now towers above us, etched across the sky in the waning sunlight.

From the train station it is a steep uphill climb to reach the entrance and looks like a difficult walk so late in the day. Instead, Suzanne and I make a loop around the deserted streets and then manage to find our motel located in a shopping mall on the edge of town. We decide that further exploration will have to wait until morning and spend the evening preparing for interviewing and volunteer training.

As we discuss our research plans, Suzanne worries we might not find enough people to get an adequate sample of users.

"*We'll just have to wait and see what we find,*" I reply, disappointed with the start of our field trip. "*We will do everything we can to learn about the new park and whether it works.*"

Early next morning we arrive at Walkway in brilliant sunshine on a perfect autumn day. Our plan is to meet with a group of "Ambassadors," members of the Friends of Walkway Over the Hudson Historic Park, a nonprofit organization that supports and promotes the park. They maintain a website with a calendar of activities and events, raise money for improvements, and run an active volunteers' group of mostly retired people, some from IBM and Vassar College, but also including bike advocates and youth groups. We agree that it is best to have local volunteers take on the job of collecting the survey while we focus on training and conducting "walking interviews."

Suzanne proposes using digital tablets to enable interviewees to record their own responses as we walk with them. Visitors can type in what they see and how they feel about their experience using a text program on an Apple iPad, while at the same time taking photographs and making voice memos at different points along the route. This "walking interview" records a photographic glimpse of the bridge

from the interviewees' point of view and offers an opportunity to record their own comments and insights.[6]

The Ambassadors plan to meet us on the Highland side, across
the bridge from the Poughkeepsie entrance, so we set off to walk
it for the first time. The concrete deck is 25 feet wide and enclosed
by a 4.5-foot-high railing that provides most adults an unobstructed
view of the Hudson Valley and sufficient safety for small children.
Backless benches line the edges, especially in the center where the

Figure 4.1 Interviewee Using Mobile Phone to Record Experience, Walkway
Over the Hudson, New York

pathway widens. Along the railing, posted placards convey local history and facts about the ecology. In addition to reading the information on the placards, there are signs about accessing historical information by listening to the "Talkway" program that can be reached by cell phone.

The ample width accommodates a lively social scene and various forms and velocities of movement. On this Saturday morning the deck is filled with skateboarders zipping by and passing individuals, while couples and small groups stroll at a leisurely pace. People often stop to look over the side, take a photograph, put a small child back onto a tricycle, or clean up after a pet on a leash. Cyclists weave through the groups, sometimes calling out to walkers to warn them of their approach. A unicyclist moves back and forth smiling and waving

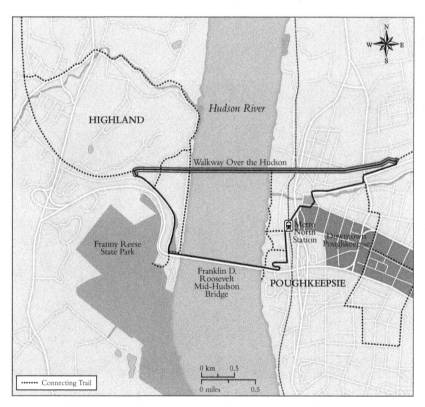

Map 4.1 Walkway Over the Hudson from Poughkeepsie to Highland, New York

to other visitors. A dog in a frilly dress sits in a baby stroller greeting on-lookers. Some visitors are dressed in comfortable clothing and footwear prepared for a long walk. Others wear party attire suggesting that their visit is part of attending another event, or that they view their visit as a special occasion.

The scene at the two entrances is active as well, with people using the concession stands, picnic tables, benches, bathrooms, and drinking water for pets. On the Poughkeepsie side there is shade where couples

Figure 4.2 Different Ways to Move Across Walkway Over the Hudson, New York

chat over cups of coffee at tables and individuals relax on benches, check guidebooks, or just sit for a moment. Larger groups hang out in the parking lot: we see a Harley Davidson motorcycle club meet up and families waiting for other members to arrive for a communal excursion.

On the Highland side, in addition to the concession stands, picnic tables, and a bathroom, the Friends of Walkway maintain the West Pavilion, a shed serving several functions. The Ambassadors meet here before heading onto the bridge. We watch visitors ask for information, borrow wheelchairs, and purchase Walkway memorabilia. The pavilion also provides a location for holding special events such as craft fairs, fundraisers, and musical performances. A community group sets up microphones to amplify their message that drowns out our attempts at conversation—and precludes interviewing.

The Ambassadors eagerly greet newcomers and talk with regular visitors, many of whom they know. They add an animated vibe to the socializing and laughter—creating a place where relationships are forged. By the time our Ambassadors appear—three men and two women of retirement age—we know they will be great at gathering survey data from Walkway users.

While Suzanne works with the Ambassadors setting up a training schedule and practice time, I venture out with an iPad to try a walking interview. It is difficult to catch people at the West Pavilion, so I walk to the midpoint of the bridge. This wider area offers several lookout areas and more benches where visitors linger, take pictures, and strike up conversations. It is a prime spot for people-watching as well as observing the boats and trains passing underneath the bridge. Some sit on the ground, without waiting for a spot on a bench, and enjoy the view.

I approach two young women, Beth and Julia, getting ready to resume their walk who agree to be interviewed. As they slowly move along photographing and recording our conversation, they talk about how important their Saturday walks are to their sense of health and well-being. Beth, who has been living in Poughkeepsie for twenty

Figure 4.3 Food Stand on the Highland Side of Walkway Over the Hudson, New York

years, tells me: "*It's great to get out of the house and away from my family. Sometimes my responsibilities are too much and so . . . It really helps me to stay on track and keeps me in touch with my friend, Julia.*" Julia adds that they walk every weekend as part of trying to lose weight and come as often as they can.

Beth points out the homes where they dream of living, close to the water with a river view. Below us are large houses with grassy yards, willow trees, and out-of-ground swimming pools backing up to the

Figure 4.4 View of Idealized Home from the Bridge, Walkway Over the Hudson, New York

river edge. They make up stories about the people who live there imagining their expensive lifestyles. Julia pretends to put a diamond collar and leash on her designer dog, while Beth giggles as she gets in her BMW. Laughing they remind each other of the beauty they share all around them. Their photographs record scenic views, including one with a tugboat chugging down the river, a restaurant with a boat dock, and a garden behind a large house with trees and a swing. At the end they ask me to take a picture of the two of them.

"It was an amazing experience," I tell Suzanne when I return to where she is working with the trainees. *"They enjoyed taking pictures and talked about what they feel and imagine as they do their weekly walk . . . I had no idea that Walkway would offer such an incentive for improving people's lives."*

★ ★ ★

With the help of the five volunteers, we collected 182 interviews that gave a sense of the range of visitors. Over half were from the two local counties of Ulster and Duchess with a quarter from Poughkeepsie alone. Fifteen percent came from other areas of New York and New Jersey and the remainder from elsewhere in the United States and other countries. The interviewees were predominately white, but included 20 percent who self-identify as African American, Asian, Native American, and Latino residents and visitors. Self-identified men outnumbered self-identified women, and the age distribution was strikingly older than other park surveys we have completed, with older adults over sixty-one making up 41 percent of the users. About half of the visitors came with family members.

When asked what they did in the park, 69 percent said they were walking. Dog walking, running, cycling, and other sports such as rollerblading made up only 27 percent of the responses, probably because it was harder for them to stop and take the questionnaire. Our participant observation fieldwork notes record that the visitors who wanted to walk or run faster maneuvered around the slower ones, snaking their way through the crowd. Half of the visitors were there for the first time, but all the rest came frequently, several times a week or month in all seasons. The majority said they looked at the scenery, watched the river and birds, took pictures, and socialized with other people.

After a couple of weeks of interviewing and observation, patterns began to emerge. Weekends were like our first encounter, with lots of local users, tourists, and crowds. During the weekdays, however, it was mostly pairs of women, older adults—both men and women—walking, and small groups of shirtless male college students jogging. Women pushing babies in strollers or pulling them in wagons moved briskly across the bridge as exercise. At lunch time, groups of men and women in work attire strolled along the deck deeply engaged in conversation. Later in the afternoon teenagers appeared on bicycles and middle-aged dog walkers came out for a stroll.

★ ★ ★

We were interested in learning more about the impact of the historic bridge renovation. If the park was successful, then creating parks based on deteriorating railway beds and bridges could enhance other communities in the region. The expensive, landscaped High Line in Manhattan became a global model for regenerating urban downtowns, but could a more modest endeavor, funded and supported by residents, rejuvenate an economically depressed small city? To answer this question, Dana Taplin joined us to complete a series of interviews with the longtime residents and local activists involved in the restoration.

When the Poughkeepsie-Highland Railroad Bridge opened in 1889, it was the longest bridge in North America, and the first to cross the Hudson between Albany and New York. "*It's phenomenal what they were able to achieve during that period*," said Mr. Melewski, a partner in the engineering firm Bergmann and Associates (who designed and supervised construction of Walkway). "*It's quite a landmark. It had a lot of firsts*."[7] The steel and iron structure facilitated the movement of raw goods from the west to industrial centers in New England. But once the interstate highway system was built, traffic on the railroad bridge declined.

Sparks from a train started a fire on the creosote-soaked wooden planks around the tracks on the then-poorly maintained bridge in 1974. Firefighters could not pump water fast enough, and it destroyed the rail bed. The owner at the time, the bankrupt Penn Central Corporation, petitioned the Interstate Commerce Commission to permanently close it.

Although trains could no longer cross, residents of Poughkeepsie and Highland never lost their emotional connection to the remaining ruins. By the mid-1980s, dirt trails to the bridge were covered by overgrown bushes, and trees from the riverbank were growing up through the remaining train tracks. Nonetheless, locals continued to visit, disregarding the danger of walking on the decrepit structure even though pieces of rail ties falling on boaters raised safety concerns.

In 1992, concerned residents formed an association to transform the bridge into a walkway and a safe place to visit. They worked tirelessly for the next fifteen years to create support and to raise funds for the reconstruction. During this time, the organization gained control over the bridge, becoming its primary source of maintenance and protection. In the late 2000s, they formed a public-private partnership with the Dyson Foundation and the New York State Office of Parks, Recreation, and Historic Preservation to rebuild for contemporary pedestrian use. Construction began in 2008, and the redesigned and reinforced bridge officially opened in 2009.[8]

Walkway Over the Hudson continues to gain regional attention as a tourist destination. An elevator was installed on the Poughkeepsie side so visitors arriving by train or from downtown Poughkeepsie can easily reach the entrance. Walkway is connected to the Duchess County rail trail in Poughkeepsie and extends into the town. Hundreds of thousands of tourists arrive every year, fueling a miniboom in local development including new apartments and artists' lofts.[9] Reasonable housing prices attract new buyers even though Poughkeepsie continues to struggle with relatively high poverty and violent crime rates. Highland is also experiencing economic and population growth, increasing 13 percent from 5,647 residents in 2010 to 6,385 in 2020 with housing prices still below nearby towns, and the number of house sales almost doubling since 2018–2019.[10]

Walkway, however, is much more than a tourist attraction and a site where community members came together. It is a symbol of social progress and a beacon of hope for long-awaited economic development in the region. This "blue space," that is, a public space with visible water such as a riverbank, harbor, lake shore, canal path, or ocean beach, contributes to the well-being of individuals just as much as the highly coveted "green space" of a park with trees and meadows. By encouraging walking as well as promoting economic activity and attracting new residents, the blue space of Walkway contributes to individual well-being and community resiliency.

★ ★ ★

Residents and visitors frequently talk about how Walkway improves their physical health by encouraging them to exercise. I watch a man, about fifty-five and wearing a navy jacket, gray sweatpants, and comfortable running shoes, execute a smooth-running stride, though I notice that he favors one leg as he quickens his pace. He stops for a moment to look over the railing. The dark green shores of the riverbank frame shimmering strips of water from the wake of a passing boat. The slanted afternoon light and gentle waves lapping on the shore evoke a sleepy, peaceful scene.

As he pauses, I introduce myself and ask him about his experience of being on the bridge. He replies "*the greatest values of Walkway are the physical benefits and beautiful scenery that enhance my experience. I run religiously to prevent another stroke.*" A middle-aged woman in a jogging suit overhears our conversation and adds, "*I pick up the pace of my run when I get to the bridge because the air is cool, and the wind makes me feel alive.*"

A younger woman powerwalking in black tights and a red tank top passes us and then returns to impart her impressions. She is from Highland and uses the bridge to add variety to her exercise regime. She smiles and says, "*I love looking at the boats and down at the water, and the houses. I love being outside like this. It's a backup plan for not going to the gym. Sometimes it's too nice outside and I don't want to be inside, so I come here.*"

In addition to the benefit of physical exercise, the bridge is therapeutic in other ways. Although Walkway is creating new opportunities, parts of Poughkeepsie remain rundown with buildings shuttered due to the decline of its industrial base. Retirees and families struggle to survive, and many commute to find a job. The stress of supporting a family, of aging and illness, or not being able to fulfill one's dreams is doubly difficult without places for healing. Thus, the value of Walkway to those who face adversity is more than physical and contains an emotional and spiritual component of uplift and hope.

An older man in a heavy sweater and slacks sits on one of the backless benches that line the bridge railing. A cloud passes, darkening the ripples in the water below: a cold breeze sweeps across the walkway. I pull my sweater closer, feeling chilled by the rising dampness. The man, who I learn is turning eighty next week, closes his eyes as if meditating and then opens them, waving at me to come over. "*The bridge is my sanctuary,*" he tells me. "*I love the water. I don't want to go in the water, but I love looking at it. It helps me think, make sense of my life.*"

I also contemplate the splendor and scale of the pastoral river landscape. Dark green pines dot the hillsides above entangled shrubs and vines along the river's edge. In the distance hills and low mountains flank the riverbed. Dried grasses line the shore, shaking noisily in the wind, and blackbirds caw as they fly overhead. Interviewees say the dramatic scenery prompts them to think about the fragility of the natural environment while the changing seasons remind them that time is marching on.

For some, the bridge evokes happy times in their lives, and they visit to reconnect with those memories. An older couple wearing matching gray windbreakers and tennis shoes recollect: "*We look at the foliage, the water, and we try to locate the church that we got married in. This is the backdrop to our wedding.*" A twenty-nine-year-old woman reminisces about her past as we sit looking out at the churning water. "*The walkway is sentimental. It's one of the places I used to go to a lot with my ex-husband and my son. We loved coming here. It's kind of a neutral place where I still come with my son. It's so beautiful. It makes for a better time and for peace of mind.*"

The natural beauty makes people feel better. A sixty-year-old man in work overalls from Poughkeepsie says, "*I enjoy its beauty. It's soothing, makes me feel high. I enjoy the beauty of God's creation more than I used to because I appreciate it more here."* Another middle-aged resident offers his point of view. *"It's just an amazing walk. You forget your problems; it's such an amazing view."* He adds, *"Even my friend who has a fear of heights can get on the bridge. It's not a problem because the scenery is so alive!"*

Safety and accessibility play a part in the promotion of health and well-being. In a city that is economically depressed and physically deteriorating, an accessible and well-used public space takes on new meaning especially for young women. An avid college student in a Vassar tee-shirt emphasizes that the walkway makes her feel safe compared to other places she occasionally goes for exercise. She chuckles and says: *"Everybody here is very friendly too. Luckily everyone I come across lets me pet their dog and even the dogs are friendly. In some of the parks I go to I worry about the people there. But I've never come across anybody who made me feel uncomfortable or unsafe on Walkway."*

Parents comment they feel at ease having their children run freely at Walkway because the railings are designed so that they cannot crawl under them. Families with strollers and people in wheelchairs are everywhere due to the flat and open entrance that is accessible for everyone on wheels. The "design for all" environment encourages visitors of all ages and abilities to participate and feel part of the action.

The safety and sense of security that people experience at Walkway increase its popularity in the context of Poughkeepsie, where there still is a high crime rate. One resident who runs over the bridge several times a week recognizes the faces of other visitors, which allows her to feel more relaxed. As another young woman puts it, *"I think it's just that there are types of people who walk here to have a peaceful experience and to free their mind of whatever is on it, especially when you're working out. I think one of the reasons I come to the Walkway is because I feel secure, and I can get lost in my thoughts; it's a very peaceful place."*

Another apparent reason is the number of friendly dogs. A young man a baseball cap and jeans says he appreciates Walkway because he can interact with dogs without owning one: *"The dogs are friendly here when I pet them. One dog wanted to go with me over the Walkway. This makes it a different park in that anyone can use it. Some are running, some are jogging, some are with dogs, and there are a lot of different people. And it feels secure to everyone."*

Without a doubt, the bridge is a symbol of community pride and resiliency for residents. People who grew up in the area are proud that they turned it into a historic site. An older man who lived through the economic hardships of Poughkeepsie recounts, *"I grew up in the area and I remember this place when it was a railroad bridge. I remember the fire in '74. So, I have thirty-five years of memories of trains going over. I've seen a lot of development in this area, but now it's just exciting to walk the bridge, and you know, just look at the scenery, enjoy the four seasons, and watch the leaves change in the fall."*

A much younger Highland resident shares this sense of pride at the results of the community effort. She recalls, *"I used to work at a retail outlet in Poughkeepsie, and having handouts for the Walkway way back when they were making plans to rebuild the bridge. It's kind of nice to see that all the hard work paid off."*

Residents who participated in the Walkway Over the Hudson association feel they are part of the process that reclaimed not just the bridge, but their community. An older man talks about his own transformation during the restoration: *"I was in the salvage business, and one of my dreams was to tear the old bridge down. Since I used to be a salvage driver, I knew how to do that type of job. But I found myself here four to five years before the Walkway was built with my truck removing planks and ties, putting in lights. There were probably a couple of hundred people in the volunteer group, and thirty to forty of us were workers. It's ironic, a strange coincidence that I went from wanting to tear down the old bridge to now walking on it and loving it."*

The sense of accomplishment and working together to achieve a goal contributes to the increase in resiliency experienced by residents. Both Highland and Poughkeepsie suffer from deindustrialization, a lack of new jobs, few commercial opportunities, and the subsequent loss of younger residents leaving to take jobs closer to New York City. With each recession they lose population, and there is a lingering concern that the towns will never flourish as they once did. Building Walkway Over the Hudson restores the towns' pride as a place with people who get things done. It supports their sense of efficacy and ability when facing other economic and social challenges.

Even visitors from outside the region remark on the transformation of Poughkeepsie. A middle-aged man visiting from Saratoga County had the opportunity to get out on the bridge before it was restored. He is astounded by the transformation: "*You have here one great engineering feat! The scenery here is beautiful and the people of Poughkeepsie are alive and well!*" Another visitor who is familiar with the community's role in the development of Walkway adds, "*Poughkeepsie is a place that has been overlooked, but democracy works. The people saved their own great walkway. They honored it by saving it.*"

Public Space and Health and Well-Being

Suzanne and I should not have been surprised at the impact of Walkway on the health and well-being of local users or the large number of older adults safely using this new public space. The evidence that public space improves health and well-being through physical activity such as walking or running, experiencing "natural environments" that reduce stress, or spending time with people is well established. In the past twenty years, large-scale studies have confirmed qualitative observations such as our own of public space's health-enhancing impact.[11] The 2020–2022 lockdowns during the COVID-19 pandemic prove that living in isolation without social contact leads to depression, anxiety, and loneliness.

The history of the modern relationship between the physical environment and health began in the 1600s, when *miasmic theory* was widely accepted.[12] Vaporous poisonousness substances produced by particles of decaying matter, or "bad air," were thought to be the cause of devastating epidemics of infectious disease. It took more than two hundred years until physician John Snow traced the source of a

London cholera outbreak in 1854 to a contaminated water pump and stopped its spread by removing the handle.[13]

The developing science of epidemiology became the basis of early city-planning strategies. Even though the notion of *miasmic theory* was discredited, the underlying association of the urban environment with disease was reinforced. Overcrowding, polluted water, and filthy streets contributed to high urban mortality that by the 1940s was finally controlled by changes in zoning, water-system protection, and food provision prior to the use of modern antibiotics.

In the twenty-first century the major killers—heart disease, stroke, cancer, and diabetes—are due to chronic diseases of which the leading risk factors are obesity, physical inactivity, poor diet, and smoking.[14] These precursors are often considered moral or personal failures rather than attributed to inequalities in the urban environment. A resurgence of research produced an evidence-based consensus on the importance of the physical and social environment in encouraging healthy lifestyles. Public policy and planning initiatives advocate for the proximity of parks, recreational facilities, and other forms of active urban public spaces for their health-enhancing properties available to all.[15]

A significant milestone is the 2016 World Health Organization publication that identifies the benefits of urban green spaces on improved mental health; reduced cardiovascular illness and death, obesity and the risk of diabetes; and improved pregnancy outcomes. The mechanisms for these positive changes include psychological relaxation, increased physical activity, and reduced exposure to environmental hazards such as pollution, noise, and excess heat.[16] The report highlights that contact with nature is restorative and relieves high levels of stress by shifting attention to a more positive emotional state and improves performance on cognitive tasks.[17] These results support the "biophilia hypothesis" that there is an evolutionary human need to connect with the natural environment.[18] While many scholars question whether biophilia is innate in humans, there is neuroscience evidence that place, in terms of spatial location, is a critical dimension in neuron processing and that green space is associated with improved immune-system functioning.[19]

The strongest case that can be made linking green space with health is via its capacity to facilitate physical activity, which improves fitness and reduces the incidence of obesity. The relationship of physical activity to cardiovascular, mental, and neurocognitive health as well as general well-being is most visible among older adults who find it difficult to maintain moderate levels of physical activity. Other positive aspects include noise buffering, pollution reduction, heat island reduction, exposure to sunlight, and pro-environmental behavior. All these effects show differing degrees of benefit depending on the age, gender, ability, ethnicity, and socioeconomic status of the individual. For example, urban green spaces have the greatest health benefits for economically marginal communities, children, pregnant women, and older adults.[20]

Living near a river, beach, or lake—"blue space"—and walking along it are also associated with better health and well-being.[21] In fact, interventions that take advantage of a riverfront have direct benefits, especially for mental health and greater social connectedness, similar to our findings from Walkway interviewees.[22] Becoming involved in reconstructing, monitoring, and maintaining a public space appears to increase overall community resilience and promote a sense of social cohesion.[23]

Urban planners, landscape architects, and environmental designers who renovate public spaces or construct new ones also suggest that there is a relationship between the designed environment and its health and well-being outcomes.[24] Matthew Carmona's work on "place value" explores the health benefits of urban tree canopy and other aspects of green space, confirming that the percentage of green space within a neighborhood is significantly related to perceived general health.[25] Place quality, including people's perceptions of their everyday street-level environment, contributes to their mental and emotional well-being. Like the Walkway users, inhabitants of more scenic environments report better health,[26] while residents who

Figure 4.5 Walkway Over the Hudson Spanning the Hudson River, New York

perceive litter and graffiti in their neighborhood experience greater anxiety and depression.[27] These mental-health studies of how perceptions and experiences of the environment impact psychological well-being complement the physical-health findings.

The health and well-being benefits of public space are often mediated by social interactions.[28] Informal friendly chatting, what earlier generations refer to as "schmoozing," promotes a sense of belonging and ontological security, leaving people feeling more comfortable in the world.[29] Interpersonal relationships that offer social support and networking, and neighborhood and community factors including social cohesion and social capital, are key elements in determining many health-enhancing behaviors.[30]

For older adults the psychological importance of self-determination plays a critical role in motivating public space use, but also in providing a sense of well-being.[31] A sense of competence and safety is fundamental to encouraging people to walk. Yet many public spaces endure substantial impediments to their use: heavy automobile and truck traffic, reckless cyclists and drivers, unattended dogs, and poor roadway or pathway surfaces.[32]

Considering public space use from the perspective of embodied experience—the way in which the human body interacts with the environment—offers insights into the differences people feel when confronted with various kinds of public space.[33] A steep climb to the entrance of a bridge might deter a person with different abilities or physical restrictions from using it, while an elevator such as the one at Walkway makes the entrance accessible to all. The same is true in terms of the social environment, where subtle social cues or more obvious signs of exclusion affect users' motivation to walk or socialize.

The New Urban Agenda contains nine paragraphs describing the importance of public spaces for improving physical and mental health, urban resilience, household and ambient air quality, and reducing noise and other environmental stressors. The United Nations Sustainable Development Goal 11.7 aims to provide access to safe, inclusive, and accessible public spaces particularly for women and children, older persons, and persons with "disabilities."[34] The policy implications of adding public space as a source of individual and community health is transforming the way that we think about the significance of urban and environmental planning.

The ethnographic findings from Walkway and other qualitative studies augment this conclusion by establishing that this positive relationship is not attributed solely to the presence or absence of green space. Equally important are the social aspects of having a place to walk, socialize, and be with other people. For physical- and mental-health benefits to accrue to a neighborhood, town, or city, there are the indispensable conditions of safety, accessibility, and community resiliency that must be met. The design and planning of the public space should consider both the physical and social dimensions of the local context and population needs. This recipe for health and well-being contributes to flourishing for all.

5

Playing in the Fields of Lake Welch, New York

Spending time at Lake Welch reveals how public space promotes play and recreation for the entire family. Here, visitors find a special place where children learn culturally appropriate behavior and youth play team sports while parents, grandparents, and extended family members and friends enjoy being together and relaxing. Being able to run freely, examine plants and insects, encounter strangers, and discover hidden landscapes, children are encouraged to explore new ideas and activities. Adult visitors often accompany their children in these pursuits, but also experience "getting away" and "moments of reflection" that enable them to imagine different worlds and reflect on larger questions not contemplated during the busy hum of everyday life. Play for children and "re-creation," in both the traditional sense as well as the ability to get away and re-create oneself, are essential aspects of psychological flourishing that this public park and natural environment encourages.

Play is an essential part of children's social and cognitive development and sparks early creativity and patterns of thinking that persist throughout a person's life.[1] Pediatric research establishes play as the foundation of healthy children's growth and maturation in that it stimulates brain structure and function, regulates responses to stress, and nurtures prosocial behavior.[2] The American Academy of Pediatrics was so concerned by the erosion of play opportunities in the city that it commissioned a series of papers about the importance of play based on comparative studies that illustrate children's lives worldwide.[3]

Children's access to public play and recreational space has declined in New York City since the 1930s. Public disinvestment in parks and playgrounds, the perception that play spaces are not safe, and increasing commercialization and privatization of playtime activities has limited opportunities for free play, especially near public housing projects and in low-income areas.[4] Parenting fears also contribute to the limitations on free play. Even adults who grew up in the 1970s are overprotective and do not let their children roam as widely as they did when they were young.[5]

Parks and larger public spaces offer occasions for socialization and personal growth in the context of diverse people and multifaceted activities that are not easily accommodated in small homes and on narrow sidewalks for many urban dwellers. Children growing up in older, poorer, and more densely populated central sections of a city are at risk for a variety of negative developmental outcomes, some due to limited play environments. But when children have access to outdoor spaces with grass and trees, most (73%) get involved in some kind of play.[6] In relatively barren spaces, however, the incidence of play is significantly lower. Even in marginalized neighborhoods with multiple health risks, positive child development outcomes can be achieved through access to quality play areas.[7]

Through playing in groups—with family members, friends, schoolmates, neighbors, and strangers—a child learns to become a social and cultural person. Socialization occurs in a myriad of locales, much of it at home or in homelike spaces. Nonetheless, acquiring the skills to navigate school, neighborhood, and city spaces requires a wider range of settings. A sense of place attachment and cultural identity are cultivated through the interplay of the social and physical relationships children encounter.[8]

Public spaces act as co-educators through the spatial segregation of play areas and the rules of who is included and who is not. Children learn to identify qualities of a built environment such as whether it is safe or friendly and negotiate ways of being and behaving that are carried with them throughout their lives.

★ ★ ★

Lake Welch, located in Harriman State Park, is a unique setting with expansive fields, tree canopy, barbeques, and tables for large groups and various activities. Only a half hour drive from New York City, there is room for celebrations, picnics, and playing fields for families who otherwise share small apartments near few public space amenities. It is one of a few mass visitation sites within the area, most of which is rugged, rocky woodland utilized for hiking and camping.

Edward H. Harriman, one of the more prominent figures of the post-Civil War period, made a fortune through controlling the Union Pacific, Southern Pacific, and Illinois Central Railroads. Harriman, who as a boy had worked in an iron mine in the Ramapo hills, amassed an estate of 30,000 acres named Arden between the Hudson and Ramapo Rivers. At the time the land contained exhausted iron mines and some pasturage.

Harriman Park is predominantly a gift to the state from Mary Harriman, who inherited Arden upon her husband's death. It was the result of a deal reached in 1910 whereby the state agreed to give up their plan to build a prison and instead establish a state park in return for the 10,000-acre donation. Both Bear Mountain and Harriman State Parks owe their existence to this early example of the "not in my backyard" (NIMBY) development strategy.[9]

Lake Welch is a recent addition to Harriman Park: plans were made in the 1940s, site preparation and filling of the lake got underway in the 1950s, and it opened to the public in 1962. The original approach from Willow Grove Road climbs from 400 feet above sea level at Exit 14 on the Palisades Parkway to 1,000 feet near the eastern lake shore. The road offers pleasant views over the water, as does the dam that controls the water level. After crossing two short causeways over the lake's southern reaches, the visitor arrives at a fishing boat launch and then the original main entrance. Fields 1 and 2 were the first parking

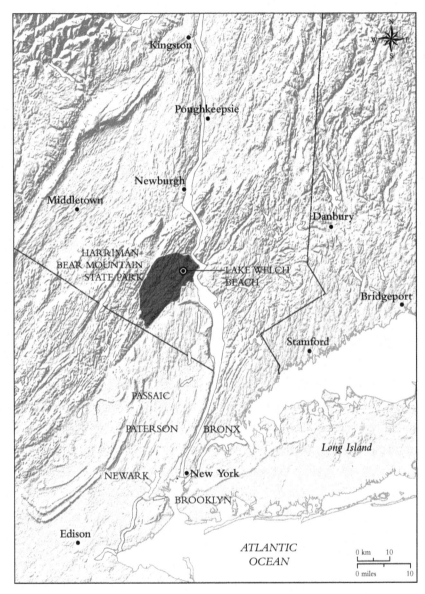

Map 5.1 Location of Lake Welch, New York

lots to be built. These lots give access to hilly, rocky, wooded terrain with picnic tables and grills under the tree canopy. Trails then go down through the picnic groves to the lakeshore.

The park access road leaves Fields 1 and 2 and the picnic groves to the right before descending to level terrain at the northern edge of the lake. Most of this area is devoted to a large parking lot, Field 3, and the park's main visitor facilities including the beach, beach house, and picnic grounds. Another approach to Lake Welch was built later from Exit 16 of the Palisades Interstate Parkway and is now the main approach to the lake.

The beach, a long, wide crescent, forms the entire northern shore of the lake. While the lake itself might pass for a natural formation, no natural lake would ever have so much beach, and so conveniently situated at one end for swimming. The beach has a dozen or so guarded sections, each with a lifeguard tower. Most of the time only those closest to the bathhouse are open, and visitors are not allowed to swim anywhere other than in guarded sections. The far ends of the beach are used mainly on Saturdays for baptisms performed by evangelical and Protestant churches.

Along the beach is a concrete promenade without railings, benches, awnings, or any other furnishings. At the center of the beachfront is the bathhouse, a 1960s modern wooden structure with spacious shower, restroom, and locker facilities. The bathhouse has a side entrance under a large roof overhang where people take cover when it rains.

Next to the side entrance is the manager's office where staff come and go in four-wheeled vehicles. The food concession is located to the right of the bathhouse with a long walk-up counter, like an elongated hot dog stand. In front, on an elevated concrete surface, is an area of picnic tables with umbrellas for shade. Next to the food concession is a convenience store where they sell beach and cooking supplies. The concessionaire says he does a good business, which seems remarkable considering how many of the visitors arrive with their own food and supplies. "*They always forget something,*" he tells us.

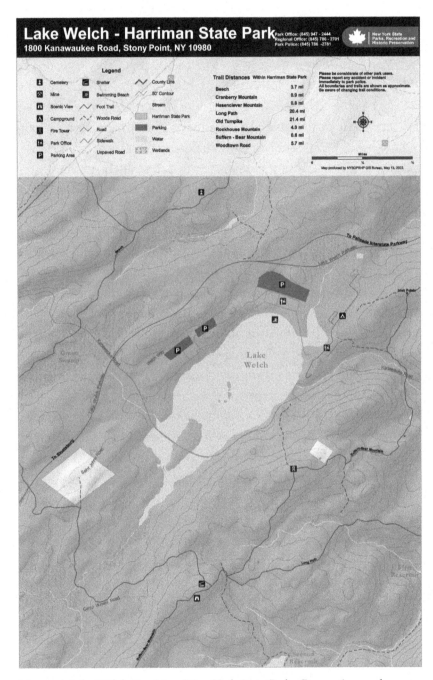

Map 5.2 Lake Welch Site Map (New York State Parks, Recreation, and Historic Preservation)

Figure 5.1 Picnicking at Lake Welch, New York (Photograph by Dana Taplin)

East and west of the bathhouse are level square fields enclosed with privet hedges. The field west of the bathhouse is known to park staff as the "manager's panel," the one to the right as the "concession panel." The concession panel has several shade trees and picnic tables and is a favorite place for family and church groups to set up. Beyond the concession panel is a larger level area with a lagoon that separates the public day-use area at Lake Welch from Beaver Pond Campground. The lagoon also has some trees and many picnic tables and is another popular place for people to spend the day. The manager's panel is less popular as it has less shade. All three areas have very dry, coarse, patchy grass, the victim of too many feet and Canada geese.

There is a noticeable presence of trash due in part to the way that people linger at tables loaded with food and disposable plates, napkins, utensils, and cups. Trash barrels are distributed throughout, although we found that there were not enough in the most heavily used picnic

Figure 5.2 Leaving the Beach Before the Rain, Lake Welch, New York
(Photograph by Dana Taplin)

areas. Staff often circulate among the picnickers offering plastic garbage bags to help clean up.

Observing children playing with friends, running in and out of
the water, or racing up and down a gentle hill under the watchful
eyes of their families makes it easy to understand Lake Welch's
popularity. Residents from the northern sections of New York
City (53% of visitors), especially the West Bronx and northern
Manhattan that house many of the city's Hispanic and Latino[10]
residents, come for the open and healthy environment. Children
and teens are safe to hang out and enjoy themselves, something
hard to replicate in the city with its stop-and-frisk policing that
discourages neighborhood park use.[11] A significant number come
from Rockland, Westchester (21% of visitors), and other New
York counties, and from New Jersey (19% of visitors). Based on
our survey sample of 488 visitors, three-quarters self-identified as

Hispanic/Latino, 15 percent self-identified as white, and 7 percent self-identified as Black. There were 266 self-identified men and 222 self-identified women.

Swimming (87%) and barbecuing (62%) are the predominant activities as seen in Table 5.1. Swimming, however, is only one of many beach activities that include playing in the sand, throwing a ball or Frisbee, sunbathing, and reading. Barbecuing encompasses picnicking, meeting friends and family, playing games, and attending parties. The experience of being at the park is reported as relaxing no matter the mix of activities.

Lake Welch attracts Hispanic/Latino visitors based on a long history of welcoming large families, offering them a clean place for children to play and explore nature. Several people we spoke with remember coming as children or talked about their families coming. An older woman who was part of a thirty-person family group sitting in the concession area reminisces, "*I first came here with my uncles about forty years ago and I never stopped. Everybody has a good time here. The beach and the lake are clean.*" An older man wearing a red tee-shirt and carrying his young granddaughter on his shoulders has been coming for forty-five years: "*My parents came before me. It's a way of getting away from the city and having a place for the children to play. The air is clean and fresh. You've got water and trees. It's a getaway.*"

Hispanic/Latino patronage goes back as far as the park's first decade in the 1960s. Our survey found that 22 percent of visitors have been coming for over twenty years and 24 percent for more than five years, while only 14 percent were visiting for the first time. Families come early, establish themselves at a location, and stay several hours. On weekends people wanting choice spots arrive as early as 6:00 am. Other members of the family or group come later, and by then all the picnic tables are claimed, groups established, and the distribution of tables set. In July many visitors leave in late afternoon, while others stay well into the evening. There is a much smaller flow of nearby residents who come to the beach to swim and sunbathe, stay a short while, and then leave.

Table 5.1 Activities Today—Total Responses at Lake Welch, New York[a]

Activities Today	Responses	Percent of Responses	Percent of Cases
Swimming	426	20%	87%
Barbecuing	290	14%	59%
Relaxing	268	13%	55%
Picnic tables/grills	211	10%	43%
Picnicking	168	8%	34%
Sunbathing	149	7%	31%
Enjoying nature	94	4%	19%
Playing in the sand	82	4%	17%
Playing ball/frisbee	74	3%	15%
Soccer	63	3%	13%
Fresh air/calm	47	2%	10%
Meeting friends/family	45	2%	9%
Volleyball	44	2%	9%
Fishing and/or boating	28	1%	6%
Playing games	27	1%	6%
Reading	24	1%	5%
Baseball/softball	21	1%	4%
Food concessions	19	1%	4%
Attending party	15	1%	3%
Walking	13	1%	3%
Baptism	11	1%	2%
People watching	7	0%	1%
Football	6	0%	1%
Sports, other	6	0%	1%
Bird watching	2	0%	0%
Camp	2	0%	0%
Cruising	1	0%	0%
Playing cards	1	0%	0%
Total	2,144		

[a] From 488 interviews and includes all responses.

There is quite a bit of competition for space because of the large number of people who want to be together:

> One thing that jumps at you is how big the visiting groups are. The smallest group is ten members, while the larger—usually church groups—has more than 100 people in them. This makes tables and grills a hot commodity. Groups line up at the gate before the park even opens to assure that they get the tables they need for the day's events. There appears to be no limit to how many tables one can snatch. One church group lines up over thirty tables to form a circle, while another group assembles over twenty. This second group all wear the same shirts and bring their own volleyball net. We learn that they are one huge extended family celebrating their great-grandmother's hundredth birthday.
>
> Whether a group gets a grill or finds shade because of a tree is not as problematic as the table arrangement—after all, trees and grills can't be moved while tables can. In fact, we could see a couple of groups with both grills and shade but no table—but this is rare. For the most part everybody has at least one table because the early groups accommodate those who come later. In several instances, newly arrived visitors request a table from an adjoining group. This willingness to share things —not just tables but everything from cooking materials, to cups, to balls, and even food, is characteristic of how people treat one here.[12]

Being part of a community with roots in Latin American or Caribbean countries communicates meaningful social and cultural values. Visitors remark on how connected they feel to one another even though they are strangers. The Spanish language and familiar traditions impart a strong sense of inclusion.

There is a sense of shared norms and expectations. One middle-aged man notes that "*people here are very nice . . . Whenever I need a lighter for the BBQ, somebody lends me one.*" Another older man observes that "*this place has many Latinos. We naturally gravitate towards them when we hear people speaking Spanish. It's a normal human reaction.*" Watching the children dart about moving between their own and neighboring spots, "*No one tells them to come back or shoos them away as they play with other children. They try different foods and hear other stories.*"[13]

Given the community sensibility, it is not surprising that most people feel welcome and say that the park "*is . . . safe. They check everything. There's not a lot of drinking. This is a family place, a good place.*" A woman sitting at a group of fifteen tables adds "*People share their stuff or leave it*

for the next person. People are more outgoing here. We talk to each other. More
outgoing and friendly than Orchard Beach (a beach in Pelham Bay Park in
the Bronx)."[14] A man comments that "*Lake Welch is a large Latin com-*
munity. Nobody is offended by other's people's music. The only thing we fight
over is tables and grills (laughing)."

In many ways the park serves as an extension of people's living
rooms, kitchens, and backyards. People perform food preparation,
cooking, and socializing over dominoes, and other games in full view.
The privacy of domestic functions sequestered in homes and backyards or in private clubs and vacation houses is not evident. Here, little
is hidden; there is no embarrassment at hanging out in this public
setting. Children allowed to play every is recognized and reciprocated.
The scene is similar from one location to another.

> *A volleyball net has been constructed, and a large group of men and women*
> *are engrossed in the game. Across the trail I count a total of nine groups, all of*
> *whom have barbecues going. At this hour only one group has music playing, that*
> *I recognize as the famous Mexican* corrido, "*I Continue to Be King," an old-*
> *fashioned song that speaks to the identity of many Mexican men.*
>
> *Here and elsewhere, children wander in and out of groups as they play,*
> *making friends and ignoring the concept of personal space that most adults take*
> *more seriously. A woman comes down from the hills with a bunch of dry branches*
> *to be used for cooking, and as she approaches her group's spot, another man is*
> *borrowing lighter fluid from a neighbor. I sit and watch them struggle to get the*
> *fire going, fanning it with a piece of cardboard gathered from trash on the ground.*
>
> *Nearby, a family has a nice view of the lake from their spot as the barbecue*
> *and table are located close to the edge of the cliff. The family is using only one*
> *table but has several camping chairs set up. Two women are busy cooking chicken*
> *on the barbecue, and three young children are playing hide and seek around the*
> *site exploring the area. Later, during an interview with the mother, the children*
> *move down the hill to the next group and begin making a fuss over an infant*
> *there. As I walk by, some of the women are eating* tortas de jamon *with avo-*
> *cado, and almost immediately upon arriving they put a sandwich together for*
> *me. The family all laugh when I agree to adding* jalapeños *to my sandwich.*[15]

Another aspect of children's play and socialization is having contact
with animals and learning how to treat "nature." One woman visiting
with her daughters tells us that for her family, "*The best day was finding*

a turtle in the road on the way here. I took it out of the road and brought it back to the park rangers. They thanked me, then took the turtle and released it into the lagoon as we watched. You could see they cared about the environment and were there to teach our children as well."

For some visitors the park triggers memories they want to share with their children and grandchildren. As a couple explains: "*It reminds us of playing outside in Mexico when we were children . . . we want our children to have these same experiences.*" A mother remembers "*coming here with my parents when I was a kid on Sundays. We'd have four or five cars of family in a caravan. Just having all the family together every Sunday, knowing it would happen. It was something to look forward to.*"

Informal sports at Lake Welch develop cooperative play and social skills ancillary to time spent on the beach or in the picnic areas. Since there are no organized teams, youth and young adults form their own "pick-up games," meeting new people and learning to play together. These pick-up games provide another arena for social interaction and team building.

Such games also offer an opportunity to exhibit skills and confidence for individuals who may not enjoy such opportunities in other areas of their lives. While people are drawn to sport by the pleasure of playing, the privatization of space through enclosure and as a consequence of urbanization has done much to destroy traditional forms of play. Social control measures helped to remove sport from streets, beaches, and other public spaces. The creation of the modern sporting world with its network of clubs and associations depends in large measure on the construction of dedicated sporting facilities. Such facilities ordinarily involve exclusivity, and the high cost prohibits joining a sports club and competing in organized sports. Without a dedicated facility, sports clubs are left to compete with each other and with other users for space in public parks. What is left then is the informal recreation of sporting practice in imitation of formally organized sport.[16]

Even though Lake Welch does not have dedicated athletic fields, people still come to play soccer, football, volleyball, and baseball, and softball. Some of this activity is on the beach near the shore-line, but most of it takes place in open areas of level ground such as the manager's and the concessions panels, where impromptu games compete with family encampments. Pick-up soccer is par-ticularly popular among young men who form teams based on who is there at the time, and then as players drop out, those who have been watching join in. The atmosphere is one of goodwill with little conflict and lots of teasing. Volleyball, however, is the most popular sport:

> *A volleyball net is strung from tree to tree, and young men and women are laughing and playfully chiding anyone who misses a shot is a common scene. I watched a group gather over thirty park tables, put up volleyball nets, several sun tents, and six barbeques right in the heart of Field 2. I thought this was a church group, both because of the size of the group and because they were wearing the same shirt. It turned out to be a family reunion including extended family and friends—145 people in all!*[17]

Free play, cooperative play, team sports, and cultural socialization are important for young adults, youth, and children, but for older adults, relaxation and reflection seem more significant. These affective states are appreciated especially by those visitors who experience the pressures of working multiple jobs, juggling children, and caring for elderly parents. Enjoying a day outside in nature with a chance to decompress allows visitors to think more clearly and creatively. More than half of visitors who answered our survey find the park "relaxing" (268 of 462 responses), a place they can slow down and escape the stresses of everyday life. Many express some form of "nature appre-ciation" including "enjoying nature," "smelling the fresh air," and "feeling calm."

As a young mother put it, one can *"get the stress off by relaxing with others here in nature with a highly sociable setting."* A woman in her seventies, resting by the lagoon with several younger family mem-bers, points to the contrast between the outdoor environment at Lake Welch and their daily life in the tiny room where they live. The park gives her the chance to clear her mind (*despejarse*). She says, "... *we like the beach, the water and we live closed within a room (encerrados). Here, we get to go out to relax and unwind."*

While the park offers time for relaxation and reflection away from the stress of the city for some, for others the experience is religious and involves a retreat from everyday life. Lake Welch has a long history of accommodating church meetings and Sunday dinners as well as life-cycle rituals and other ceremonial occasions. The natural setting creates an affective atmosphere where congregations gather to attend baptisms held in the shallow water at the far end of the shoreline. It is seen as a sacred site by many church members as well as by some visitors who want to get away from secular distractions.

Being together with one's congregation on a church outing arouses great emotion. For a sixty-year-old man, it reminds him of his initial experience of finding God surrounded by church members. He tells us that: *"The first time I came here was for my sister's baptism. I was new to the church, but it was a special day. It was the first time I knew for certain that I could commit myself to God. It happened right over there."* These profound religious experiences are embedded in the landscape of Lake Welch and re-emerge offering a sense of connection and spirituality.

With so much public concern about declining budgets, closing public facilities including parks (e.g., nearby Lake Sebago beach was closed in 2012), corporate sponsorships, and privatization of other state park facilities, we ask users whether they thought it important that Lake Welch remain public. The majority answer "yes," adding that people with limited means should have beautiful, welcoming places to get together with their families and friends and for their children to have a chance to play outdoors.

A middle-aged man wearing a soccer shirt responds, *"We need places for people without a lot of money—it's very important for our families. Without spaces like Lake Welch, we would have very few options as this is the only place that city dwellers can come to."* An older woman with her grandson in her lap explains, *"We come from New York City and there is no place like this there . . . where everyone can come, regardless of their race or culture."* Like the sentiment at Jones Beach, a young man comments that *"public means everybody can come in. If it is private only white Americans would be allowed and we Latinos would be excluded."*

Lake Welch is an unusual blend of the ingredients necessary for a child- and family-friendly public space. It offers an expansive natural environment and social setting where children become culturally proficient and behave in ways that might not be possible in the restricted confines of the city. The open playing fields encourage team building, cooperative play, and social skills across groups through sports such as soccer, football, and volleyball. The natural vegetation, trees, water, sun, beach, and light enhance people's sense of being away, relaxing, reflecting, and retreating from everyday life. It is not surprising that Lake Welch is also a religious site where families and congregations come together for ritual events such as baptisms and celebratory dinners.

Parks provide significant benefits for children and youth, but these benefits are tempered by their quality, amenities, maintenance, and safety.[18] Lake Welch offers a close look at public life in a park where these are apparent, yet there is much more to why it is such a satisfying recreational experience. What many studies leave out is the substantial role of culture and social context in framing children's interpersonal and social interaction through play.[19] Public settings including parks such as Lake Welch offer common ground for "the harmonious intermingling of children of different backgrounds, races, and ethnicities and that encourage their social interchange, play, educational development, and collaboration."[20]

Another addition to the usual list of why particular public spaces matter is that people form attachments to their play spaces, whether based on a specific sporting activity, makeshift fields used for volleyball and soccer, or the allure of the natural environment.[21] The materiality of the setting—the varying landscapes with their smells, sounds, and physical textures—provide a context for building social relations and feelings that become embedded there.

★ ★ ★

Certain kinds of play, particularly pretend play and some forms of free play, facilitate the insight necessary for divergent thinking and thus the development of creativity in children.[22] Indeed, in the 1990s researchers were worried about a "creativity crisis" when they observed a downturn in children's creativity due to increasing use of video games and more limited opportunities for pretend play.[23] Pretend play uses the child's experience of the world and fantasy to reconstruct past experiences and knowledge in unique ways.[24]

Play and creativity are interconnected, involving similar cognitive and affective processes.[25] Play is characterized by excitement and positive affect such as interest, enjoyment, and surprise, and motivated by satisfaction, spontaneous behavior, and exploration free from rules.[26] Creativity is the ability to make something through imagination or bring something new into existence.[27] Central to both is divergent thinking, the ability to generate a variety of ideas and to represent a range of alternatives symbolically.[28]

Even when the odds against a neighborhood seem overwhelming, recovering public spaces for children to play can have a transformative impact on their creativity. On a trip to Nairobi for a workshop with public space activists, I visit Dandora, a predominantly Kikuyu neighborhood located next to a waste dump in the Eastlands area of Nairobi. My fieldnotes reflect the community's resilience and resourcefulness in their efforts to take back a neglected spatial resource—similar to the case of Walkway Over the Hudson in Poughkeepsie—but with the additional excitement, mastery, and creativity that emerges when children and youth join in restoring their neighborhood.

Finding the entrance to the Dandora courtyards is tricky when you don't know the way. A member of the Dandora Transformation League guides us along a busy street lined with make-shift shops where everything from recycled plastic containers to machine parts is sold. Many residents collect recyclable materials by picking through the trash on the adjacent dumpsite to make a living, then selling what they find in this market.

About 142,000 residents live in a housing project planned and built by the World Bank in 1977, but that deteriorated over time. Residents and youth groups in collaboration with UN Habitat and the Making City Together Coalition cleaned previously trash-filled open spaces to create courtyards, walkways, and playgrounds for play and relaxation.[29]

Gleeful children crowd around, holding my hands and arms as I listen to their stories of getting rid of the trash built up over decades and the difficulty of convincing other residents to participate or at least cooperate. Low-cost play structures and chairs from abandoned tires line areas of painted cement pavement surrounded by freshly planted flowers and grass. I sit comfortably with Michael and Cecilia[30] *on a handmade bench as the youth leaders explain Dandora's history and marvel at the background of children running, laughing, and playing tag.*

Employing only materials collected from the waste dumpsite, community leaders encouraged the children to find ways to furnish the gardens and playgrounds with what they could find. The results are delightful and artistic, resembling art installations that reveal unbridled creativity and humor. Tire chairs arranged in a semi-circle are filled with mothers back from work, relaxing in the early evening as the heat of the day dissipates and a breeze cools the grounds and shakes the few, leafless trees.

Even in this relatively barren and dry landscape, flowers and small shrubs grow when carefully tended by the garden caretakers. Youth gardeners are paid

Figure 5.3 Learning about Dandora Garden, Nairobi, Kenya (Photograph by Joel Lefkowitz)

by collective donations of Dandora residents with good results. The community garden has vegetables just beginning to poke their heads through the crusty soil that the youth carefully tend by dripping water slowly and carefully on their roots to not waste a drop.

The hand-built play structure reminds me of a jungle gym but is hard to see with all the children climbing all over it. They stop to wave hello and shout "What is your name?" I smile calling back "Setha," which they repeat, and then clamber down to show me their handiwork along the paved path. A seven-year-old boy in bright yellow shorts and no shirt calls me over to see his sculpture/ planter made of an old boot, painted white and red and filled with a small purple flower. A girl of about five takes my hand and drags me to see her painted red and white striped stone, one of many lining a small "creek" that holds a trickle of water. There is a makeshift bridge on the "creek" suggesting that during the rainy season, the trickle quickly turns into a torrent, requiring the wooden plank placed there to get across.

The ongoing restoration of Dandora and the struggle to reclaim the landscape still faces the continuing threat of poverty, precarity, and government neglect that led to the loss of public space initially.[31] Collectively, however, the local community restored much more than the playgrounds, sitting areas, vegetable and flower gardens, and cleared walkways. It is now a place where children can play safely on equipment produced by their own hands—a testament to the power of a low-income neighborhood to transform their built and natural environment.

Dandora is a model of what is possible with few resources and local determination, even in what is perceived by outsiders as a dangerous and poor urban area. In this case, recovering the public spaces contributes not only to the well-being of children, but to the local community and city as a site of inspiration and imagination for what urban life for children, youth, and families should and can be. It also offers another example of how social contact within a neighborhood can be transformed into collective action through the development of a public culture focused on children and youth. The mobilization of the joy and energy of children and youth generates an affective atmosphere that further enhances the ability of public space to con-tribute to flourishing for all.

★ ★ ★

The centrality of play and recreation is acknowledged in the 1959 Declaration of the Rights of the Child, which states, "the child shall have full opportunity for play and recreation" and "society and public authorities shall endeavor to promote the enjoyment of this right."[32] The Convention on the Rights of the Child of 1989 focuses greater attention to providing play and recreational activities appropriate to the age of the child as well as participation in cultural life and the arts.[33] But even with the implementation of programs for organized children's activities, there is little investment in public space. In 2013 the UN reiterated the need for play space, especially with respect to girls, poor children, children belonging to minorities, and children with disabilities.[34]

The importance of public space for play and socialization is in-commensurate with the level of public space funding and the number of playgrounds and unstructured play areas that exist in many cities. Their marked absence in low-income areas, informal settlements, and refugee camps is striking considering the multitudes of children growing up in these physically marginalized and underserved envir-onments.[35] The lack of commitment to providing playgrounds and green and unstructured open space is an often-unremarked failure and threat to children and their families globally.

6

Improvising Public Space and the Informal Economy

Sidewalks, Streets, and Markets in Buenos Aires, New York City, and Baguio City

Public spaces play an important role in supporting and promoting the informal economy, especially in rapidly growing cities straining to provide economic opportunities and adequate employment. The inability to create enough jobs accompanied by increasing municipal deficits is contributing to widespread labor informality. More than half of the global workforce is informally employed in the Global South, dependent on streets, sidewalks, plazas, parks, railroad lines, bridges, and passageways, as well as other interstitial spaces as workplaces.[1] While many have written about the social inequality and hazards of informal work, I focus here on the necessity of maintaining safe and inclusive public spaces to accommodate these unfairly stigmatized, hard-working, and economically productive small-scale entrepreneurs.

The use of public space by waste collectors in Buenos Aires, Argentina, and street and market vendors in New York City and Baguio City, the Philippines, offers insights into how urban spaces accommodate a variety of jobs and working conditions. Vendors improvise and rely on defensive strategies to adapt to their fragile social and spatial position. Waste collectors use evasion and courtesy to avoid being barred from middle-class sidewalks in Buenos Aires. Street and market vendors in New York City utilize the news media, local politicians, and the American Civil Liberties Union to retain their foothold. Baguio City market vendors practice guerilla urbanism and protest to claim more workspace.

Streets, sidewalks, and public markets occupied by a plethora of informal workers reveal how essential public space is to individual flourishing and a thriving informal economy without which a large segment of the population would not have a place to earn a living. To give some sense of the magnitude of this workforce, around 200,000 people were working in the public spaces of Bogotá in 2018, while informal labor made up 48 percent of the workforce in all of Colombia.[2] In cities in sub-Saharan Africa and Southeast Asia, the proportion is as high as 70 percent.[3] Street trading, for instance, provides the means for generations of poor and marginalized urban residents to sustain some kind of livelihood.[4]

The informal sector of the economy "is the diversified set of economic activities, enterprises, jobs and workers that are not regulated or protected by the state."[5] Originally the concept was used to characterize self-employment in small unregistered businesses but now includes any wage employment that falls outside the formal economy and tax system.[6] Informal work is often stereotyped and stigmatized as illegal, underground, or part of the black or gray market even though most informal workers pay taxes and obtain municipal licenses.[7]

The kinds of work and workers vary by region and include more than 61 percent of the world's employed population—2 billion in 2018—mostly in low- and middle-income countries.[8] Women in Informal Employment Globalizing and Organizing (WIEGO) defines informal workers by their occupations or trade.[9] They support a global network of community organizers and facilitators who assist domestic workers, home-based workers, street vendors, and waste pickers to demand better working conditions, access to health care, and the right to work in public space.

In the U.S., the informal economy refers to temporary or occasional work that is not reported to the Internal Revenue Service and considered supplementary to a formal sector job. After the Great Recession of 2008–2009, researchers found that 44 percent of respondents from 2011–2013 reported participating in informal work to earn money.[10] While well below the percentages for the Global South, these figures indicate that there is a sizeable informal economy in the United States that includes everything from street performers to restaurant delivery workers and office messengers who add to the ranks of street vendors, day laborers, and domestic and home health care workers.

While the increase in informality is often attributed to the recent international restructuring of the global economy, informal work has been a strategy for economic survival throughout history. However, the increasing precarity of workers is a product of pervasive neoliberal policies that reduce protections for poorer and homeless individuals and reinforce patterns of marginalization.[11] Working in public spaces under these conditions puts vulnerable populations at greater risk of physical violence and theft as well as police surveillance and incarceration.

During COVID-19 streets and sidewalks took on new importance when commercial activities moved outdoors to reduce the risk of contagion. In New York City, shops and restaurants with proximity to sidewalks expanded their footprint into public walkways. Arguments about the privatization of public space and the exclusion of vendors, buskers, and other informal workers became more nuanced and less dogmatic in the face of the risk that mom-and-pop stores and neighborhood restaurants would not survive COVID-19 closures.

The fear that all restaurants would close—and the NYC restaurant scene cease to exist—changed the way the media, urban planners, and city officials reacted to spatial incursions during the crisis. The new mix of outside places to sit and eat transformed some of the city's rulings about the location and number of sidewalk vendors, food trucks, and other informal economic activities. In fact, the acceptance of restaurant tables on sidewalks and in parking spaces on streets opened opportunities for informal establishments to gain access to public spaces that heretofore had not been available.

The COVID-19 pandemic and the lockdown of cities and national borders also increased the number of unemployed and underemployed throughout the world. In countries already experiencing severe economic contractions such as Argentina and Venezuela, the impact of COVID-19 exacerbated the situation. Argentina is estimated to have lost 850,000 salaried jobs, and the formal economy is expected to contract between 8.2 and 10 percent.[12] In Venezuela, 33 percent of the population is suffering from food scarcity. The crisis of inadequate food production and distribution, loss of jobs and income, shutdown of non-essential businesses and industries, and closing of schools and universities amplified the pressure to accommodate the growing numbers of unemployed people. This shift highlighted the conflicts over who has the right to use public space and the role of government in the regulation and protection of informal workers.

Streets and Sidewalks as Improvised Workplaces

A visit to the pilgrimage city of Varanasi in India reveals sidewalks and streets jam-packed with people informally working in some capacity. Every kind of public space imaginable including the steep banks of the Ganges River and the ghats, the stone slabs where pilgrims perform ritual ablutions, overflow with people. Women in canary yellow, peacock blue, and scarlet saris stand on the ghat steps washing clothes or knee deep in the river washing their bodies while being careful to cover themselves. They look like beautiful birds from a distance, their colors reflected in the murky water.

The narrow alleyways are full of locals offering bicycle repairs, haircuts, cooked meals, incense, and custom-sewn clothes. Hindu priests wearing white dhotis with bare chests are located high above the river tending to small shrines where they perform funeral rituals for the dead and dying. On a tiny lane lined with houses and shops that extend into the street I step carefully around and sometimes over animals, foodstuffs, bedding, and arrayed items for sale. I smell saffron, hear vendors calling out their wares, and feel the thick smoky air while everyday life and death fill every inch of public space.

Originally an important industrial center for muslin and silk fabric, Varanasi is the holiest of seven sacred cities in Hinduism and Jainism, and an important site in the development of Buddhism. It is the preferred place for Hindus to die as the rituals of death and cremation on the banks of the Ganges enable one to attain salvation. Bathing in and drinking the water is believed to be health-enhancing, and pilgrims come from all over India to partake of this sacred elixir. Everything necessary for maintaining life as well as the rituals of death-—boats to take the ash remains to be poured into the Ganges, wood for funeral pyres, and priests who can observe the proper death rituals—are found, and purchased, on the street.

One morning during another field trip to India, I stand in front of the Mumbai train station to watch men exiting with large wooden carts filled with what look like stacked cans. Some are wrapped in bright cloth while others are unadorned with clamps on either side. Men wearing white kurtas strain to pull the carts onto the sidewalk where hundreds of other men wait on bicycles. One calls out what turn out to be addresses, as the bicycle men come forward to claim their cans. I am intrigued by the elaborate orchestration of parcels given to the couriers who then pedal off in different directions balancing tall stacks on their bike racks with rope and red cord.

Later I learn that this performance occurs every workday morning. The men on bicycles are "dabbawallas" (one who carries a box) who deliver an estimated 80 million lunches a year. They pick up home-cooked meals packed in a round tiffin from workers' wives, sisters, or mothers, then use the train and bicycle to deliver them to family members. The intricate choreography of dabbawallas picking up and dropping off each tiffin box by color and location produces a human infrastructure saving office workers money, time, and the risk of eating unclean food. At the same time this complicated delivery system provides a meager living for the dabbawallas who depend on the informal economy.

Streets and sidewalks offer rich opportunities for the complex routines and improvisations that characterize the informal economies of today's turbulent cities. Public spaces are employed both as the sites of circulation of goods and services and as a physical resource where access to clients is ensured. While selling and delivering may represent the most common uses of public space, there are other urban resources exploited by the informal workforce.

Waste collection provides jobs for many hundreds of thousands if not millions of people in low- and middle-income cities. While much of the collecting occurs at night, informal workers can be seen throughout the day collecting, dumping, and sorting in public areas. In cities without industrialized garbage disposal, "trash-picking" is a respected profession. Urban residents accommodate workers' presence since "rag-pickers," "bottle-collectors," and *cartoneros* (paper and cardboard collectors) provide a necessary service by disposing of trash and recycling valuable materials, cleaning, sorting, and reselling what would otherwise be lost. The relationship of waste collectors and public space becomes fraught, however, when cities modernize and mechanize trash collection as a municipal service, thus making the task more difficult.[13]

In Buenos Aires, Argentina, attitudes toward waste collectors changed when roughly 35,000 scavengers began roaming the city streets due to the 2002 devaluation of the *peso*.[14] The flood of impoverished people from informal settlements created a moral panic among the middle-class, who began to invest in security equipment and demand militarized public security.[15] The "ordering of the chaos in the streets"[16] became the political agenda for Mauricio Macri, the chief of government in 2007. Macri decried the "thousands of criminals who 'steal from the trash' that people put out on the sidewalk,"[17] and promised to take them off the street and put them in prison. In 2008 he created "plaza guardians" to ensure "proper" behavior in public space that led to the removal of *cartonero* settlements, street vendors, dog walkers, fair vendors, trans sex workers, and sidewalk café operators.[18]

Mariano Perelman's ethnography of *cartoneros* in Buenos Aires from 2002 through 2011 describes the juxtaposition of workers who perform tasks publicly and their need to be recognized by people in those spaces to carry out their work.[19] The relationship between the *cartoneros* and *vecinos* (neighbors) is constantly re-negotiated through everyday encounters based on current attitudes, norms of behavior, and strategies of governance. Perelman offers an insightful vignette from his fieldwork:

> During the collection periods, cartoneros deal with the inquisitive looks of the residents. Both actors [in public space], they must learn to live together. For many vecinos, the collectors are dangerous invaders. They blame them for the robberies occurring in the neighborhood, for the dirtiness of the streets, for traffic

problems (as they circulate with large carts or leave them parked in the middle of the street).

The same ideas are expressed by some cartoneros. One afternoon, talking with Pedro, the forty-five-year-old waste collector told me, "It's not easy to walk down the street. I feel a knife in my back all the time. People look at me with contempt. They cross the street when they see me, and when I want to talk to them, they hurry by."[20]

The conflict over public space is about who has the "moral" right to be there and whether *cartoneros* are seen as legitimate workers. With increased numbers of people on the streets and governmental policies of criminalization, the *cartoneros* originally depicted as "deserving workers" became "criminals" and were forcibly removed. New laws imposed middle-class norms of public behavior that excluded waste collection, street vending, and other forms of informal

Figure 6.1 *Cartonero* (trash collector), Bueno Aires, Argentina (Photograph by Mariano Perelman)

work. *Cartoneros* attempted to circumvent the fear and antagonism of middle-class residents by adopting a deferential and courteous self-presentation and becoming less visible, working at night and in interstitial spaces where they were less likely to be seen. But when working conditions require visibility and trust for access to discarded materials—for example, getting permission to enter a side yard or asking a resident if she has bottles or cans to recycle—and at the same time require invisibility to avoid personal attack or imprisonment, there is no real solution.

In 2017–2018 street vendors and *cartoneros* in Buenos Aires protested their removal from public space. "*We are workers*" they chanted, and "*as workers deserve the opportunity to earn a living wage.*" The right to work in Argentina is upheld by the National Constitution and grants protections for all forms of work. The protestors won that struggle and re-entered the public sphere, but it was a short-lived victory. New laws and regulations were put in place creating a patchwork of policies even more difficult to navigate. There was no clear victory, but only an ongoing battle that continues to this day.

Street vendors in New York City always had to fight to retain the use of streets and sidewalks. According to a recent survey, there are approximately 20,000 carts selling hot dogs, flowers, tee-shirts, street art, gourmet foods, ice cream, and more. Most are owned or leased by immigrants and some vendors are military veterans who work long hours in harsh conditions subject to police surveillance and ticketing. When interviewed about their job, many say that they prefer to work for themselves and do not have the necessary capital to rent a space or shop, or they inherited a cart or stall from other family members. What they want is greater access to places where they can sell their goods, protection from theft and vandalism, and more legal permits to reduce the harassment.[21]

Pushcart vendors in New York City were historically regulated with licenses and permits and allotted to spaces in pushcart markets. Inspectors would visit these markets to make sure vendors were in place, while ambulatory pushcarts traveled farther into residential

Figure 6.2 Ambulatory Vendors on Strike for Right to Work, Buenos Aires, Argentina (Photograph by Mariano Perelman)

neighborhoods selling scissor and knife sharpening services, notions, and dressmaking wares.[22]

In the 1980s, Mayor Ed Koch capped the number of food vendor permits at 3,000 (5,100 today). This cap fueled a black market in the illegal leasing of permits that cost as much as $30,000 a year.[23] The situation was exacerbated from 1994 to 2000, when street vendors became the victims of Mayor Rudolph Giuliani's aggressive "quality of life" crackdown. Streets, plazas, and sidewalks were closed because of the powerful business lobby and the rise of Business Improvement Districts (BIDs) that regulated the use of public spaces in designated areas. BID regulations and the increasing quasi-privatization of streets, plazas, and sidewalks by corporate interests limited street vendors' access to many of the locations where they traditionally worked.

These policies imposed a heavy burden on street vendors trying to make a living. An example is Ahmed Ebrahim and his brother, who inherited the family business of selling hot dogs, knishes, and soft pretzels from their mother, who immigrated from Egypt thirty years ago. They also inherited the debt of $20,000 every two years to illegally lease a permit for their cart located near Rockefeller Center.[24]

The inability to get low-cost permits and burdensome restrictions and regulations resulted in the creation of the Street Vendors Project,

Figure 6.3 New York City Street Vendor, Manhattan

an association organized in 2014 to expand the number of permits as well as improve working conditions. With growing political pressure and the loss of jobs during the COVID-19 pandemic, a victory was declared when a new vending law was passed by the City Council on January 28, 2021. Intro 1116 adds 400 new food-vending permits annually over the next ten years, creates a dedicated unit—rather than the police—to enforce vending laws, and regulates the locations where vendors can operate and how close they can be to brick-and-mortar stores.

Public Markets and the Integration of Immigrants

Public markets were seen as a solution to street vending as early as 1928, when the New York City Department of Markets' Annual Report decried open-air pushcart markets as "fire hazards and a health menace." The first enclosed public market, "La Marqueta," opened in

1936,[25] followed by four others, including Moore Street Market in 1941. An article published at the time claimed that public markets would end "the obnoxious features of the pushcart while preserving its principal benefit, inexpensive wares, and giving the consumer more protection."[26]

During the 1940s and early 1950s, Moore Street Market vendors were Jewish, Italian, Irish, and Polish immigrants, reflecting neighborhood demographics. Starting in the late 1950s, though, market vendors began to come from the Caribbean and Latin America. The first wave immigrated from Puerto Rico and joined New York City's labor force as young adults. "*They all lived nicely together,*" one of the Moore Street merchants explains. "*They respected each other.*"[27]

In the 1970s, Puerto Rican workers were adversely affected by deindustrialization resulting in high levels of poverty and forcing many into the informal economy. A Puerto Rican vendor describes this transition as a positive force in his life.

> *My first job was in a factory when I was seventeen years old . . . The factory moved to the South at the end of the 1960s. After that job I "took a rest" and then began to work as a security guard in a kindergarten in Brooklyn. Later, I began to work as a street vendor (vendedor ambulante). I worked in different places "because I liked, and I still like it, that's why I do it." I enjoy doing business (me gusta el ambiente de los negocios), "because every day I learn a lot. At my age, it is a motivation. . . I don't have the profits that I would like, but I have the motivation or the spirit to do business" (tengo motivación).*[28]

Other market vendors were initially small business owners outside the market, and one a former employee of the grocery store he now runs with his wife and family.

The second wave of Moore Street Market vendors came from Mexico, due to the deterioration of the rural economies in Puebla, Oaxaca and Guerrero in the mid 1980s.[29] In the ethnically and racially segmented labor force, Mexican workers filled the jobs abandoned by Puerto Ricans. One older Puerto Rican vendor observed, "*Mexicans work too many hours. They do the work we don't want to do. They work harder than we do.*"[30] Others working in the market were Dominicans, Ecuadorians, and Nicaraguans who came because of urban poverty, the oil crisis in Central America, and the various wars and civil conflicts of the 1980s.

Unfortunately, Moore Street Market jobs provided only subsistence wages. A female vendor complained: "*I only gain an income to buy the food and pay the bills.*" Another vendor worried about the rising price of food and housing, and declining wages: "*Have you seen how food prices are rising? Today it is impossible to buy a house.*" Others, however, were successful, and at least two vendors established businesses that were profitable for more than twenty years.

Thus, Moore Street Market incorporated successive waves of first-generation Caribbean and Latino immigrants and served as a vehicle of social and economic mobility. This was especially evident with the second generation, as children born to first-generation migrants often attended college and obtained white-collar jobs. The market offered greater stability and was physically safer than street vending, especially for women.

In March 2007, however, New York City's Economic Development Corporation (EDC) announced that the market would close June 15 due to the decreasing number of shoppers and vendors and poor financial management. The vendors were not given prior notice of EDC's plans and were shocked to learn of this decision.

With the pending closure, the Public Space Research Group (PSRG) joined the Project for Public Spaces (PPS) to develop design and economic alternatives to forestall the forced closing. The field team included Babette Audant, Bree Kressler, and Rodolfo Corchado, who spent six months gathering data to make the case for the continuation of Moore Street Market as a Latino public space supporting a locally endorsed initiative. A research process based on dialogue with the community produced a revitalization plan responsive to the needs of the vendors, the cultural context, and the diverse neighborhood. Since stakeholders, residents, and visitors did not agree with any single vision of the future, it was vital to involve as many groups as possible, including government officials, Moore Street Market vendors, local street vendors, nearby business owners, residents and visitors,[31] developers, and religious and secular leaders.[32]

While the ethnographic study of Moore Street Market focused on the desires of stakeholders, it also included insightful stories of the market's importance as a supportive infrastructure when compared to street vending. For example, at the nearby intersection of Broadway and Flushing Boulevard, Mexican, Ecuadorian, Puerto Rican, and Dominican immigrants, and African American street vendors were selling flowers, fruit, ice cream, cold water, belts, sunglasses, and books from carts. The majority were women from Ecuador and Mexico who had formerly worked in manufacturing.

When interviewed, they said that working conditions were difficult due to police harassment, a serious deterrent to continuing in their current location. The women reported that they have been beaten and robbed and were left without adequate protection. Further, the relationship between the Latino vendors and the African American population in the neighborhood was tense, shaped by conflicts and fear.

Within the public enclosed market, working conditions were better. A policewoman at the entrance protected vendors from threatening customers and robberies. It had heat in winter and air conditioning in the sweltering summer, a café and bathroom, and coolers in the basement.

Most Moore Street vendors said that the market should stay open and keep its pan-Latino identity. As one put it "*We have a lot [of] plans for the market. This is a very important and strategic place for the society in general, not only for the Puerto Ricans, but for the whole society . . . The place [the market] is strategic because [it] is surrounded by the Latino population and the products that we sell here are very well liked by Latinos.*"[33] They wanted to retain their pan–Latin American identity and continue as a Latino public space.

In 2019 Moore Street Market received a $2.7 million renovation grant for the market and outdoor area, Humboldt Plaza, as well as weekly and monthly classes run by El Puente de Williamsburg, a

Figure 6.4 Moore Street Market Vendor and Customer, Brooklyn

human-rights institution that serves as Moore Street Market's community partner.[34] The neighborhood continues to gentrify, but newcomers support it as a historical and cultural site that lends character to the area. Many of the original vendors have retired or left, but online applications are open and encourage immigrants to apply. And a few of the original businesses, the barbershop, tailor, and Ramona's café with Caribbean cuisine, as well as the fresh fruits and vegetables stands, remain. Though slow in coming, investments in infrastructure and programming enabled vendors, residents, and visitors to benefit from this cultural center and public marketplace.

The use of ethnographic research, political activism, and media coverage to keep Moore Street Market open is only one strategy for contesting the closure of a valued public space. At Baguio City market in the Philippines, vendors employed insurgent public space practices to protest their disenfranchisement in the redevelopment process.[35] When the redesign constrained their ability to work, the vendors moved their businesses onto the bordering streets and expanded their stalls into the aisles to recapture the economic vibrancy they had lost.[36] Their "guerilla urbanism" reversed the previously marginalized street vendors inability to assert their rights to make a living and claim their legitimacy. At another public market in Baguio City, vendors succeeded in drafting new governing strategies and forming the necessary associations to obtain government permission to establish a legal used clothing market on a main city artery.[37]

Parks for Caregiving

Parks, as well as sidewalks, provide opportunities for informal workers, especially caregivers who use the playgrounds for entertaining children and benches and shady paths for eldercare and assisted walking. For Caribbean-born nannies working in Brooklyn, the neighborhood streets and parks become "quasi-offices . . . rendering them visible to the rest of the community and ultimately their employers."[38] As more parents work from home, childcare providers are expected to take the children to the park and be out of the house all day long regardless of the weather. Thus, public space becomes their workplace where they struggle to keep their charges occupied and try to avoid constant surveillance due to being in public all day long.

A combination of salaried employees and informal workers also clean and maintain public spaces. While in the past, park staff were mainly unionized public servants, today a much greater amount of park work is done either for free or informally at much lower cost.[39] In New York City, park workers are made up of a variety of volunteers, welfare-to-work assignees, unionized city employees, summer youth workers, private workers under contract for a conservancy, community-service workers, and short-term workers hired on a seasonal basis.[40] This army of workers includes a mix of formal and informal employees, some with city benefits and others who are minimally paid with no job stability. Informal workers increasingly supplement the dwindling number of full-time park employees because of limited municipal finances and the low priority of parks and recreation for most administrations.

Parks, sidewalks, streets, plazas, and squares are also places for informal workers to get together, relax, and socialize, as well as care for one another. One Sunday afternoon walking in downtown Hong Kong, I discovered streets packed with Filipina domestic workers sitting on blankets strewn across the pavement.[41] This weekly sharing of meals and exchanging news at Statue Square has since spread to nearby streets, skywalks, and even the lobby of the Hong Kong Shanghai Bank.[42]

The migrant appropriation of Statue Square stimulated businesses for sending remittances, buying clothes, and purchasing foods, and it became a center of Filipina mutual aid and worker identity. Political organizing based on shared concerns resulted in demonstrations on labor issues such as maternity leave and a minimum wage. Statue Square remains a visible site of informal immigrant workers' integration into the social and political life of Hong Kong.

The stories of waste collectors in Buenos Aires, market vendors in New York City and Baguio City, and domestic workers in Brooklyn and Hong Kong highlight many of the important ways that public spaces contribute to maintaining the informal economy. In these places workers meet one another and their customers and employers, and it is where relationships are nourished, and networks sustained. In this sense, public space offers more than just a workplace, but also a field of social relations that enhance the workers' sense of self, access to goods and services, and the financing necessary to transform informal work into more stable lives and permanent jobs. These workspaces become social centers that develop workers' social capital.

Another insight that emerges is the significance not just of public space, but of "people as infrastructure."[43] AbdouMaliq Simone observes that when faced with the difficulties of making a living, people use whatever resources and assets are available.[44] In the rapidly urbanizing cities of Johannesburg, South Africa, and Jakarta, Indonesia, marginalized youth employ a variety of strategies to survive, drawing upon a wide network of contacts to improvise temporary cash solutions. He offers the example of a transport depot in Abidjan, Ivory Coast, where:

> Hundreds of young men function as steerers, baggage loaders, ticket salespersons, hawkers, drivers, petrol pumpers, and mechanics. There are constantly shifting connections among them. Each boy who steers passengers to a particular company makes a rapid assessment of their wealth, personal characteristics, and the reason for their journey. This reading determines where the steerer will guide the prospective passengers, who will sell their tickets, who will load their baggage, who will seat them, and so forth. It is as if this collaboration were assembled to maximize the efficiency of each passage, even though there are no explicit rules or formal means of payment to the steerers.[45]

Public space supports an ever-changing human infrastructure that generates economic value through a "transaction economy" based on the exchange of goods and services as well as information and care.[46] For example, *dabbawalas'* delivery of midday meals in Mumbai and the network of workers at the train station in Abidjan illustrate how innovative informal systems solve complex delivery and transport problems in dense urban environments. Public spaces are the physical platform of this transaction economy that depends on informal workers' improvisation, local knowledge, and exchange.

Fluidity of spatial occupation in response to the ebb and flow of police surveillance and enforcement also encourages constant adaptation and swift modifications in informal worker practices. These tactics create transient spaces in which the dynamics between informal workers and state agents show "how people, goods, rules, and regulation are in continuous change, incessantly constituting space anew."[47] For example in Taipei, Taiwan, popular night markets have gone through multiple cycles of removal, reorganization, and relocation, yet throughout, vendors have found ways to evade eviction, hide their merchandise, pay criminal syndicates for police protection, and invent innovative strategies for continuing to sell their products.[48]

Working together in public spaces, warding off police detection and surveillance, developing systems of resource and client distribution, organizing to gain access to spaces and markets, all while trying to make a living, generates strong alliances. These connections are initially between people in the same family, country, or language group, but over time extend to broader cultural and political groups. As these networks include other people encountered in public space or through more distant ties, reciprocal vertical and horizontal associations evolve, along with additional resources and greater social capital.[49]

Informal workers exploit their socio-spatial knowledge of public space to improve their daily lives.[50] The psychological and cultural processes of place identity and place dependence also contribute to the formation of worker communities, collective empowerment, and political participation.[51] Certainly Moore Street Market, Baguio Market, and the streets of Buenos Aires demonstrate the multiple ways

Figure 6.5 Flushing Sunday Street Market, Queens

that powerful place-based relationships and social capital in the form of contingent networks develops among the informal workers who spend their days there.

★ ★ ★

Public space enables informal workers to thrive and flourish. It provides a venue for all kinds of improvised work and innovation in addition to all its other contributions. When we think about public space, it is usually in terms of its sociality, cultural events, and recreation. But for much of the world, public space is a place of work or looking for work and building social capital to find a better or more stable job. Without public spaces, these supportive centers of exchange and solidarity might not exist, increasing the precarity of informal workers.

Indeed, part of the increased attention to public spaces is their perceived contribution to economic outcomes,[52] especially in terms of providing added value to a particular location by increasing real-estate prices through the provision of a public asset. Increased real-estate values contribute to the wealth and assets of a city but are less critical to the global informal economy than providing workplaces for the marginalized, unemployed, and underemployed.

Public spaces offer some of the most open, flexible, and accessible workplaces that exist. One notable aspect of Moore Street Market is its ability to integrate immigrants into the formal economy by developing a set of relationships and skills that can lead to entrepreneurship and a better job. This occurs through the mentoring, knowledge, and expertise, as well as financial support that immigrants offer one another. But finding places where immigrants are culturally accepted, able to establish social ties, and gain the trust necessary for learning an informal job or skill can be difficult, as the previous ethnographies and stories illustrate. Inclusive public spaces such as sidewalks, streets, markets, plazas, and train and bus stations offer environments where this transfer of skill and knowledge can happen.

While social and spatial inequalities continue to plague newcomers, immigrant workers are still able to transform space, producing an emergent migrant urbanism that includes physical, social, and political strategies of evasion, appropriation, and solidarity. Immigrant entrepreneurs, for example, carved out a space for themselves in the suburbs of Washington D.C. through the local farmers' market.[53] Pickup soccer games at the Mar Vista Recreation Center, a public park in West Los Angeles, re-created social ties and enabled immigrants from Latin America to find "off the books" construction, painting, and gardening jobs through their team participation.[54] Visibility in public space is a critical component of societal integration, reducing precarity by establishing migrants' right to the city and political voice.[55]

7

Green Guerillas, Seed Bombs, and Granite Gardens

Environmental Sustainability and Public Space in Paris and New York City

A yellow alert blasts my iPhone, warning residents of a tornado accompanied by hurricane-force winds and high tides. It is a storm alert for Hurricane Henri barreling north on the east coast of the Carolinas. I go outside and feel the wind already picking up as I retrieve anything that could blow away or be ruined by what I expect to be torrential rains with high-velocity winds. I cover the outdoor sofa, lay the umbrella down on the bluestone patio, and sequester potted flowers behind the shed. As the weather report worsens, I consider covering the largest windows with plywood.

In the northeastern United States, we live with extreme weather events attributed to climate change and, in this case, a shift in the Gulf Stream that channels tropical storms to the northeastern Atlantic coast. We also suffer from scorching summer temperatures and brown-outs while wildfires tear through the western United States as part of the new "hot" summer.

Growing up in the hills of west Los Angeles, I experienced the fear of all-consuming fires, watching my house burn from the algebra classroom window. Its incineration was inevitable as the fire roads and empty land along the ridge were built on, adding more houses to fuel the flames. Contemporary brush fires or a misplaced match now turn into infernos that burn for weeks and sometimes longer destroying indigenous groundcover, trees, and small animals. Water supplies, already stressed by encroaching desertification, are further depleted by the conflagration.

Overdevelopment and a lack of understanding of a local ecology that requires burning to regenerate continue to be ignored by local urban planners. Real-estate interests are paramount in the Los Angeles basin. But now there is the added impact of global warming caused by the increase in urbanization and unbridled energy use and resource deterioration. Concern about climate change and the impact of our recent geological era, the Anthropocene, is now commonplace in everyday life.

At a conference sponsored by the Center for the Future of Places (CFP) in 2019, I talk with scholars about the role that public space plays in environmental sustainability. Late spring in Reykjavik, Iceland, is perfect, with long days for discussions and warm enough to visit the glaciers and explore this geothermal-energy-sufficient country.

My colleague Michael Mehaffy reminds me that "while we may not have clear answers, there is good evidence that public space is critical to environmental sustainability." "That may be true," I counter, "but 'environmental sustainability' is frequently used as a linguistic cover for larger and more expensive urban developments rather than a prescription for a healthier planetary future. How can you argue that public space contributes to the mitigation of climate change when the term is coopted and lost its meaning?"

Julian Agyeman, injured from working out, hobbles over to join us on the glacier viewing platform as Michael and I debate the issue. He advocates using "a just sustainability framework to expose the lack of social justice in many environmentally sustainable plans and designs. Instead of employing sustainability as a discursive strategy to signify some vague environmental goals, let's redefine those goals to be inclusive and fair."

The term "environmental sustainability" is found everywhere these days, in advertisements for affordable and luxury developments with green space to media reports on remediation of public spaces destroyed by "natural" disasters. Sustainability has become a metaphor for any good that is threatened or at risk and thus in need of preservation in the face of rapid globalization, economic restructuring, and technological transformation. It highlights the importance of maintaining and continuing human institutions and biological life in a world that values progress and urban development over damage to the environment and the people and animals who live there.

The United Nations World Commission on Environment and Development defines environmental sustainability as "meeting the needs of the present without compromising the ability of future generations to meet their own needs."[1] This presupposes the goal of improving the quality of human life while remaining within the carrying capacity of current ecosystems and stabilizing the disruptive relationship between human culture and the biophysical world. Due to the ecologically destructive and materialistic practices of wealthier nations and transnational elites, the Earth's resources are being consumed at a rate that jeopardizes continued existence.

The concept of "ecological sustainability," by comparison, emphasizes the interconnectedness of the Earth's ecosystem, including the stability of the climate systems; the quality of the air, land, and water; land use and erosion; biodiversity of species and habitats; and ecosystem services. Nine environmental problems—climate change, stratospheric ozone depletion, atmospheric aerosol loading, ocean acidification, biochemical flows, freshwater use, land-system change, biosphere integrity, and novel entities—have been identified as planetary boundaries that if succeeded risk the production capacity of ecosystems.[2] These planetary boundaries are "scientifically based levels of human perturbation of the Earth system beyond which Earth system functioning may be substantially altered."[3] I focus on only a few of these risks, including water (pollutants, groundwater levels, salinity, temperature, and alien species), air (pollutants, particles, ozone layer, climate system, and noise), land (pollutants, erosion, land use, and alien species), biodiversity (species and natural habitats), and ecosystem services (pollination, photosynthesis, water purification, and climate control).[4] Public space can play an important role in the mitigation of the risk to these essential and life-supporting processes.

Confusion and obfuscation in the application of these terms has led to their misuse. Indeed, it is helpful to distinguish the values orientation of environmental sustainability that has discursive and political power, from ecological sustainability that refers to the scientific measurement of planetary boundaries.

"Sustainability" has been transformed into an empty signifier used to justify a wide range of practices and contemporary ideologies.[5] In the early 2000s it was a keyword in urban and social policy, reflecting increased concern about climate change and a catch-all for a general turn toward the environmental issues and problems wrought by the geological age of the Anthropocene.[6] But there is little agreement about what sustainability actually means and why it has become the commonsense way to talk about modern life and its disparate ideas and practices.[7]

One way to understand why sustainability has become such an important watchword is to consider its history. In the early nineteenth century environmentalism emerged as a scientific strategy for understanding the impact of industrialization and economic growth and became part of the New Environmental Paradigm for progressive urban planners in the 1960s and 1970s.[8] Black intellectual leaders such as Nathan Hare and Dorceta Taylor and activists such as Hazel Johnson brought attention to the concept of ecology and an environmental justice paradigm for Black liberation and civil rights equality in the 1970s.[9]

In 1983, the UN secretary general created a commission to study the failure of aid programs and the environmental degradation that occurred. The resulting 1987 UN Brundtland Report coined the term "sustainable development" as a strategy to meet the social and ecological needs of contemporary populations by better management through private services. Sustainable development linked technology and capitalism for the more productive and efficient use of natural resources to ensure future growth and stimulate national economies.[10]

The UN Conference on Environment and Development passed Agenda 21 in 1992, laying out a series of action plans and guidelines to protect ecosystems and vulnerable groups. But while instituting important changes such as Copenhagen's commitment to carbon neutrality by 2025, the guidelines ignored racial inequalities and issues of environmental injustice.[11] Thus, economic prosperity based on renewable natural resources, and sustainable growth continued to bypass poorer nations and marginalized regions.

Green public spaces contribute to ecological sustainability and neighborhood flourishing directly through community gardens, sustainable parks, and environmental justice programs, and indirectly through ecological planning and design approaches that protect eco-system services. Strongly held environmental values support a public culture of defending community gardens, advocating for trees and green space, recycling trash, composting organic waste, and protesting when deleterious land uses threaten neighborhood open spaces. Research on brownfield remediation or restoring deteriorating parks and fragile ecosystems, however, also reveals how greening accelerates gentrification.

The gentrification risks of environmental interventions in low-income neighborhoods are well documented and substantial, but to ignore disease-causing particles in the air, repeated flooding, and build-up of mold in house basements, deterioration of healthy tree cover due to drought conditions, and other hazards in low-income neighborhoods is problematic as well. We need strategies so that neighborhoods surrounding a new environmental amenity such as Domino Park or Brooklyn Bridge Park in Brooklyn do not result in sky-rocketing housing prices, gourmet markets, and high-end restaur-ants that increase rents and taxes and accelerate evictions for local ten-ants.[12] Developments that utilize public spaces as greenways, gardens, ecologically resilient systems, and biodiverse refuges must include policies that protect the human as well as the biophysical ecology of a neighborhood for the future. While there are risks there are also social and environmental benefits from environmental interventions that mitigate climate change and reduce global warming.

★ ★ ★

Running through sprinklers is a summer pleasure that city children enjoy at many New York City playgrounds. Sprouting water from the mouth of a bronze hippopotamus in Riverside Park or a granite boulder at the 89th Street playground in Manhattan cools everything including, the hot pavement, kids, parents, and vegetation. Water draws people together and reduces the impact of the "heat islands" gener-ated by high-density buildings and asphalt surfaces designed without a green infrastructure of trees, water, plants, and permeable paving.

Two hours at my grandson Gavin's birthday party at Playground 89 watching four-year-olds as they spray each other with water pistols while eating pizza and cupcakes highlights how cooling water is on a hot summer day. This is the first time his friends and family are together because of COVID-19 restrictions now reduced in July 2021. I ask him if he is enjoying himself and he stretches out his arms to encompass the entire space. "Of course," he exclaims with a smile, "everyone is here." The moisture-laden breeze reminds me of suburban sprinklers set in an expanse of trees and green lawns that cooled the high temperatures of Los Angeles summers.

Across the street is a verdant oasis of gardens and people watering flowers and vegetable plots at the West Side Community Garden (WSCG). "Is

Figure 7.1 Children Playing on Hippos in Water at Riverside Park, Manhattan

this community garden an important public space for the neighborhood?"
I wonder, going over to investigate. "What role does it play compared to
Playground 89?"

Entering through a wrought-iron gate, I hear birdsong and rustling trees, and
smell the moist soil and fragrance of herbs and flowers. Rectangular garden plots
arrayed in concentric circles descend to a sitting area that defines the central space.
People are spread throughout, some individuals sleeping on benches or resting in
wheelchairs, couples laughing as they enjoy lunch at a small table, while most are
watering their plots. The garden includes small flower beds as well as large areas
of neatly trenched rows of vegetables with stakes and protective fencing.

Figure 7.2 Westside Garden Neighborhood Context, Manhattan

Figure 7.3 Westside Garden Vegetables, Manhattan

The WSCG is one of many community projects that grew out of the 1970s urban renewal that left city-owned abandoned buildings and vacant lots scattered throughout Manhattan neighborhoods including the West Side, Lower East Side, Hell's Kitchen, and East Harlem. Residents worried about children playing in these trash strewn and often dangerous places and the physical deterioration of the neighborhood. In response, grassroots neighborhood movements began to reclaim these areas and turn them into safe and productive places. But their land tenure was uncertain, and with the increase in the value of properties and gentrification of the neighborhoods there was the constant threat that the city would sell the property to developers.

Initially most neighborhoods leased their vacant lots through the political activism and support of the Green Guerillas. The Green Guerillas organized on the Lower East Side of Manhattan by removing trash, adding topsoil, and lobbing "seed bombs" to beautify the area. In 1974 they convinced the Office of Housing Preservation and Development to lease the first community garden, Bowery Houston

Community Farm and Garden, and became a model of what could be accomplished with volunteers.

The city became interested in these grassroots revitalization projects initiating the Green Thumb program to coordinate neighborhood leases for city-owned vacant land for a little as $1 a year in 1978.[13] By the 1990s Green Thumb had become the nation's largest urban gardening program supporting more than 550 gardens throughout the city and accounting for more than 100 acres of public open space.

The WSCG took a different route to secure their land and with the help of the Trust for Public Land became a 501(c)3 with a board of founding members able to negotiate with the city and the prospective developers to develop a plan. The terms of the agreement included that the garden remain open every day and that all events would be free. Initially WSCG had a long-term lease, but in 1988 they were able to purchase the deed if the garden remained open and run as a nonprofit organization.

WSCG provides a refuge and place for relaxation; supports volunteers who plant, clean, and harvest; offers movie and concert evenings; and organizes a tulip festival and an annual fundraiser. It has a unique governance structure as a private nonprofit run by a board committed to keeping it open and accessible, yet like other community gardens, it functions as a public space that enhances the environmental quality of the neighborhood.

Urban gardening is part of the public space movement. Activists and residents argue that gardens are accessible outdoor community centers that need to be defended against the use of public space as a mechanism for increasing real-estate values and as an amenity for wealthy buyers.[14] The significance of community gardens as social centers and green infrastructure should not be underestimated.

Gardeners are deeply attached to their gardens; grow valued flowers, fruit, and vegetables; understand their cultural importance for the neighborhood; and encourage democratic processes in decision-making. A 2019 study of thirty-five community gardens in East Harlem found that of the 18,000 square meters of garden space, at least half was open green space.[15] These East Harlem community gardens contribute environmental benefits, including moderating heat islands, reducing runoff from heavy rains, and contributing to food supplies and better nutrition.[16]

Community gardens in New York City continue to face threats as the price of land skyrockets, putting pressure on the city to use these valuable lots for affordable and luxury housing. But the benefits of community gardens—environmental, social, cultural, and political—are increasingly emphasized as urban gardening becomes a way for low-income neighborhood residents living in food deserts to obtain fresh produce. While community gardens started in Manhattan through political action, Sharon Zukin writes that of New York City's 700 gardens, 316 are in Brooklyn, where residents are mainly Black and Latino and many are immigrants who use their gardens to supplement their income by selling products in local markets.[17] In southwest Philadelphia, Sankofa Community Farm at Bartram's Garden increased access to fresh fruits and vegetables for older African American families and new West African immigrants. By managing farm stands and affordable grocery partnerships with 4 acres of land, 1,500 volunteers, and 20 paid high school interns, they were able to grow and distribute 15,000 pounds of food each year [18]

The shift in scale from community gardens to urban agriculture to supply basic nutritional needs in marginal communities; supplement food shortages during economic crises, disasters, and pandemics; and support community revitalization and social solidarity is escalating.[19] Programs are found in US cities with a history of urban renewal and abandonment or progressive programs of revitalization such as Detroit, Chicago, Seattle, Portland, San Francisco, Los Angeles, and Washington D.C. In post-Hurricane Maria Puerto Rico the food sovereignty movement is working to revitalize local food production and reverse the harmful effects of the colonial pattern of US food dependency.[20]

As far back as the 1980s while participating in a five-year longitudinal study of a resettled *barrio* in Guatemala City, Francis Johnston and I found that even a few corn, bean, or tomato plants impact a child's growth and cognitive development.[21] A tiny garden or selling produce in the local market helps children to thrive even in the worst socioeconomic situations including those at risk for malnutrition.[22] Today, urban agriculture programs are expanding in response to food shortages due to failing economies and the COVID-19 pandemic.

For example, Argentina's third-largest city, Rosario, was recognized by the World Resources Institute for its sustainable and inclusive approach to urban farming.[23] After the 2001 economic collapse, the municipal government worked with 700 families to grow their own food using underutilized and abandoned urban land. Twenty years later they have created 74.1 acres of community *parque huertas* (garden parks) and another 37 acres of agricultural family gardens offering food and employment for residents.[24] Urban agriculture programs are important in cities as varied as Nairobi, London, Ahmedabad, and Monterrey, creating green belts of gardens and open space to address environmental and social inequities.[25]

Community gardens and urban farms add to the green infrastructure of the city, providing public spaces that increase environmental sustainability by reducing heat islands, recapturing stormwater runoff, rehabilitating abandoned and vacant land, and creating green spaces where animals, birds, trees, plants, and people can flourish. They fulfill many of the UN Sustainable Development Goals such as improving water and air quality, mitigating climate change, increasing biodiversity, and protecting fragile ecosystems.[26] Community gardens and urban agriculture offer models of how to rethink the role and purpose of nature in the city as not solely for beautification or real-estate value, but as a strategy for producing a greener city and providing the necessary ecosystem services to reduce the impact of global warming.[27] Putting together the social dimensions of gardening with the fundamental nexus of food-energy-water-people of urban agriculture connects strategies from individual gardens to city-scale strategies.[28]

★ ★ ★

Sustainability is becoming an increasingly important component of public space design with the recognition that parks and greenways can reduce resource use and support critical ecosystems and ecos-ervices. In 2004, Galen Cranz[29] and Michael Boland added the Sustainable Park as a fifth urban model to modify Cranz's historical park typology of Pleasure Ground (1850–1900), Reform Park (1900–1930), Recreation Facility (1930–1965), and Open Space System (1965–present).[30] Sustainable parks increase ecological performance and emphasize ecological values such as using native plants, restoring streams and wildlife habitat, composting and recycling, and utilizing energy-saving technologies and renewably resourced construction materials.[31] Their study of 125 parks found that Sustainable Parks at-tempt to be resource self-sufficient, integrate with the surrounding environment, and generate new aesthetic forms. Specifically, they minimize the ecological costs of construction, encourage self-generating woodlands, plant indigenous trees and bushes, institute compost production, and employ on-site stormwater retention basins and permeable asphalt to reduce erosion and recapture rainwater.[32] Nonetheless, Cranz and Boland were unable to determine whether these parks simply used environmental discourse and symbolism or reduced resource use.[33]

Building and designing a sustainable park is a complicated political project. Andrew Newman's ethnography of the Jardins d'Éole located in a low-income immigrant neighborhood of Paris illustrates these complexities by tracing West African and Maghrebi residents' activism to transform a brownfield site into a ecologically sensitive park.[34]

Newman argues that the neighborhood mobilization to construct a green space was a way to express the long-standing social demands of this marginalized community.[35] Yet their vision of a "new green space" was explicitly linked to the need for cleaner air, a safe place for children to play, a gathering space outside of deteriorating apart-ments, and a community space for culturally diverse residents to come together.

The architects and municipal agencies responded positively with a green design and supported transforming the former toxic industrial site into the residents' vision. At the level of the resident's lives, this change mitigated pollution and added green space, but also bolstered the political clout of West African and Maghrebi residents.[36]

The Éole mobilization began in the late 1990s led by middle-income public workers of non-immigrant and Maghrebi origins with a wider membership of West African residents representing the working-class, immigrant neighborhood.[37] When an abandoned SNCF (the French National Railway System) rail station was to be leased for a new industrial use and the current warehouse space expanded, the Éole mobilization countered these proposals as environmental hazards, demanding a park as an environmentally beneficial alternative. A weekly news publication revealed the dangers of the diesel fumes of SNCF trains and trucks to local families and children and that toxic waste had been stored there. The report justified the argument for constructing a sustainable park to reshape the politics as well as the environment through a public space intervention.

Residents also faced a housing crisis and were living in crowded apartments. They needed a green space where they could raise their children. Mothers and children called for a community garden, a safe playground, and natural places for healing the neighborhood. Other residents used the language of ecology and pollution, arguing that a park would give them a "space to breathe," "let in light," and be the "lungs of the neighborhood."[38] The mayoral election in 2001, and a Socialist Party and Green Party coalition offered an opportunity to place their claims, and by 2004, 4.2 hectares and $26 million were set aside for the planning and design process.

The activists articulated their desire for an organic and resource-efficient design that would use no chemical fertilizers or pesticides and promote sustainable practices. The designers also focused on sustainability, but only as a design principle that communicated their alignment with the globalized environmental discourse that included energy conservation and renewable resources. A miniature turbine, the use of natural materials and reappropriated stones from the site, a gravel garden for the recycling of water, and a plant-filled connecting canal as well as an aesthetic of minimalism reflected the designers' sustainable intentions. Environmental elements such as using water instead of fencing as a border to be more inviting and to allow more visibility from the street offered some of the green benefits that residents requested.[39]

The management structure of the park reflected the collective principles espoused by the neighborhood and the municipal authorities. Residents had a central role in the community garden and the refreshment stand, and the residents' committee which included representatives of all the cultural, youth, and neighborhood associations worked with the Paris Parks and Environment Department to manage park problems.[40] The new park provided open spaces for Maghrebi and West African teenagers with outdoor concert venues for hip-hop performances on summer nights and neighborhood-wide festivities. The main plaza was open twenty-four hours a day, contradicting the usual Parisian practice of locking parks at sundown, emphasizing it was "their park"[41] where residents would monitor safety rather than resorting to gates and police.

Figure 7.4 Jardins d'Éole, Paris, France (Photograph by Andrew Newman)

Yet there were contradictions and conflicts that arose. Citing safety concerns and noise complaints by residents, city authorities began closing the esplanade at night in the mid 2010s. The architects chose species of plants that would attract birds to contribute to biodiversity. But the birds never came due to the extensive lighting used for night security and the loud noise of youths playing. Similar problems emerged because social, ecological, ideological, and political goals associated with the park were often in conflict with each other.[42]

While sustainable parks may fail to offer ecological transformation and increase housing prices and rent, they do improve the overall environment as in the case of Jardins d'Éole. This new green space reduces toxic hazards that existed when the space functioned as a rail station and remediates existing air pollution. It adds plants, trees, and flowers that increase biodiversity, and water features cool the environment with gravel drainage to slow runoff. It reuses materials that were on the site and employs local workers. The community garden offers locally grown food and offers programs for neighborhood youth about plants and fruits and their propagation.

At the same time, this sustainable park—while not necessarily addressing all its ecological potential—provides a socially inclusive setting for other aspects of public life. Even with the night closure, it includes a place for children to play; for seniors to sit and talk; for teenagers to hang, dance, and play music; and most importantly for the neighborhood to demonstrate their pride and mastery and claim it as their own. Like Walkways in Poughkeepsie, and the children's garden and playground in Dandora, Jardins d'Éole redefines the neighborhood and gives residents a greater sense of control and political autonomy, even though there remains some degree of contestation with creating such a space.

★ ★ ★

My first experience with ecological planning and design was a study of Sanibel Island, Florida, in 1978. Residents were worried about whether they could get off the island if there was a hurricane. Working with an ecologist and a landscape architect, I learned that the island's carrying capacity and the one narrow bridge linking Sanibel to the mainland were not sufficient to evacuate all the residents. In fact, with the current rate of housing and commercial development, they were courting a future disaster.

Human ecological thinking argued for very low population density, limited growth, and development restrictions to mitigate this problem. Our plan for ecologically sensitive public space proposed streets lined with grass paths rather than paved sidewalks, interconnected nature reserves for biodiversity, natural drainage systems with water retention ponds, and restrictions on clearing of wetlands along with limits on the number of visitors at any one time. We presented our plan to the community and planning board and then waited for their decision.

During a visit in 2020, the small beach parking lots closed as soon as the maximum number of cars was reached to keep day trippers from adding to the resident population. The bridge was reconstructed to hold more automobiles as developers had persuaded the planning board more housing was necessary to pay for the large areas of ecologically fragile reserve. Multiple biodiverse reserves dotted the island linked by greenways to protect the birds and animals, providing safe wildlife corridors, yet I wondered whether we had done enough to protect the island.

When nearing the end of my doctoral research in Costa Rica, there were few anthropology positions, and like many in my cohort I was looking for other opportunities. One day a man from the farm behind my house came running saying that there was a Professor Ian McHarg on the telephone who wanted to talk to me. I remember sprinting through the pasture, dodging cows and chickens and wondering who might be calling. Once on the telephone, a melodious deep voice with a thick Scottish brogue offered me a job as an assistant professor in the Department of Landscape Architecture and Regional Planning at the University of Pennsylvania. At the time I did not even know what landscape architecture was, much less what a medical anthropologist would have to offer, but McHarg was adamant. Needing a job to finish my dissertation, I accepted a position to teach human and environmental health as an outcome of ecological planning.

Ian McHarg was a student of Lewis Mumford at Harvard University, whose thinking was grounded in ecohumanism, an educational philosophy with the objective of moving society toward a more ecological culture.[43] Mumford's classes emphasized the complexity of human ecology and its importance as a framework for understanding people and their environments. Ecohumanism emerged from integrating the scientific knowledge of ecology and social values[44] with the connectiveness of human and natural systems on earth.

Drawing on this philosophy, McHarg promoted a vision of a harmonious world where both natural and social environments were planned and developed in relation to their best and highest use.[45] He called this multidisciplinary approach "human ecological planning" and developed a method that examined the physical, biological, and cultural characteristics of a landscape in terms of their opportunities and constraints.[46]

McHarg had the leadership skills, support of the administration, and funding to reimagine the field of landscape architecture and regional planning as a means for creating a healthier world through a scientific approach. In 1969 he wrote his paradigm-breaking book, *Design with Nature*,[47] laying out his method of mapping and analyzing the local ecology, geology, limnology, geography, structural engineering, geomorphology, and anthropology of a site to find the best fit for each piece of land. The so-called layer-cake method, the overlaying of natural and social data maps to identify the most and least fragile ecosystems,[48] produced an evidence-based approach.

Using transparencies and then GIS computer programs to overlay the collected survey data, human ecological zones and patterns could be identified. The planner or designer could then locate and protect existing ecosystems by devising interventions that would have the least impact and greatest social value. Here is where I came in—my charge was to identify the human ecological relationships that would result in health for the greatest number of people.

The social-values component included an examination of who would benefit and who would suffer with the implementation of proposed planning and design scenarios. McHarg argued that by using scientific evidence the best plan for human and environmental well-being would emerge. One of the criticisms of this method, however, was that the application of the values framework and evaluation of impacts tended to be environmentally determinist based on the belief that the physical environment determines and shapes patterns of culture and social development.

This was not always the case, of course, in that both physical science and ethnographic data were open to interpretation. Further, the power dynamics of any project depended on who we were planning for—the client, the current residents, the future residents, or the environment—and who was paying for the project or intervention. In 1985 I completed a content analysis of the design outcomes of publicly versus privately funded projects and found, not surprisingly, that publicly funded plans and designs more frequently addressed the needs and desires of the local community.

The idealism of the enterprise, however, was contagious, and it was exciting participating in a planning and design studio with an ecologist, geologist, and landscape architect. Together we struggled to create an evidence-based foundation for regional planning and landscape design. Some of our projects focused on public spaces such as Farnham Park or the development of interlocking greenways and runoff systems to protect the fragile ecosystems found on Sanibel Island.

Human ecological planning and design as imagined and practiced by McHarg and the faculty at the University of Pennsylvania did not win over the planning and design fields. Some ideas lingered, but once McHarg retired and Ann Spirn became the new chair, the orthodoxy of method and theory declined. Spirn was intrigued by ethnography as she had been involved in a social values study of Powelton, a low- to middle-income neighborhood in west Philadelphia. But she had questions about ethnography's usefulness at the scale of landscape design.

Her contribution presented in *The Granite Garden* was that the city is part of nature, and that the urban landscape is made up of a complex interaction between human beings and biological and physical processes. These processes include "the movement of air, erosion of the earth, the hydrologic cycle and the birth and death of living organisms."[49] Spirn recommended the use of vacant lands and abandoned buildings to create an infrastructure of public spaces that would accomplish many objectives including recreational and aesthetic amenities; stormwater retention areas landscaped as parks; woodlands, meadows, and constructed wetlands to treat wastewater; and sewage sludge for soil amendment.[50]

The potential of public space contributing to a human ecological infrastructure remains. The theory and method of human ecological planning and design, regardless of its flaws, offered a way to plan and design for ecological sustainability. One wonders, if human ecological planning had been more successful, whether fewer fragile landscapes would have been lost and marginalized peoples displaced in the intervening years.[51]

★ ★ ★

Green infrastructures comprise parks, gardens, forests, and other private and public green spaces make up an interconnected network that conserves natural ecosystems and provides benefits to human populations.[52] This network extends into every aspect of plant and animal life from the interdependence of trees[53] to urban infrastructures that provide the connectivity and livability of cities. The concept of "ecosystem services" developed by the Millennium Ecosystem Assessment (MEA) working group describes these direct and indirect benefits to human health and well-being.[54] They provide a framework to assess the consequences of ecosystem change and produce a scientific basis for sustainable use.[55] The four types of ecosystems services include:[56]

1) **Provisioning**—any benefit that people can extract such as plant and animal materials, drinking water, and natural resources to produce energy

2) **Regulating**—any process that makes life possible such as pollination, decomposition, water purification, climate regulation, carbon sequestration, and erosion and flood control

3) **Cultural**—non-material aspects of ecosystems that change or guide cultural, intellectual and social development

such as recreation on green spaces, economic benefits of green
infrastructure, and creativity from interactions with nature

4) **Supporting**—any process that sustains basic life forms such as
photosynthesis, creation of soils, and water cycling

The ecosystem service model provides a clear and useful link between ecology and sustainability outcomes.[57] For example, the MEA
working group tracks the rapid disappearance of land cover and the
growing demand for food, fresh water, timber, and fiber that have resulted in substantial loss in biodiversity with 60 percent of ecosystems
now degraded or used unsustainably.[58]

Henrik Ernstson working with the Stockholm Resilience Center
and the African Center for Cities at the University of Cape Town
modified the MEA model to relate ecosystems services to environmental justice since the benefits to humans are entangled in social
and political processes.[59] Biophysical processes should not be viewed
objectively but include how an ecological network articulates with
struggles over land use and which ecological outcomes are given
value.[60] He employs two interlocking frameworks: a social-ecological
network analysis with a city-wide perspective, and a local values analysis based on place-based struggles and local planning goals. Many
cities have used the MEA assessment model and Ernstson's social-
ecological and values analysis to influence decisions about parks,
greenways, biodiversity reserves, and stream corridors as a way to improve environmental sustainability.

One example is the Jardins d'Éole, but similar citizen-led green
infrastructure is occurring throughout the world. These projects
range from regional reserves to protect biodiversity hotspots essential to habitat loss and indigenous peoples' displacement in the Malay
Archipelago,[61] assessments of urban stream corridors for their ecological impact and potential human use in Texas,[62] and citizen-led
adaptive re-use projects featuring a park with streambed-like features,
pollinator gardens, and bioswale and rain storage in Atlanta, Georgia.[63]
Even small-scale pop-up parks such as Grasslands in Melbourne,

Australia, made of planters with native grasses put in place for six weeks, or a pocket park using a hole in the ground left by a previous property owner in Wichita, Kansas, heighten biodiversity, pollination, and nutrient cycling—as well as social interaction—essential to the ecosystem.[64]

Ecosystem service improvements, however, usually occur in wealthier neighborhoods organized by middle-class and professional environmental groups so that they are not equally available. More importantly, some low-income and working-class neighborhoods prefer not to participate in these programs because of the risk of negative impacts. Potential hazards include transmission of insect-borne disease with the increase of ponds and streams, falling branches or trees in poorly maintained areas, and dense and impenetrable plantings where residents want open visas for safety.[65] Detroit residents in predominately Black and brown neighborhoods opposed the 2014 "greening of Detroit" tree-planting program. During the 1960s the city routinely ignored the maintenance of sidewalks and streets destroyed by tree roots, and excluded residents in the decision-making process. With that history in mind, these communities declined the city's offers to plant more trees, even though they understood and appreciated the health benefits of having more trees in their neighborhoods.[66]

Beyond Detroit, campaigns to stem climate change by planting a million trees have not always been successful.[67] Many programs focus only on getting the maximum number of trees planted regardless of whether these young trees can survive harsh urban conditions. In Copenhagen, newly planted trees were not adequately protected so people bashed them with their cars and bicycles, or they were poisoned by the salt used to de-ice winter roads. Planting trees does not have much of an effect unless they grow to maturity, and there are carbon costs to tree-planting as well. The right soil, temperature, climate, watering schedule, and species diversity and characteristics as well as protection from harsh chemicals and physical injury are necessary for trees to survive.[68]

Susan Gooberman, who retired as the director of Trees New York in 2013, explains these failures. "Not all tree planting programs are equally successful," she says. "The New York City Million Tree effort launched in 2007 was especially well thought out. They engaged many nonprofit greening organizations such as the New York Restoration Project, the Green Guerillas, and Green Thumb to work with the NYC Parks Department under the leadership of a group of young graduates from the Yale School of Forestry."

"What difference did these young leaders make?" I ask. Susan answers:

"They correctly insisted that community organizations and city-wide groups like Trees New York be partners in the endeavor. Including community stewardship projects was vital to making sure the trees would be watered and given nutrients during the first few years to be able to thrive."

Susan's organization, Trees New York, trains neighborhood volunteers to take care of their trees. I have wanted to participate in their programs to learn how to prune, water, and protect existing street trees in my neighborhood in Brooklyn.

"But it was not just Trees New York," Susan continues. "A major effort was undertaken to get community gardeners and school children in underserved areas involved. These types of community-based tree-planting programs are slower, but with this collaborative approach many more trees survive."

"The NYC Parks Departments was also adamant that a 'right tree, right place' protocol was followed, as it makes little sense to plant a sun-loving tree on a shady street." She adds, "and they were careful about the nurseries where they purchased saplings to be sure they were healthy before even going into the ground."

According to Susan, community stewardship programs are still ongoing, and tree inventories find city tree survival keeps increasing. The NYC Parks 2015 tree census counted 666,134 street trees citywide, a 12.5 percent increase from 2005.[69]

Tree planting is often seen as a panacea for global warming and improving ecosystem services because of their ability to store carbon.[70] Along with other plants, they transform carbon dioxide into oxygen, thus generating the most basic ingredient for healthy air and sustaining life. Trees provide shade and cooling in hot climates and reduce the impact of urban heat islands, while deciduous varieties offer insulation during winter in colder climates.[71] They provide food, nesting materials, and protection for birds and other animal species and play a critical role in photosynthesis, pollination, and regulating biochemical processes. Root systems form a network of nourishment that filters rainwater and provides nutrients for fertile soil.[72] Trees create places for leisure and recreation and are revered for their beauty and sacred symbolism in many cultures.

The Greening the Gateway City Tree Planting Program in Massachusetts targeted areas where there was less tree canopy. The program promoted neighborhood equity, reduced environmental racism, and integrated place, people, economic processes, and environmental remediation.[73] This intervention is particularly important in the United States, where a majority of people living in poverty have 25 percent less tree canopy and wealthier neighborhoods have as much as 65 percent more. These statistics represent current environmental inequalities that exist and result in differentials in environmentally induced illness and deaths from heat, acute respiratory diseases, polluted and contaminated water, and toxic landfills.[74]

★ ★ ★

Many tree-planting programs attempt to address environmental justice issues inherited from centuries of neglect in providing any kind of public space, much less green public space, to low-income and racially minoritized urban neighborhoods. It is not surprising, then, that Black and brown communities are skeptical about the intentions of these programs. As a Detroit resident put it, *"Environmental justice is not just about the distribution of bad stuff, like pollution, or good stuff, like forestry projects across disadvantaged communities. It's also about the distribution of power among communities that have historically only been the subjects and experiments of power structures."*[75] Equally problematic is that the outcome of public space greening or any improvement of the environmental quality of a poor neighborhood usually results in gentrification and higher rents that displace long-time residents.[76]

Melissa Checker calls the current reality the "sustainability myth" perpetuated by "sustainaphrenia," the belief that "we can stimulate economic growth while mitigating the effects of climate change, without any sacrifice."[77] The sacrifice is the degradation of those communities

that can least afford it in terms of health and life chances, but without
the money and power to stop environmentally deleterious incursions.
When low-income communities organize to fight for environmental
improvements, and succeed as in Jardins d'Éole, the long-term impact is neighborhood gentrification and residential displacement. It
is therefore not surprising that tree-planting programs in Detroit and
the restoration of neighborhood parks in New York City as part of the
One NYC 2050 Plan are met with skepticism and resistance. The Plan
NYC 2030 that funded the One Million Trees campaign and planted
new trees on every block in Harlem accelerated the green gentrification of the neighborhood. With the addition of new and upgraded
parks, a Whole Foods Market, and other street amenities, the number
of white professional residents increased, and housing prices soared.[78]

Frustrated with the lack of success at addressing environmental
justice and equity issues with improvements in sustainability, a group
of researchers in the United Kingdom began to advocate for a new
planning and design approach they call "just sustainability."[79] Just sustainability advocates argue that sustainability solutions that do not ensure equity rights cannot succeed because equity and sustainability are
inextricably linked. Building on a definition of environmental justice
as the right to live in a clean and healthy environment with equal
protection and meaningful involvement of people reiterates the importance of procedural justice. Communities should have the right to
participate in decisions about where environmental hazards will be
located.[80] Sustainability then becomes "the need to ensure a better
quality of life for all, now and into the future, in a just and equitable
manner, whilst living within the limits of supporting ecosystems."[81]

For Julian Agyeman a just sustainability perspective acknowledges
that planning tools such as urban renewal, redlining, deed restrictions,
and exclusionary zoning are racist strategies that impoverish and destroy Black and brown communities and reinforce white supremacy
and privilege. Further, financial instruments such as mortgages and
loans initially denied to Black and brown homeowners because of
their perceived financial "risk" are now available but in the form of

predatory lending that created the 2008–2009 housing collapse in the United States.

Agyeman is explicit about his desire for an anti-racist form of planning that respects Black, Indigenous, and people of color (BIPOC) and his insistence that all planning projects be based on co-production between the professional planners and community members. He includes four conditions for just and sustainable communities including: 1) improving quality of life and well-being; 2) meeting the needs of the present and future generations; 3) ensuring justice and equity in terms of recognition, process, procedure, and outcome; and 4) living within ecosystems' limits.[82] In many ways his just-sustainability mandate integrates the six goals of the Public Space and Social Justice Evaluation Framework and adds respecting ecosystem limits and planetary boundaries.

Other environmental-justice scholars emphasize the distributional as well as the procedural justice issues involved by focusing on "fairness" in terms of equity and/or equality. Equity and equality are often treated as if they refer to the same thing, yet they reflect different aspects of justice. Equity corresponds to procedural justice concerns having to do with the fairness of the decision-making processes, while equality refers to the distributional fairness of outcomes.[83] This distinction between procedural processes and distributional justice outcomes has become the focus of environmental justice movements especially in the United States.

★ ★ ★

A group of citizen scientists is mapping the way that heat is pooled in different sections of the New York City. Volunteers with sensors measuring air temperature and humidity find that on a tree-canopied block of West 94th Street near Central Park the sidewalk temperature is 84 degrees. The trees provide shade but also reduce the temperature through transpiration that occurs when water evaporates from the leaves, creating a vapor that consumes atmospheric heat. On a treeless lot where sanitation trucks are parked farther north the street surface reads 115 degrees. These heat differences are the result of the lack of trees in poorer neighborhoods and an abundance of green public spaces with mature trees and plantings in wealthier neighborhoods. This combination of socioeconomic in-equalities and racially discriminatory planning practices exacerbate health risks and ability to thrive for some neighborhoods and not others.[84]

There is a long history of socially inclusive and environmentally sensitive planning and design since the 1960s beginning with human ecological planning and design that evolved into urban ecology models that value, create, and restore public spaces as sustainable living ecosystems. Sustainable parks have emerged as a new kind of public space that foreground designing healthier and ecologically robust relationships among plants, animals, water, air, materials, and people. New ways to measure ecological sustainability in the form of evaluations of ecosystem services offer a clear and dramatic picture of how global warming and environmental change are occurring, and at what pace. Green planning strategies, though they remain entangled in neoliberal municipal policies, are making a difference in a few cities in North America and Europe.[85]

Some argue that it is too little too late to stop the melting ice-caps or the pollution of our oceans. Yet there is promise in the urban gardening and agricultural movements transforming abandoned and underutilized public space (and private space and rooftops) into green, productive, and racially and socially inclusive community places. Public space continues to play a leading role in providing social, psychological, and physical benefits, but it also offers a way to rethink how cities can become ecologically sustainable, carbon neutral, nutritionally productive, and environmentally just.

8

Place Attachment and Cultural Identity

Monuments, Parks, and Neighborhood Public Space in San José, Costa Rica, and the Statue of Liberty and Battery Park City in New York City

From the palisades overlooking Santa Monica beach traveling eastward to downtown traces my life history. A short drive from the coastline is San Vicente and Hamburger Hamlet, father's favorite restaurant for entertaining his distracted children. Then onto the corner of Westwood and Wilshire, the entrance to Westwood Village, where teenage friends spend Saturdays at the Bruin Theater or the more exciting Westwood Bowl, a space both derelict and forbidden.

Farther east almost to Beverly Glen is the Dorchester, a twelve-story condominium building where mother spent her last years only a short block from the apartment where fifty years before the family recovered from the Bel Air fire. East again to Fairfax: the boulevard of Cantor's Deli, the Farmer's Market, and the Los Angeles County Museum of Art (LACMA), formative to a love of modern art. Reaching downtown brings memories of visits to the jewelry mart with mother, and visiting father at the Biltmore near MacArthur Park.

Driving Wilshire Boulevard back and forth integrates the past with the present. With each visit, the same feelings re-emerge despite long absences and changes that have taken place. Even years after residing in New York, I still say I am "from L.A." Place attachment is about holding on to the people who lived there, and the relationships nourished, through the natural and built environment.

Place attachment is the symbolic and embodied relationship that people have with a particular place or territory. Most definitions refer to this connection as a psychological and cognitive bond that occurs developmentally through living in a location over time.[1] The rupture of this relationship through disaster, immigration, forced relocation, and even a desired move often generates a sense of personal loss and dislocation of those affected. Place attachment is also produced through the cultural practices of everyday life. Patterns of walking, sleeping, eating, working, playing, and other aspects of daily living are inscribed by repetitive movements, creating physical and emotional ties to a particular locale.

The concept developed out of the psychological construct of "place identity," which is a personal identification with places that are emotionally and socially significant. The environmental psychologist Harold M. Proshansky (1920–1990) first used the term "place identity"[2] to suggest that social identity and place identity are both the basis of a person's self-identity. Place identity situates psychological development in the life spaces, home spaces, and neighborhood spaces as well as the national and global spaces where people live. It highlights people's individual conceptions of themselves as located in a specific space and time.

While place identity focuses on sites of everyday experience, place attachment refers to a wider range of linkages including a sense of group or ideological belonging and national mythmaking. Place attachment is not only personal, but also cultural such that there is a transformation of the experience of a space or piece of land into a culturally meaningful and shared symbol.[3]

In 2004, the National Park Service asked the Public Space Research Group to study cultural associations to the Statue of Liberty and Liberty Island (LI) as part of a plan to protect those relationships during the statue's restoration. Liberty Island was originally named Minnissais ("Lesser Island") by the Delaware Nation as part of three "Oyster Islands" known for their shell beds and a major source of food. Dutch colonist Isaac Bedloe was awarded a land grant in 1667 and renamed it Bedloe's Island. The City of New York acquired the island in 1738, establishing a quarantine station to inspect incoming ships for disease and constructing a hospital in 1759–1760. During the American Revolution it was used as an asylum for Tory sympathizers and then ceded to the federal government in 1800. The US Army used Bedloe's Island as a military post and built Fort Wood from 1807 to 1811.[4]

In 1875, Édouard de Laboulaye commemorated the upcoming centennial of the Declaration of Independence and recent abolition of slavery with a gift from the people of France to the people of the United States.[5] The architect Frédéric-Auguste Bartholdi's "Liberty Enlightening the World" (the Statue of Liberty) was commissioned and erected within the fort in 1885–1886. The statue was declared a national monument in 1924, and in 1933 the National Park Service acquired the island and then took over its administration when Fort Wood was decommissioned in 1937.[6] Today the 14.7 acres encompass the Statue of Liberty Monument, the Statue of Liberty Museum, food concessions, picnic areas, a central plaza, and places to walk and recreate. Housing and offices for the National Park Service remain on site, but most staff commute daily.

From 2004 to 2005, Gabrielle Bendiner-Viani, Yvonne Hung, and I made fieldwork trips to interview personnel and conduct participant observation. We mapped the movement of people on LI and spoke with staff and visitors regarding their experiences.[7] Interviewing schoolteachers and leaders of school groups with children, we learned about their feelings regarding the statue and special places on the island. By accompanying visitors on the Circle Line ferries, participating in their first viewing of the statue, watching the video introduction, shopping in the gift shop, and purchasing food at the concessions, we gained insights into the tourist experience.

In addition to interviews, movement mapping, and participant observation, the Ellis Island Library and Museum collections offered a wealth of artistic representations of the statue as well as documentation of historical and political events. The Ellis Island Oral History

Project was a great resource for discovering people who lived and worked on LI, especially those in the early part of the twentieth century. Based on fieldwork and archival research, we learned that people and groups developed significant cultural ties to the site.[8]

At the heart of discussions of place attachment are questions about who owns the past and who has the right or responsibility to claim and preserve cultural remains and artifacts. These questions raise important ethical issues associated with the preservation of cultural property. Cultural repatriation, reparations, and/or return of property for those whose cultural property was taken, utilized, controlled, or erased rests on legal, moral, and international conventions that cultural groups have rights to their heritage and home places. The same argument can be used to emphasize the importance of maintaining the visibility of diverse cultural identities and histories at public heritage sites.

The Delaware Nation retains ancestral and historical connections to Liberty Island and a strong sense of place attachment based on their continuous occupation and use for oyster collecting and hunting since 994 CE.[9] In 2003, shell middens were uncovered on both Liberty and Ellis Islands. Representatives from the Delaware Nation, Delaware Tribes, and the Stockbridge Munsee, including Chief Brooks and Linda Poolaw, participated in the reburial of their cultural patrimony. The repatriation of cultural objects to the Delaware Nation ancestral home and the recognition of claims based on tribal identity, stewardship, and cultural use of the land reaffirm the indigenous history and settlement of the island.

People living, or who have lived, on LI, such as National Park Service staff and park managers, are also "deeply connected to the land" as Bendiner-Viani, Hung, and I found in our analysis of the data.[10] Living and working together created a "culture of care" that was familial in its expression. The Statue of Liberty was perceived as a mother or a child to be cared for. This ethic of care was reflected in discussions of how the residents and workers participated in "her" protection from cleaning and repairs to guarding against vandalism. Fictive kin ties contributed to the affective tenor of both past and present residents' expressions of place attachment and reinforced the interpersonal relationships that animated and sustained them.

Place attachment to the Statue of Liberty often occurs through the practice of pilgrimage, that is, making the trip to visit the statue for educational, social, ritual, or spiritual reasons. The owner of Circle Line, the ferry company designated to bring visitors to LI, was the first person who referred to these trips as "going on pilgrimage." Many interviewees mentioned the symbolic importance of the water voyage. Sustained cultural relationships formed among the people who visited regularly, or annually such as the Ladies Auxiliary. People who journeyed to the statue after a lifelong dream of doing so re- ferred to their trip as a journey to a sacred site such as Jerusalem or Mecca. Older adults recalled visiting as school children and wanted to re-create their childhood experience including the thrill of seeing the statue for the first time.

A more explicitly spiritual attachment is created when the Statue of Liberty and/or the land of Liberty Island plays a central role in a group's belief systems including military brigades, secret societies, religious organizations, and civic associations. The Masons, for ex- ample, incorporated statue symbolism in their iconography and secret-society practices. They felt connected through their financial contributions to the building of the Statue of Liberty and the statue's historical meanings—republicanism, freedom, and liberty—that re- flect Masonic values.

Some people integrate the cultural symbol of the statue into their lives without ever visiting the island.[11] The "Statue of Liberty Club" (formerly the "Statue of Liberty Collectors Club") is an organization that claimed an association through their enthusiasm for the symbol of the statue and the collection of images. The 77th Sustainment Brigade of the US Army located at Fort Totten, Queens, established a longstanding relationship when they chose the imagery of the statue for their official shoulder patch embroidered in gold and blue. Towns that quarried the stone to construct the monument's foundations re- tained a symbolic tie. Cities with replicas utilize the statue's symbolic meaning by placing her in civic public spaces or near the entrance to the town hall.

Others feel symbolically linked to the statue, even if they are excluded from the dominant immigrant story. For example, African Americans look to the statue's broken shackles as celebrating the end of slavery. There were visitors who were not aware of the connection between the statue and abolition, and yet found narratives of inclusion to relate to their own history and struggles for emancipation in the statue's symbolism.

Artists and poets often sent their work to the Statue of Liberty National Monument and created art pieces in homage to what the statue represents. In an art exhibition, Native American artists interpreted the statue as a Native American icon, seeing in the sculptural details a quintessential Native American woman who incorporates aspects of their beliefs. The statue waving to people in the harbor is a popular film representation of New York City in which she is the "greeter."

> As the F train to Brooklyn emerges from under the East River, the panorama of the statue standing high atop a small island in the middle of the harbor unfolds—I imagine the experience of father in 1907, catching his first glimpse of this symbol of welcome, standing on the deck, shouting, waving, arriving at his new life.[12]

Only a few public spaces have the cultural salience of the Statue of Liberty and Liberty Island. Place attachment at this heritage site developed in different ways depending on people's histories, length of residence, visitation frequency, and symbolic or artistic identification. Despite its uniqueness these cultural forms of place attachment reappear in relationship to many public spaces. Place attachment is part of the reason why public spaces retain cultural resonance and significance for diverse groups of people.

* * *

Public space is a stage for the enactment and experience of the underlying cultural system[13] and the symbolic terrain for representing the power relations inherent in it. Cultural institutions and their effects are visible in the design and use of the material environment and through the kinds of social activities and relationships that are possible. They are microcosms of the larger society, providing a window into its social structure and organization.

In pluralistic and multicultural societies there are many cultural frameworks and diverse forms of cultural expression. Thus, a crucial part of understanding public space is to untangle the power dynamics of whose culture is represented, celebrated, and valued. Often it is only the dominant culture—for example in the United States white middle-class culture—that is visible and revered.

The struggle for recognition, cultural identity, and continuity in the United States is a product of a settler colonial past that decimated indigenous peoples and ignored their territorial and cultural rights. Indigenous claims to land, self-governance, and autonomy continue to be contested, overlooked, and rejected through legal, cultural, and governmental policies. African Americans unwillingly brought to North and South America as slaves struggle against social injustice, cultural erasure, and structural racism even with emancipation and the Civil Rights Act. The BLM movement manifests this ongoing battle. Immigrant groups fight, some more successfully than others, for cultural representation and citizenship in the face of exploitative labor relations and ethnic discrimination. A system of racial capitalism that extracts social and economic value from a different "racial" identity maintains and reinforces these historically produced inequities.[14]

Public space alone is not able to redress all forms of oppression and erased histories, but it can be a place to start the processes of repair and recognition. When a public space is in front of a governmental building or in a centrally located open space, activities accrue political and cultural significance through visibility to those in power. In these central public spaces, material representations that symbolize national identity, history, power, and state control are often present.[15] National and civic culture is expressed by monuments, statues, plaques, flags, and other symbols that signify a particular view of the historic past or ideological and political interpretations of the present. In some cases, these cultural symbols denigrate people who use the space and thus become a source of cultural and political conflict over their legitimacy as well as barrier to a shared sense of belonging.[16]

The violent protest over the removal of a statue of Confederate General Robert E. Lee that stood in Lee Park in Charlottesville, Virginia, illustrates these tensions.[17] The Confederate statue was erected in 1924, one of many commissioned long after the Civil War, to reinforce a Southern confederate—and white supremacist—identity in the face of the emancipation of African Americans and their increasing access to political power. The placement of Confederate statues and monuments in civic public spaces signified a continuation of the glorification of a political movement and the people who fought to retain slavery and continue its racist trajectory. The decision to remove the statue and to rename the space Emancipation Park provoked a "Unite the Right" rally on August 11, 2017, that resulted in three deaths and thirty-three casualties. Protesters included self-identified members of the alt-right, neo-Confederates, white nationalists, neo-Nazis, Klansmen, and right-wing militias who were opposed by a small crowd of counter-protesters.[18]

The forceful remaking of the symbolic landscape associated with slavery and racial oppression throughout the United States is an important reminder of the potency of public space to reflect civic and political goals. To date 130 confederate statues and monuments have been removed, many in contentious circumstances.

In the analysis of how to achieve more socially justice public space, cultural representations and expressions at the civic and national level are critically important, leading to large-scale disputes about deeply meaningful aspects of national culture. In New York City an ongoing conflict to remove a statue of Christopher Columbus and rename Columbus Circle based on demands that it is offensive to indigenous Americans was contested by politically powerful Italian Americans who celebrate Columbus as a national hero. Women advocating for monuments representing them finally succeeded with the recent installation of suffragettes Sojourner Truth, Susan B. Anthony, and Elizabeth Cady Stanton in Central Park.[19] In Santa Fe, New Mexico, the ongoing erasure of the Tewa past in the central plaza—brought to the city's attention when activists forcibly took down an offensive monument—is being addressed by a city-wide process of truth, responsibility, and reconciliation.[20] Monuments and other symbolic representations located in central public spaces are enmeshed in local history, politics, and power relations that establish whose history and culture are most significant.

★ ★ ★

The everyday life of a publico space reflects culture not just through civic and architectural symbols. People are more likely to feel welcome if they see others like themselves, activities open to all with broad appeal, and events accompanied by food or music that can be appreciated by diverse visitors. The social and demographic make-up of a public space communicates whose culture is important and included in the national or local narrative.

Culture in this sense refers to the complexity of social life on streets, sidewalks, plazas, or any open space where people congregate. It is struggled over in ways like the statue and monument removals and can happen through the disruption of a fragile social ecology. Often the culprit is the redesign of a public space to "make it safe" and "clean" to meet class-based or tourist-oriented cultural aspirations and demands.[21] Many redesigns, executed for the benefit of those who govern rather than for those who use them, undo the cultural life and vitality already occurring. Redesigns accompanied by a long-term closure restrict the diversity of users and the multiplicity of cultural representations to create a more manageable and controllable space.

For example, the vibrant cultural life in Parque Central of San José, Costa Rica, was damaged by the 1993 redesign that forced the relocation of street vendors, shoeshine men, pensioners, and religious practitioners who had been there for over sixty years.[22] By replacing comfortable three-person benches and shady mature trees with single

Figure 8.1 Parque Central After Redesign, San José, Costa Rica (Photograph by Querine Kommandeur)

seats, telephone booths, and curved planters; prohibiting vending, loitering, and working; and opening the space for walking rather than
resting, the character of the space changed dramatically.[23] Crime levels
increased due to the absence of traditional users who kept the space
safe, and locals stopped coming to what used to be a comfortable
place where they felt they belonged.

A similar removal of users and physical clean-up was undertaken
in 2017 at the Plaza de la Cultura, two blocks from Parque Central.[24]
In this redesign all seating and greenery were removed, and an extensive list of rules and prohibitions posted. The cultural and recreational
activities of the youth and children who used to gather there were
specifically prohibited.

The architecturally designed plaza that younger Costa Ricans
and older North American pensioners, vendors, tourists, and mothers with children quickly adopted upon its opening became instead
an extension of a shopping street, a passageway with a fountain that

It is forbidden to feed the pigeons in all the area covered by the Plaza de la Cultura project (including the entrance to the museums), therefore, it is also forbidden to sell corn or any other type of food for pigeons.

Any event or audio-visual production for commercial purposes must have the prior authorization of the central bank's museum foundation.

The handrails in the stands and the ramps on the stairs for people with reduced capacity must remain free of obstacles. Therefore, it is not allowed to sit on the stairs.

It is not permitted to climb, run or jump on elevated walkways and stone benches.

The use of skates, skateboards or bicycles on the square is prohibited, to avoid affecting pedestrians.

It is forbidden to drink alcohol or to carry any type of weapon.

The Plaza de la Cultura is a smoke-free area, it is therefore forbidden to smoke.

Any type of irregular behaviour of persons that can harm the security of others, especially children, must be indicated to the security guards.

Used with Permission from Querine Kommandeur 2021

Figure 8.2 Plaza de la Cultura Guidelines, San José, Costa Rica (Graphic by Erin Lilli and original photograph by Querine Kommandeur)

curtailed wading or children's play.[25] The intent was to create a *sano* (clean, healthy) open area where people could walk to reach the nearby tourist hotel, the Teatro Nacional, and global franchises such as McDonald's or Starbucks; but the rich cultural life of the "plaza of culture" lost its inhabitants and everyday forms of expression. Cultural events are now scheduled solely by the Teatro Nacional, and the addition of special police and surveillance cameras limit children playing and youth hanging out.

This prohibition of almost every activity that the original public space encouraged was funded and implemented by the Banco Central, which owns the Plaza de la Cultura and the Museo de Oro located beneath. The original plaza was a place where youth played soccer and hung out in the evenings, children chased pigeons while their parents watched them from shady benches, religious groups came to sing while others came to protest, and evening pick-ups were still possible.[26] This was not the image that the Banco Central or the museum wanted to project. The decision to transform this previously "public" space into a version of "culture" that was tightly controlled and programmed to accommodate theatergoers, museum attendance,

Figure 8.3 Smart Surveillance on Plaza de la Cultura, San José, Costa Rica
(Photograph by Querine Kommandeur)

and consumption was not that of the city or Josefinos in general, but
of the Banco Central and the administrators of the adjacent cultural
institutions.

Ironically, the municipality of San José supports urban space policies that encourage the "collective character of culture," and the
2017–2020 Municipal Development Plan focuses on "coexistence and
a culture of peace."[27] It emphasizes democratization and citizen participation as a strategy to foster local cultural identity and heritage.[28]

Indeed, the municipality's plan insists that culture—in terms of cultural identity, continuity and collective memory, and cultural expressions such as festivals, rituals, and celebrations—are the *raison d'etre* of public space.

★ ★ ★

The drums in use range from large and small bass drums, to congas, bongos, and talking drums. The drummers are a multi-ethnic mix of people. Most of the dances observed in the circle are Yoruba (Nigerian language and ethnic group) movements. Generally, one of the bass drummers starts a "baseline" rhythm, and as the baseline becomes consistent, other players pick up the beat and perform variations on the rhythm. The cacophony soon becomes syncopated as more and more people "catch" the emergent rhythm, and the sound and intensity of the drumming increases until a "groove" is reached. They then hold this "groove," especially if the onlookers and dancers are intensely involved. Eventually, the rhythm decreases in intensity until it stops entirely, or until only a few drummers are left playing. If these few drummers continue playing, then they often set the tempo for a new rhythm, which begins in the same way—other drummers slowly begin to fall in line with the new baseline or central rhythm.

    Most of the drumming rhythms are of an African variety, mainly Nigerian, but some rhythms sound Haitian, and some seemingly of an Afro-Brazilian derivation. The drumbeats are often associated with Vodun (Yoruba based Afro-Caribbean curing practices), and there are offerings in evidence. The drumming is not simply a gathering of musicians, but also an event of religious and cultural significance.[29]

The role of culture expressed in collective events such as festivals, concerts, fairs, and art shows is foundational to a sense of social inclusion in public space. Dana Taplin, Suzanne Scheld, and I first wrote about the significance of cultural celebrations in our ethnography of Prospect Park in Brooklyn, New York.[30] The southeastern corner of the park, near the Parkside-Ocean Avenue entrance, is a focal point for West Indian and African American cultural activity. A local folk artist had carved human images into a tree stump by the lake shore, and this site of the "Grumbwa" ("grand bois" or "head") became a place where people went to play Haitian roots music. The carved image is no longer recognizable, but Haitian Americans still gather

Figure 8.4 Cultural Practices in Prospect Park, Brooklyn

on logs that circle the old stump, and religious offerings are left at the site.

During a recent walk—heavily masked for COVID-19 safety—I encounter two culturally distinct drummers' circles across from one another, one made up of mostly men playing drums and two women twirling inside the circle of participants reminiscent of Charles Price's original 1996 observations. What is different from twenty-five years ago is a group of musicians across from the drummers' circle playing cumbia and salsa on drums and guitar with electronic back up. A few couples dance to the rhythms and songs reminiscence of dancing with friends in Costa Rica and Mexico. Hearing people speaking Spanish, I stop to talk.

Many of the musicians recently moved to Brooklyn, bringing their cultural traditions, music, and dancing to Prospect Park. Some newcomers are from Mexico living near Ninth Street in Park Slope, while others are from the Spanish-speaking Caribbean and live in Crown Heights and Flatbush, a gentrifying Afro-Caribbean and Orthodox Jewish neighborhood. Soccer players organize pick-up games every afternoon and especially weekends accompanied by the sounds of celebrations nearby. Even though it's early spring, it's quite cold, but because of COVID-19 the park is full of groups too large to safely be inside.

The landscape is affectively shaped, first by one soundscape and then another, creating a cultural conversation and music competition like Moore Street Market or the New Central Bus Station in Tel Aviv, where music vendors crank up their speakers and blast popular songs to attract shoppers. Here the competition is friendly, drawing large crowds, and adding to the animated and friendly atmosphere.

Prospect Park is the center of endless numbers of cultural events from weddings, concerts, and birthdays to solemn prayer vigils, Eid celebrations, and the ritual throwing of bread in the lake during the Jewish New Year (*Tashlich*). Cultural identity is constructed within this multiplicity and celebrated in music, dance, song, theater, sports competitions, parades, and religious festivals. These secular and ritual events are characterized by collective effervescence—a sense of meaning and connection that comes from these events—that helps to explain how the gatherings add joy to life.[31] Emile Durkheim proposed this concept to describe the way that rituals reinforce social

Figure 8.5 Visitor Groups Wearing Masks in Prospect Park, Brooklyn

bonding and solidarity through the affective arousal of an assembled crowd.[32] In terms of cultural expressions and celebration—as well as affective bonding—Prospect Park is successful as a place to feel included and offers a model for other public spaces that strive for cultural diversity.[33]

Collective Memory and Cultural Continuity

While interviewing Battery Park City residents about their return after 9/11, I am surprised when a middle-aged woman in a grey sweater and skirt turns to me and emphatically exclaims, "we don't want to live in a graveyard." She suggests we go for a walk along the promenade to point out the existing monuments—the Irish Potato Famine memorial, a memorial to New York Police Department officers who died in the line of duty, and the New York City Holocaust Museum. "We're like a dumping ground for memorials," she complains. "We need more commerce and better services, places to visit and not a World Trade Center memorial built here!"[34]

Battery Park City (BPC) occupies a 92-acre site of reclaimed land in lower Manhattan along the Hudson River between Battery Park and Chambers Street. Landfill operations began in the 1960s using material excavated to build the foundations of the World Trade Center. BPC's planned community is divided into two sectors separated by the World Financial Center: these are informally called the north and south neighborhoods. Construction in the south neighborhood began with Gateway Plaza, between Liberty Street and Rector Place, in the late 1970s. The north neighborhood includes Stuyvesant High School (a highly competitive city-wide school that draws students from across the entire city), a hotel, a cinema, and a handful of completed residential buildings.

BPC contains 35 acres of waterfront parks with streets and buildings occupying the remaining 57 acres. The parks are characterized by a naturalistic style of horticulture, high-quality materials and furnishings, and numerous pieces of public art. Plantings are both lush and simple—the Battery Park City Parks Conservancy avoids showy floral displays, instead providing perennial herbaceous plants, shrubs, and many substantial shade trees along the walkways.

The playgrounds, dog runs, flower gardens, and sculpture exhibitions are strung along the waterfront linked by a Cooper Eckstut designed esplanade with benches and other places to stop and enjoy the spectacular water views and the skyline of Jersey City.[35] Each section is the collaboration of a landscape architect, architect, and artist with art elements, architectural structures, and plant materials integrated into the overall scheme. Two large playing fields located on land originally designated for housing still remain due to the community's desire to keep them for neighborhood use.[36] The parks are patrolled by Parks Enforcement Patrol officers—on foot, bicycle, and in electric powered carts, and are considered very safe even for women walking home from the subway at night.

Not only was the excavation of the World Trade Center the material substrate for the foundations of the planned community, but it was also built right next to it. On the day of the September 11, 2001, terrorist attack and its destruction, 6,000 of the neighborhood residents fled for their lives, and eight residents died. In fact, all the residents of Battery Park City had to leave their apartments for at least a week. Immediately after the towers fell, the waterfront became a Dunkirk-like scene of ferries, tugboats, and other vessels evacuating tens of thousands of residents and office workers fleeing the destruction and the smoke across the Hudson. Some residents fled on foot to the north, along West Street. BPC residents were processed in triage centers and provided with temporary places to stay.

During the initial weeks martial law was enforced throughout the neighborhood; residents were not allowed to enter their homes without being accompanied by security personnel. Frantic about their pets and belongings, desiring a return to normalcy and their previous lives, residents who returned to their homes fell between the cracks in the aftermath of the clean-up. Most residents returned to the area after the dust, debris, and smoke were finally gone, and weathered the difficulties of living in a disaster zone: the search for human remains, debris removal, the lack of basic services, and severe access restrictions. Others were so traumatized that they could not return.

For those who returned they found tourists clogging their public spaces, trying to get close to "Ground Zero." In these early days, conflicts and concerns were about air quality and other health hazards, obtaining financial and legal assistance, and dealing with the emotional consequences of witnessing death and destruction so close at hand. By the ninth month, however, rental apartment buildings that had been 25–75 percent vacant were again filled, in part by the many newcomers attracted by rent incentives and subsidies.

The 9/11 terrorist attack shook the social and cultural underpinnings of all of New York City, but had the greatest impact where residents were evacuated and then lived with the clean-up and fear. Fieldwork completed in 2002–2003 with Mike Lamb and Dana Taplin[37] and subsequent ethnographic studies by Greg Smithsimon[38] and Elizabeth Greenspan[39] documented how the neighborhood responded.

The research was undertaken to understand how residents coped with returning to their homes and adapted to the human loss and disrupted landscape.[40] What we learned was that the process of decision-making about the World Trade Center memorial and concern about newcomers who were using their public spaces contributed to a stronger community identity, sense of place attachment, and political and social activism than before the 9/11 attack.[41]

While most residents conceded that the World Trade Center memorial issue was important, the main topic of conversation in the playgrounds, dog run, and esplanade was that they did not want another memorial placed along their daily walking routes. As an older male resident put it, "*It is not healthy for me to live in a cemetery.*" Instead, they wanted to preserve their public space for events and buildings that would create more positive collective memories.

Their suggested designs and memorial ideas—such as an active recreation park, children's museum, or social center—that would bring life back to their neighborhood were ignored by the design selection committee.[42] Regardless of the outcome, however, residents' participation and increased local activism helped to produce a socially cohesive neighborhood.[43]

Communities that suffer a disaster often change in character and social structure. This shift at BPC was reflected in the number of newcomers and tourists who used the parks and walkways that previously contained neighbors who knew one another. With the loss of pre 9/11 residents and the influx of others, new social groups and forms of contact emerged.

For example, one long-term male resident tried to explain the "eerie" feeling in the neighborhood by dividing the post-9/11 residents into three groups: *"(1) those who live and work at good but demanding jobs; (2) the 'week-end picnickers,' and (3) the rich, who do not need to work, who become activists due to their increased leisure time, and design and run the park. These three entities are at different points, socially and economically. They don't mix much . . . We are isolated but civil. [But] people are great about sharing the park . . ."*[44]

Long-term residents said that pre-9/11 there was a sense of community based on being a relatively socioeconomically homogeneous group. The influx of newcomers who were perceived as less wealthy and only interested in work rather than in community building was troubling.[45] The pioneer residents, who were the mainstay of community organizations pre-9/11, also worried about a loss of community control.

New forms of social contact were commented upon again and again. *"There were people who you would have waved to before September 11th,"* remembers a south-side resident in her sixties, *"Now you hugged them."* A heightened sense of warmth in heretofore more distant neighbor relations was a common theme. *"People greeted you like a long-lost relative,"* said an older woman who lived in Gateway since its construction. *"And the feeling has stayed."* As the new and old residents fought the memorial plans, advocating for their health and a vibrant public space, a new community identity emerged expressed

Figure 8.6 Families in Battery Park City Playground, Manhattan (Photograph by Gregory Smithsimon)

through social activities, neighborhood organizations, local blogs, and newsletters.[46]

One outcome of this increased solidarity was the BPC Block Party first organized in September 2002 to celebrate "*the best small town in the Big Apple*" and to reinforce a sense of shared community as well as to help local commercial establishments that were struggling. Larger than a typical block party, there were the usual food and games but also booths reserved for local businesses and community groups.[47]

The BPC block party turned into a secular festival backed by the post-9/11-created Battery Park City Neighbors and Parents Association. Broader mobilization during the second BPC Block Party in 2003 made explicit the community-building efforts. As issues arose over the redevelopment of the neighborhood and the design and location of the World Trade Center memorial, these festivals took on even more of an activist tone, rather than simply being a celebration of community strength. Other events such as collective dinners in the public spaces and fundraisers were mounted to support political causes benefitting the well-being of residents.[48]

Using public spaces—especially the dog run and the children's playgrounds—the diverse groups of people living in BPC after 9/11 reconstructed a sense of collective identity and continuity. Expressed at first by opposing the use of BPC public spaces for the World Trade Center memorial, local activism targeted the city's disregard of the polluted air and post 9/11 health hazards. As a newly active resident put it: "*It is a great place to live. After 9/11 there were issues that brought us together. It was a force for community activism. A lot of people felt abandoned by the officials and the government, such as with asbestos and financial issues.*"[49]

In the end, long-term BPC residents incorporated the newcomers, created new associations and community-affirming rituals that marked the return of the "original" community culture. Ironically this reassertion was based on the loss of their right to decide about the memorial, yet their activism and sense of purpose increased the social cohesion[50] of otherwise disparate resident groups, business owners, and real-estate interests. The daily use, symbolism, and appropriation of BPC public space played a major role by providing a resource for the expression of these unifying activities. More importantly it was through the struggle to control the design and use of public space that residents encountered one another, developed a public activist stance, and reinstated a collective vision of what and how their community should be.

The New York City and San José case studies illustrate the many ways that public space promotes and sustains cultural identity, continuity, collective memory, and cultural expressions such as music and dance. Public space is also an important site for the formation of place attachment through various forms of place-making. Civic public spaces inscribe culture, cultural diversity—or a lack of it—and the power dynamics of these interrelations through symbolic and artistic means from graffiti chalk drawings to statues, monuments, flags, and commemorations. They offer a rich resource for reading culture as well as sociocultural inequalities in who is present and whose cultural traditions are visible.

Architectural elements are also a means by which cultural diversity is enhanced and protected. For example, the landscape park Superkilen in Copenhagen includes artifacts selected by residents of the surrounding immigrant enclaves to assert their sense of ownership and belonging.[51] Designed by Big-Bjarke Ingels Group, Superflex, and Toptek I in 2012, it received the 2014–2016 Aga Khan Award for Architecture for promoting integration across different religions and cultures and creating a safe meeting place in Denmark's most ethnically diverse neighborhood. But while artifacts were selected by neighborhood residents from different cultural, national, or language groups, there was no evaluation of how each selection and site installation was interpreted or understood by the others.

Jonathan Daly takes an intercultural perspective to compare cultural design interventions and criticizes their assumed success. By "following the actors" in Superkilen in Copenhagen, Nathan Phillips Square in Toronto, and Federation Square in Melbourne, he evaluates what role design elements play in encouraging or discouraging intercultural encounters in these "multiculture" cities.[52]

Intercultural encounters are indeed shaped by meanings communicated through a combination of form, color, materials, and associations. But using objects with narrow ethnocultural and political meanings such as at Superkilen lead to a loss of meaning and even offend other cultural groups.[53] Abstract coding of ethnic diversity such as on the building facades surrounding Federation Square is also problematic and incomprehensible to residents and users. Flag-raising ceremonies at Nathan Phillips, meant to create a sense inclusion for minority groups, actually reduced intercultural encounters. Thus, design elements intended to promote cultural integration and increase inclusion did not work in the ways that the architects expected.

Instead, basic physical affordances such as seating, walkways, and open spaces influence human and nonhuman interactions and

Figure 8.7 Federation Building Façade, Melbourne, Australia

encourage intercultural interaction. Programmed events have contradictory outcomes, sometimes excluding minority participation because of scale or the lack of adequate privacy and protection for women. As we found at Lake Welch, Jones Beach, and Prospect Park, the affective atmosphere of the public space has considerable agency in shaping the nature and quality of social encounters including intercultural ones.[54]

Ruth Fincher, Kurt Iveson, Helga Leitner, and Valerie Preston go a step further by asking whether intercultural encounters become a basis for a new kind of politics. Comparing field sites in Los Angeles, Melbourne, Toronto, and Sydney, they found that everyday urban encounters with difference—at home, at work, in transport, and in public spaces—encouraged egalitarian political formations.[55] Riding the trains in Sydney, gathering in the local mall in Melbourne, and singing with workmates in Toronto developed into a "being togetherness with difference."[56]

These shared experiences and forms of participation produced new micro-geographies that became the basis for egalitarian politics and policies. Many of these egalitarian sites were public spaces such as streets, promenades, and parks or quasi-public spaces such as food courts in malls, workplace cafeterias, and transportation systems. New solidarities and collaborations emerged through the ordinary practices and localities of daily life.

Public spaces facilitate intercultural encounter, a sense of belonging, and the recognition of difference. They are a valuable platform for the working out of social relationships through engagement with symbolic representations and validation of cultural differences. The resulting solidarity has the potential to generate new collectivities and thus promote democratic practices and a greater sensitivity to social justice issues. This high-stakes issue—transforming strangers into "mates," colleagues, acquaintances, and friends who come together to solve a problem, enjoy a moment, contest an injustice, or address a goal—may be the most significant contribution of public space to an inclusive and just society.

9

From the Winter of Despair to the Summer of Euphoria

Public Space During COVID-19 in New York City (2020–2021)

Throughout the centuries epidemics and contagious diseases have had an impact on the use and function of public space. Daniel Defoe describes his experience of the London plague of 1664–1665, and much of what he describes mirrors changes in New York City during COVID-19. His neighborhood between Aldgate Church and Whitechappel Bars had not yet been affected, but he recalls wagons and carts with goods, women, servants, and children leaving the city, with crowds pressing for passes and certificates so that they could travel abroad. Worried about his business, Defoe remains in the city and records how London is transformed: "It was a most surprising thing to see those streets which were usually so thronged now grown desolate, and so few people seen in them . . . and nobody to direct me except the watchmen set at the doors of such house as were shut up."[1]

He goes on to recount that while the wealthiest fled, most middle-class and poor residents adapted by walking in the middle of the street so as not to mingle with those coming out of the houses. Watchmen were assigned to keep sick residents confined, a method enacted during the 1603 plague, while doctors visited only to declare cases

hopeless and to call for a wagon to come for the cadaver's immediate burial. Municipal orders were passed on cleaning and sweeping
the streets while idle assembly, plays, feasting, and open "tippling
houses" were not allowed. "Loose persons" such as "beggars" were
thought to spread the infection and warned to stay off the street or
risk imprisonment.

Defoe's account reminds us that disease has always played an important role in the design and planning of public space, and that the
lessons learned through each epidemic, whether smallpox, polio, or
typhoid fever, lead to social movements to restore health to the over-
crowded and dense cities of the industrial age. Large public parks,
wider streets and sidewalks are the legacies of activists who organized to improve the survival of the urban dweller through the circulation of fresh air, access to sunlight, removal of waste and garbage,
and provision of clean water. Ebenezer Howard's plan for garden
cities incorporated lower population density and improved air quality
with walkable neighborhoods filled with green spaces, and the civic
grandeur and landscape architecture of the City Beautiful movement
were responses to the dirt and disorder of cities thought to cause disease.[2] New York city constructed a 40-mile aqueduct system to carry
safe drinking water, as well as wide boulevards in response to cholera
epidemics.[3]

Infectious disease molded home environments through spatial
interventions of twentieth-century modernism that emerged in the
wake of tuberculosis and waves of cholera. Tuberculosis was the cause
of 25 percent of New York City deaths between 1810 and 1815 and
continued until the discovery of the contagious tubercle bacillus in
1882 gave rise to the sanatorium movement that emphasized strict
hygiene and exposure to sunlight and air.[4]

Epidemics in recent history including SARS, the Avian flu, and
Ebola were more prevalent in Asia and the Global South, leaving US
residents unaware of the contemporary risk of infectious disease and
the government unprepared for the COVID-19 pandemic. The last
time there had been an epidemic of this scale was the 1918–1920

Spanish flu with the number of US deaths estimated to be 650,000, requiring physical distancing, closing of shops and schools, and the use of masks to limit its spread.[5]

Missteps and delays in the handling of the emerging novel coronavirus plunged the United States into a quagmire of medical and political conflicts beginning the winter of 2019–2020.[6] The lack of coordination, botched communications, and institutional incompetence resulted in one million deaths in the United States by May 9, 2022.[7] The tragic story of why the United States, with a technologically advanced, research-based public health service, and an extensive medical system, failed to stem the spread of this infectious disease was based on governmental inaction and indecision.

Little has been written about the impact of COVID-19 on public space and its contribution to the health and well-being of urban residents.[8] While travel restrictions curtailed field work in other cities, nearby New York City, Brooklyn, and Long Island suburbs offered insights into the ways COVID-19 transformed our relationship to urban space. Interviews with neighbors, colleagues, family, and friends; journalist accounts published over the past year and a half; fact sheets published by the School of Public Health at the City University of New York, the World Bank, and UN Habitat and recently published journal articles and edited collections on public space and COVID-19 form the basis of this analysis.

Five temporally differentiated but spatially overlapping "phases" organize the materials collected from March 2020 through October 2021. These include: the initial lockdown, a series of graduated openings, the devastating second peak of cases during the winter of 2020–2021, and the reopening of New York City during the summer of 2021. Data visualizations from the John Hopkins Coronavirus Dashboard defined the phases for New York State and the New York City Health Data Trends tracked the daily cases, hospitalization, and deaths by neighborhood to generate this periodization.[9] Data from the *New York Times*, Next City, the CUNY School of Public Health, weekly surveys, and other websites produced an approximation of public space openings, especially of streets, sidewalks, and parks used to understand residents' mobility and spatial patterns. The emerging discourse about who uses public space, and the evolving moral geography of risks, rights, and stigma, offered additional insights into the way that public space was deployed to reduce isolation, segregation, depression, and sense of loss that pervaded the city.

Developing a sequence that reflects the expansion and contraction of public space use in relationship to other spatial and temporal changes helped conceptualize its role during the pandemic. Each phase produced different kinds of inequalities, social discourses, and spatial separations.

The takeaway is that greater equity in access to public space would have improved COVID-19 outcomes for low-income and marginalized neighborhoods. During the height of the pandemic, public space became a critical resource, providing much-needed space for additional hospital tents and vaccination sites; safe forms of transportation; places for children and families to be outside and socialize in open-air surroundings; locations for alternative theater, art, and other cultural events; alternatives to indoor classrooms; and sites for food distribution and places where people could socialize and eat together. Indeed, public spaces became crucial for satisfying most basic needs.

An overview of the five phases for New York City is presented and then fleshed out in greater detail:

Phase 1- In the late winter and early spring of 2020, public spaces were closed and used as spatial resources for medical and transport services. Sheltering-in-place was at its most extreme. The use of masks and protective clothing was restricted to hospitals and medical personnel and difficult to obtain. Homeless individuals moved into subways and train stations rather than remain in shelters perceived as dangerous.

Phase 2- Public spaces were partially opened, especially streets and large parks. Playgrounds remained closed. Many middle-class and wealthy residents left for the suburbs and vacation homes. Essential services remained open, including markets, gasoline stations, telecommunication companies, transportation services, and all medical facilities and pharmacies. New forms of social and racial stigma developed around the use of masks, social distancing, essential workers, and the vulnerability of older adults.

Phase 3- In the summer of 2020, Black Lives Matter protests filled streets. Police responded, sometimes with force, and there were violent confrontations between police and protesters. Public spaces became the sites of cultural performances and art festivals and played new roles as policing and social controls increased. A small number of businesses attempted to open, but "third places" such as bars, gyms, churches, libraries, indoor restaurants, and coffee shops remained closed, and people increasingly reported feeling lonely and missing everyday social contact. Neighborhoods, however, were full of local activity, adapting to the changing circumstances, and mutual-aid support increased dramatically.

Phase 4- Throughout the late fall of 2020 and into the winter and early spring of 2021, public space remained open, but COVID-19 cases were on the rise. Winter and colder temperatures increased social isolation, and businesses and restaurants moved to the streets with heaters. People waited for vaccine approval and then appointments to be vaccinated with increasing anxiety, while a strong anti-vaccination movement emerged. Economic concerns pushed city and state government to open non-essential businesses and end masking and vaccine restrictions even though cases of COVID-19 were increasing.

Phase 5- In the summer and early fall of 2021, New York
City experienced a period of euphoria and a rush to
occupy all public venues by locals, visitors, and outer-
borough residents. The parks, sidewalks, and streets were
flooded with people, including a few tourists. Conflicts
developed with the perceived "overuse" of Washington
Square and in public spaces where the users were not
"locals"; police presence increased. The opening of
businesses and restaurants increased the privatization
of public space as parking spots and sidewalks were
appropriated for open-air stalls and eating sheds. Bike
lanes and street closures were expanded. By early fall all
businesses, school, and cultural institutions were fully
open even through cases were again increasing from the
new, more contagious, Delta variant of COVID-19.[10]

Phase 1: March–April 2020

Once it became apparent that COVID-19 had arrived in the New
York suburbs, there was an initial lockdown. All parks, playgrounds,
beaches, and open spaces were closed. The first documented case in
New York City was identified on March 1, 2020, and by March 22
Governor Andrew Cuomo had shuttered all non-essential businesses,
including schools and public institutions. Residents were encouraged
to stay home and only go out for shopping and health care—not
even the hour of exercise that was included in Sydney, Australia's
lockdown—so that by the end of the month the city was silent. From
March 20, 2020, when most states told people to stay home, until
about April 30, 2020, when most states eased those restrictions, 43.8
percent of 144 million US residents stayed inside, up from a normal
20.7 percent.[11]

Streets in downtown NYC were abandoned, and even midtown
was empty with shops boarded up. There were few people using

the subway, predominantly health-care staff and the transportation workers making it possible for people to get to hospitals. People described the city as dark and surreal.

The closing of public spaces, especially those that New Yorkers went to after 9/11 and other crises, made social contact difficult except through the internet or telephone. Families hunkered down, college students came home to stay with their parents, and states monitored roads restricting New Yorkers from entering because of the state's high number of cases. Airports were quiet with few flights and even fewer passengers. The initial closure of public spaces, especially parks, walking trails, beaches, and playgrounds, took a tremendous toll on people already struggling with lockdown orders. A survey of more than 500 people in Boston, Atlanta, San Francisco, and Phoenix found at the start of the pandemic that people spent less time outdoors and reported feeling "significantly nature-deprived since sheltering began" as well as experiencing a significant drop in flourishing.[12]

Central Park converted into a medical triage center to relieve overrun hospitals, with white tents lining the edges of the park for patient beds and waiting rooms. Neighborhood parks became triage centers and were used for the distribution of information, including masks and hand sanitizer as these supplies became available for the public and not just for medical workers. Parks were widely acknowledged as medical resources, and fifty-seven of the hundred largest US cities used them as part of their critical public-health infrastructure for patient processing, COVID testing, and personal protective equipment distribution. Seventy of the hundred largest cities employed parks as centers for free meals and accessible food pantries. In Memphis, in the 168-acre city park, staff distributed bottles of water amid a boil-water advisory due to low water pressure.[13]

Tragically, the number of deaths began to mount. Large refrigerator trunks lined streets to hold the bodies that hospital morgues no longer had room for. Mortuaries and cemeteries could not handle the number of deaths, much less offer support and adequate services to the increasing number of grieving family members. From people interviewed and from media coverage, the hardest part was the inability of family members to say goodbye to their dying loved ones in the hospital.[14] Telephone and Facetime calls with family members in isolation or on ventilators were the best that the medical staff could manage under the circumstances. Nurses and aides were breaking down under the stress of losing so many patients so quickly without contact or care.

Between March 1 and April 30 approximately 5 percent of NYC residents—roughly 420,000 people—left, leaving wealthier areas or neighborhoods where students and young people were returning home to live because of closed colleges or a loss of a job.[15] These "escape artists" were reviled by other residents for jumping ship and by the towns and suburbs where they moved for overwhelming services, buying out supermarkets, and creating too much traffic.[16]

Families who left offered rationalizations reminiscent of residents living in gated communities in the 1990s and 2000s.[17] They worried about exposure to essential workers with COVID-19 and not having safe outdoor spaces for their children to play. Like the royal court leaving for the countryside during the waves of plague in medieval Europe, these families had the means to reduce any potential contact they had with contagious strangers and "gated" themselves off in greener and more open suburbs and small towns.

Most people stayed home and watched the world from their televisions or computer screens if they had them. After the initial shock, grassroots groups mobilized to install internet service in low-income neighborhoods so that families in inadequately networked areas would have access to virtual classrooms. Public spaces around Link NYC kiosks set up by the city with fast, free public Wi-Fi, device charging, and access to city services, maps, and directions attracted young users who sat around the kiosks to finish classwork and communicate with friends. Children missed their friends in school, and instead made virtual dates to play video games together.

Virtual platforms such as Zoom dominated video chat, beating other tech giants such as Webex and GoToMeeting as well as Google and Microsoft.[18] Zoom offered sending a meeting link as easily as sharing a YouTube video and beginning March 15, 2020, became the basis for most virtual classrooms including mine, as well as business meetings, fitness classes, happy hours, court proceedings, presidential campaigns, funerals, and memorial services.

Staying at home, spending the day talking only to my partner was a difficult adjustment. While still in Brooklyn, I shifted to hours on Zoom for work and teaching but also for socializing. Reaching out to old friends and becoming reacquainted with people by telephone became an important social strategy. With Zoom, I could spend an afternoon chatting with a friend in Moscow comparing notes about what was happening there or with a friend in Nairobi who was also writing a book. New groups formed, such as monthly get-togethers with junior high school girlfriends from all over the United States or weekly conversations with colleagues in Ireland and Germany to plan projects.

Starved of connection, people reached out to one another through various forms of virtual public space more than ever before. The result was that virtual public space strengthened global and distant social ties, but the absence of face-to-face interaction deepened the sense of isolation and loss leaving many uneasy and depressed. While accessible virtual public spaces helped to alleviate social isolation, studies of virtual religious ceremonies, memorials, and funerals reported that participants felt emotionally detached and dissatisfied with this form of contact.[19]

The replacement of everyday public spaces, schools, and offices with virtual public spaces, Zoom classrooms, and Webex offices produced a major cultural shift. Yet the same exclusions and injustices experienced in physical public spaces remained, this time in terms of unequal access to and distribution of technology and equipment, as well as having personal space and safe locations to explore this new social realm. Understanding virtual public space and its social justice ramifications became more important than ever .

Phase 2: May 2020

After weeks of shelter-in-place orders, US residents began to move again, with states relaxing restrictions. Based on cellphone data at the end of the lockdown, about 25 million more people in the United States went outside their homes on any average day than during the previous month.[20]

By the end of April some NYC public spaces began to open up. Large parks were lightly used, and runners and walkers with masks appeared in Central Park and Prospect Park. Yet most people did not have a way to reach these large public spaces as they were avoiding the subways and buses to reduce COVID-19 exposure. Older adults found the streets too crowded for walking and remained inside their apartments overcome with a deepening sense of stigma and isolation.

On May 2, 2020, Mayor Bill de Blasio closed more than seven miles of city streets throughout the city to encourage walking and cycling, and pledged up to one hundred miles of roads, though there was considerable stopping and starting of his "safe streets" initiative.[21] Neighbors quickly appropriated their streets for sitting in the sun or stopping to talk to neighbors. Some sidewalks, though, were still filled with long lines of people spaced six feet apart waiting to enter supermarkets while early morning senior hours provided the most vulnerable access when there were fewer people.

Mutual aid increased with open kitchens and distribution centers offering food and clothing on sidewalks. Large refrigerators showed up on neighborhood streets and corners filled with free food. Eventually over 800 mutual-aid groups, many small and informal, emerged nationwide expanding their mission to include mental-health counseling, veterinary care, and helping people sign up for health care.[22]

Sociologist Zeynep Tufekci writes that by late April some cities such as Zurich and St. Louis were still closing down public parks and outdoor spaces because of overcrowding. London closed down Brockwell Park after 3,000 people appeared on the first day of good weather. She observes that closing parks may at first have seemed

Figure 9.1 Neighbors Sitting Outside on Closed Street During COVID-19, Manhattan

prudent but was a mistake, describing a scene at Brockwell Park in South London where two policemen ticketed a lone sunbather with no one near her.[23]

Essential workers became synonymous with people of color (POC) and stigmatized because their occupations and lack of economic privilege meant they could not protect themselves by sheltering in place or practicing physical distancing. Physical distancing became a class marker, practiced easily by those who had the luxury of working from home, computers for their children to attend virtual classes, and adequate room to allow children and parents to pursue their work and school activities separately. Indeed, "*social* distancing" became the term used for keeping six feet away from other people to reduce disease transmission by coughing and sneezing or droplets and aerosols in the air. Conversations about social distancing became a moral discourse about appropriate or socially acceptable behavior.[24] Those who wore masks, stayed inside, and separated by six feet became "good citizens," and those who did not wear masks and clustered in groups to play, talk, or even share a pizza were chastised as "bad citizens."

The use of stereotyping and stigmatized language began even before these behaviors took on political overtones and were manipulated by then-president Trump and right-wing politicians. The moral ground of good or bad, safe or dangerous, quickly grew as well as the xenophobic language of the "Chinese" or "Wuhan" flu. Public spaces remained places to go that were safe and offered a temporary release from the strain of being in a workplace filled with anxiety and fear, yet at the same time, people began to treat some kinds of public behavior in socially disparaging ways.

May 2020 also marked the release of epidemiological evidence of the unequal distribution of COVID-19 cases and deaths. Structural racism intersected with public health as Black, Indigenous, and other POC were identified as the most vulnerable targets of COVID-19 and endured greater harm. Beginning in early April the *New York Times* published interactive maps of numbers of virus cases and deaths in New York City in which the lines of race and wealth were clearly demarcated. Brooklyn's 11239 zip code, a community of about 13,000 people, had a 40 percent higher death rate than any other part of the city.[25] The area is home to the highest concentration of people over sixty-five and African American residents, many who live in a large low-income housing project known as Starrett City. Many families are multigenerational, and a sick member might not have the ability to quarantine from the rest. Neighborhoods with the lowest death rates were in the richest zip codes in Manhattan, while the highest number of COVID-19 deaths were in the most impoverished areas.[26] These findings confirmed earlier reports that Black and Latino New Yorkers were dying at twice the rate of white residents.

The explanations for this large discrepancy in number of cases and deaths includes all of the factors already discussed including 1) inequality in access to health care; 2) inability to stay home when sick because of economic need; 3) predominance of essential workers being Black, Latino, and POC who were forced to work during the pandemic; 4) dependence on public transportation such as subways and buses; 5) living in multigenerational families often in small apartments; and 6) medical risk factors such as diabetes, high blood pressure, and high body index.[27] Low-income neighborhood residents already suffered from food deserts, where fresh and high-quality ingredients were scarce and expensive, and during COVID-19 the lack of access to healthy food only became worse. Ultimately, a deadly combination of increased exposure and subsequent lack of access to health care or sick leave left many frontline workers in a dangerous and debilitating position.[28]

There were other vulnerable populations overlooked in those early months. Older people living in nursing homes in the United States were vulnerable, as were those with underlying medical conditions. Differently abled people who depended on caregivers for basic needs could not physically distance.[29] Populations and groups living in contained spaces from luxury yachts to prisons were at high risk of the transmission of infection, and in the case of detention and refugee camps where malnutrition and other infectious diseases were already present, COVID-19 deaths exploded.[30] Any form of confinement was hazardous before the availability of vaccinations, adequate space for physical distancing, resources for mask wearing and testing, and the ability to institute quarantining when someone was ill.

By the end of May 2020, New York City parks were open for solo exercise, but team sports were not allowed, and children's playgrounds remained closed until mid-June. Park restrooms were open and cleaned every day with disinfectants, and park visitors were reminded

Figure 9.2 Older Adults Finding a Safe Space to be Outside During COVID-19, Manhattan

not to congregate in large groups and to maintain physical distancing. Recognition of the critical role of hospital workers was expressed each evening at 7:00 pm by loud clapping and cheering from the surrounding buildings and streets, and later used to express frustration with calls to "cancel rent" by people unable to pay their landlords as the pandemic deepened.[31]

The City University of New York's School of Public Health's weekly survey of the week ending May 4, 2020, reported that 49 percent of NYC residents said that they wanted the city to wait until June 1 to reopen non-essential businesses, and more than two-thirds of those still employed were concerned about returning to their jobs.[32] A *New York Times* editorial suggested that the city open up the beaches, keep gardens and parks accessible, close down more streets, encourage fishing and bird watching as fun activities, and plan street dance parties and movie drive-ins as safe ways to enjoy the upcoming summer. Emergency bike lanes were being created to encourage safe transportation, and streets, parking spaces, and loading bays were re-claimed for pedestrian use.[33]

Phase 3: June–September 2020

Memorial Day weekend marked two major events that would char-acterize the "summer of uncertainty." New York
City residents experienced a re-emergence of cookouts, park visits, and beachgoing even though health officials continued to plead about the need for social distancing, masking, and staying home. Governor Andrew Cuomo signed an executive order permitting "any nones-sential gathering of 10 or fewer individuals . . . provided that social distancing protocols and cleaning and disinfection protocols re-quired by the Department of Health are adhered to."[34] Many noted that Memorial Day was a subdued and somber holiday due to the increasing number of deaths among older people, including war vet-erans who were patients of the Department of Veterans' Affairs.[35] And while the beaches were open to some, new restrictions were posted, and local beaches began enforcing strict residents-only policies, citing worries about the coronavirus.[36]

The second and more significant event that weekend was the murder of George Floyd by the Minneapolis police and the street protests that followed. The circulation of the video of Floyd's struggle to stay alive, repeating "I can't breathe" while white policeman held him down, triggered an outpouring of grief and outrage. Floyd's death ignited months of protests in the United States and globally.

On Memorial Day, Monday, May 25, 2020, George Floyd died in police custody, and hundreds of demonstrators took to the streets of Minneapolis, setting fire to the police station on May 27. Street protests spread to many cities where the deaths of Breonna Taylor and Ahmaud Arbery were added to Floyd's as part of the recitation of the long history of police killings of Black people. By May 29 protesters clashed with police on the streets of New York City and Atlanta, and a crowd gathered outside the White House triggering a Secret Service lockdown.[37] Curfews were imposed across the United States on May 31 to stem the unrest, but by June 2, tens of thousands had again taken to the streets. Black Lives Matter protests filled the streets and squares worldwide following George Floyd's memorial service on June 7.[38]

Memorials for George Floyd with murals, flowers, handmade signs, and letters on the sidewalks of New York City grew as Black Lives Matter (BLM) protests continued to fill streets and squares. The use of public space for protests of police brutality and structural racism continued throughout the summer.

The BLM protests led to a rethinking of structural racism as practiced in the city, from schools to public transportation, and from access to health care and food to green public spaces and adequate housing. BLM's contestation of the status quo of police violence against Black

Figure 9.3 George Floyd Street Memorial

men encouraged policymakers to take more seriously the epidemiological evidence that low-income and POC neighborhoods were experiencing twice the level of COVID-19 cases and deaths. The city began to take steps to address these inequalities by providing targeted neighborhood health interventions and medical outreach for COVID-19 patients and later placing vaccine distribution centers in these locations .

Thus, after over two months of sheltering-in-place, New Yorkers saw a loosening of restrictions even as the nation reached 100,000 COVID-19 related deaths.[39] News articles and health blogs encouraged people to freely venture outdoors arguing that the coronavirus does not spread as effectively in fresh air as it does indoors.[40] At the same time health officials continued to worry and recommend maintaining social distancing even when jogging or playing ball. As COVID-19 cases continued to rise, the country remained divided about whether masks should be mandated, and based on the photographs of busy parks and beaches during that period, it appeared that mask wearing was still not accepted by most young people enjoying the outdoors for the first time in months.[41]

By mid-June, the city was quickly growing more social with parks full of couples and small groups sitting in socially distanced circles such as in Domino Park in Williamsburg, Brooklyn.[42] But increased police enforcement of COVID-19 regulations marred this bucolic image when more than forty people, thirty-five of whom were Black, were arrested for social distancing violations in Brooklyn in one day.[43] Increased policing and stop-and-frisk as well as 311 telephone complaints about people not wearing masks continued to push the number of arrests higher.[44]

In contrast to the policing and surveillance of some neighborhoods, large parks (Central, Prospect, Pelham Bay, Van Cortland, and others) that had always been centers for outdoor music performances expanded to include more theater and dance. Alternative art shows, performance art, stand-up comedy hours, and music events were added with hands-on activities for families and children. Attempts at democratizing arts and culture were tentative at first, but by summer 2021 supported actors, artists, and musicians who had lost their jobs due to studio, gallery, and theatre closings.

Museums and cultural institutions began to rethink their staff and audiences as BLM demands resonated with residents locked in their homes and neighborhoods. COVID-19 brought up questions about public access to libraries, museums, historical archives, and performance halls dominated by wealthy white patrons and their cultural tastes. The combination of BLM protests in the streets and the restricted sociality of everyday life forced a reimagining of a more equitable distribution of arts funding and cultural activities including greater use and programming in neighborhood public spaces.

City streets were increasingly closed, creating more space for socializing while maintaining six feet of physical distance. Restaurants that had been struggling to survive with take-out menus, call-in ordering, and outside pick-ups set up outside seating as well. Bustling avenues were transformed from being filled with cars to pedestrian walkways with cafes and restaurants where patrons could sit and enjoy quiet streets. This reversal of previous policies protecting

Figure 9.4 Restaurant on Sidewalk, Manhattan

sidewalks and streets as public space and instead giving restaurants and businesses greater control became widespread by the following summer.[45]

The number of people commuting by bicycle grew during the summer months in the open streets and next to the new cafes. While in the past traffic conflicts were between bicycles and cars, now new problems arose between bicyclists and pedestrians competing for space on a closed street or when people were seated next to a bike lane to enjoy a meal. Customers needed to be careful not to be hit by a bicycle when trying to get to their seat at a restaurant on upper Broadway, a busy avenue where automobiles, not bicycles, used to be the concern. Parking spots also took a hit as restaurants extended into the street, providing evidence that the city could be vibrant without automobile traffic.

Mayor de Blasio's popular "Open Restaurants" program enrolled more than 10,300 establishments starting in June and on September

Figure 9.5 Restaurant, Pedestrian, and Bike Conflict, Manhattan

2, 2020, announced that it would be extended year-round and made permanent. The eighty-five car-free streets with expanded space for restaurant seating would continue on designated days.[46] It was every urban planner's dream, but still most non-essential businesses remained closed, unemployment continued to skyrocket, and bankruptcies continued at an unabated rate even with the partial revival of the NYC restaurant sector.

During summer 2020, social interaction increased in cities, but not as much as in suburban and exurban neighborhoods. Vikas Mehta studied the behavior of families in the suburbs of Cincinnati and found that their experience of space was quite different from the urban dwellers who confronted crowded open spaces, difficulty in social distancing, and having to use public transit to get to work.[47] Instead, people living in low-density neighborhoods walked in public and used their sidewalks, porches, and entrances of their houses to socialize while maintaining adequate physical distance. These activities extended into the street with gatherings organized on sidewalks being used for games and children bicycling thus integrating the public and private realm. Public spaces were also used as local art galleries with children's drawings posted on fences, community events, and weekly tag sales. Numerous material responses to COVID-19 and altered landscapes grew including chalk art, graffiti, painted rocks, and public space signage globally.[48]

There were other, more sobering realities that emerged as the summer wore on and COVID-19 cases did not subside.[49] The boredom of staying at home and the anxiety of worrying whether one had work or would get COVID-19 resulted in a dramatic rise in alcohol sales during the first few months of the pandemic and remained higher than the year before.[50] While during the first month crime rates plummeted, violent crime overall skyrocketed in 2020, with gun violence reaching the highest level ever recorded in the United States.[51]

Neighborhoods that had struggled with gangs and guns found themselves facing another crisis with the large numbers of deaths of older residents from COVID-19. The loss of valued matriarchs and patriarchs, especially in neighborhoods such as South Jamaica, Queens that had just succeeded in reducing street violence, was devastating.[52]

Children suffered when the playgrounds were closed on March 25, but by June 22 Mayor de Blasio reopened them in neighborhoods with lower numbers of COVID-19 cases. Nonetheless, many parents kept their children on "house arrest," increasing the sense of social isolation and domestic stress.[53]

A study of New York City residents' engagement with urban green space during the first summer reported that the racially diverse, predominantly female respondents' level of satisfaction with parks did not change with the pandemic, but their level of use and how much they felt "at home" increased.[54] This increase, however, was primarily among the white participants and participants living in middle- and upper-income neighborhoods. There was an overall increase in the sense of belonging to parks during the pandemic both in this NYC study and in other US surveys. These differences in the level of park use and feeling at home reflected the ongoing neighborhood-level environmental inequality in NYC based on restricted access to urban green spaces and local parks being perceived as dangerous or having an increased risk of stop-and-frisk policing.[55]

Phase 4: October 2020–May 2021

The relatively open and relaxed summer of 2020 changed dramatically as the number of COVID-19 cases worsened to a peak of over 6,000 reported per day in NYC during late December 2020 and early January 2021. This second peak was higher than the original outbreak due to the cold temperatures, infrequent masking, and people moving indoors.[56] Even with schools, theaters, gyms, and most cultural institutions remaining closed and most social services moving online, cases continued to rise throughout the winter into early spring.[57]

The affective atmosphere was somber, with daily articles about the availability of virtual mental-health services and other online therapeutic treatments. From August to December 2020, symptoms of anxiety rose by 13 percent and symptoms of depression by 15 percent based on CDC surveys of the United States. There was a strong correlation between the average number of daily COVID-19 cases nationally and the severity of respondents' anxiety and depression.[58]

New Yorkers had a difficult time dealing with a lonely holiday season, and many felt hopeless and alone at a time when they most needed family and friends. Students found it was difficult to study with little structure or interpersonal motivation while elderly parents complained of not getting enough to eat or not eating because of their feelings of abandonment and fragility.[59]

Students going to high school or college for the first time met their teachers and classmates online and felt disconnected while trying to adapt to new social worlds. Many dropped out and went home, while others struggled to keep up with their classes, feeling claustrophobic from sharing tiny apartments and dorm rooms. Even though some of these measures were in place during the initial months of March and April 2020, the return to virtual learning and lack of social contact during fall 2020 signaled that it would be a long time until life would "get back to normal." Indeed, during this "winter of despair," some New York City residents began to wonder if it ever would.

The pandemic highlighted the plight of parents—particularly mothers. When the schools closed, 8,500,000 women nationwide left the workforce, four times higher than the number of men. The impact of school closings also illuminated racial and economic inequalities in the provision of a social safety net for economically struggling families, adequate and safe childcare, and alternative educational support systems.[60] Grocery store and other essential workers suffered from longer hours and the constant worry that they might bring the virus home to their children.[61]

Finding safe housing for homeless individuals became a priority in New York City after Governor Cuomo removed the thousands of people sleeping in the subways to clean the subway cars each night. In California the number of people who were unhoused jumped 40 percent to 113,000 residents.[62] In response California governor Newsom used stimulus funds to repurpose ninety-four hotels for permanent housing for unhoused individuals and families. In New York City, hotels were used as shelters, but only as a temporary solution, and is still being debated.[63]

The value of public space became even more significant as the number of COVID-19 cases escalated.[64] People used public spaces for birthdays, weddings, reunions, and memorials even during the coldest months. Large parks became sanctuaries for bird watching and observing wildlife.[65] Boxers trained at South Street Seaport and Hudson Yards showed movies and sporting events for free on a giant outdoor screen. Iceless curling games appeared at Bryant Park, and heated igloos popped up as cozy places to meet friends. As temperatures dropped, restaurants invented a new art form, the Outdoor-Dining Shelter,[66] the hut-, tent-, and shed-like structures with heaters lining the streets so patrons could eat outdoors.[67]

A hopeful moment took place on December 14, 2020, when the first dose of Pfizer and BioNTech's coronavirus vaccine was given to Sandra Lindsay, an intensive-care nurse at Long Island Jewish Medical Center in Queens. Since the start of the pandemic through December 14, 2020, New York City had recorded more than 780,000 cases of COVID-19 and more than 35,100 deaths, making it the most heavily impacted in the United States at the time.[68] The city organized a campaign to distribute vaccinations as safely and widely as possible by opening high schools, health clinics, and pharmacies as distribution sites.

Unfortunately, getting an initially scarce vaccination appointment accessed through the internet was difficult for older people and those

Figure 9.6. Shed-like Structure on Sidewalk and Street, Manhattan
(Photograph by Merle Lefkowitz)

without computers or mobile devices. The specter of social and racial inequality emerged again, with white middle-class professionals
getting the majority of the first shots.[69] Eventually, however, support
networks of social workers, nurses, college students, sons, daughters,
grandchildren, nieces, and nephews rallied to help get everyone over
sixty-five who wanted appointments registered so they could safely
re-enter the public realm. With the arrival of the vaccines, this vulnerable population began to re-emerge.

Phase 5: May–October 2021

COVID-19 cases in New York City dropped significantly in April 2021, and by the end of May 2021 had reached another low, comparable to the previous summer. The reduced rate of mortality achieved through widespread vaccination spurred the opening of New York City public spaces, creating a sense of jubilation throughout the city. People flooded into parks and plazas, filling the spaces with large crowds who were ready to party. The newspapers proclaimed this re-emergence the "summer of euphoria" with a series of city-sponsored activities. Hundreds of photographs of the "young and restless" filled the pages of the *New York Times* Sunday Style section celebrating the pent-up energy of what everyone hoped would be a return to normalcy.[70] The summer was capped by an epic homecoming concert in Central Park featuring Bruce Springsteen and Paul Simon.[71]

May 2021 was declared the month that New York "woke up" with parties, beachgoing, graduations, and people riding subway trains.[72] Festivals, both political and religious, as well as birthday parties, chorus practice, swimming pool parties, and sports audiences, were back as the city awakened.[73] By May 22, restaurant dining rooms were allowed to fill every seat for the first time since March. But many people chose to continue dining outside. Sidewalk restaurants that evolved during the winter provided all the atmosphere and contact that most people were looking for without the COVID-19 risks.[74] On the Fourth of July NYC "buzzed" with activity as tourists returned with only 193 new cases and 3 deaths a day. People started doing things they had not done for a year from traveling by plane and driving to resorts to gathering with friends and families for customary Independence Day celebrations.[75]

Inequalities in access to park space remained with low-income neighborhoods having access to 21 percent less green open space than those who lived in high-income areas. The discrepancy was even greater when viewed along racial lines with majority POC neighborhoods having 33 percent less park space than predominantly white neighborhoods.[76] The Trust for Public Land reported that while the 2,300 parks in New York City were critical to mental and physical health during COVID-19, parks in Black neighborhoods were much smaller, with an average size of 7.9 acres compared to the 29.8 acres in white areas.[77] Asian and Asian American communities continued to be threated by assaults occurring on subways and streets. Asian Americans' well-being—in addition to the pandemic stressors of financial worries, fear of infection, and isolation—created a particularly difficult situation for the large Asian and Asian American populations in Queens to use public space.[78]

Disparities in maintenance, programming, and police surveillance of parks resulted in young adults from low-income neighborhoods in the Bronx coming into Manhattan to gather and see friends. Nightclubs had opened, but many young people found them expensive and instead partied in the public spaces, streets, and sidewalks of downtown neighborhoods. Washington Square in the West Village was a prime designation for hanging out and the place to go for nightlife. But the flood of young people dancing, playing music, setting off firecrackers, and generally making a lot of noise triggered outrage from neighbors who said that they could not sleep. The city responded with a 10:00 pm curfew for Washington Square, and police officers in riot gear moved in to enforce it, arresting twenty-three people and injuring eight police officers.[79]

When interviewed, the revelers explained that the parks in their neighborhoods were heavily policed and not as nice as Washington Square. During COVID-19 there had been an increase in policing and greater surveillance with young people of color often targeted. Those who wanted to party safely, traveled downtown. But their presence, and complaints about the noise, partying and drug use animated a deeper dispute about who gets to use public space.

Washington Square Park has always been a popular destination and a recent hub for Black Lives Matter demonstrations as well as pro-Palestinian and anti-Ethiopian government rallies. It is a place for young people to gather and is heavily used by New York University students who attend classes in the area. It is both a neighborhood park controlled by wealthy West Village residents and New York University, and a city-wide resource with a history and ambiance that attracts many visitors, tourists, and youth.

The imposed curfew and violent police enforcement because of the noise seemed to be a reaction to who these young people were, that is, youth of color perceived by residents as not "belonging" in their neighborhood park. At the same time, these young people did not have safe public spaces in their own neighborhoods. Searching for a nicer place to be outside during COVID-19 created a situation where they were discriminated against for "being out of place." The conflict between residents (who see Washington Square as their park) and the new Washington Square Park users (who were using the city's public space resources to enjoy themselves and feel safe) illustrates how public space inequalities became even more problematic during COVID-19 when safe public space became essential to everyday social life.

Beyond these urban green space disparities, public spaces newly appropriated for restaurants, cyclists, and pedestrians were also challenged as cars and trucks poured back into the city with the opening of small businesses and retailers. The consensus that more bike paths, closed streets for pedestrians, and sidewalk cafes were necessary for a healthy urban environment emboldened the use of public land in new ways. The successful transformation of busy avenues into everything from children's playgrounds, roller-skate rinks, free Zumba and salsa classes, and even a pop-up circus encouraged neighborhood leaders to turn these streets into permanent linear parks.[80]

But others questioned these decisions and incursions with the resurgence of automobile traffic. New conflicts emerged including a dangerous mix of scooters, bikes, and pedestrians, while car-owning residents and shop owners bemoaned the loss of automobile parking. By November 2021, neighborhood groups were pushing back against outside seating at restaurants. Community groups with slogans

such as "outdoor dining is home invasion" attended planning meetings complaining about the rats, noise, trash, sleeplessness, and general
disruption of their neighborhoods due to the expansion of outdoor
dining. Neighbors argued that it attracted out of towners who did
not care about the neighborhood, accompanied by a loss of civic
engagement.[81]

The summer euphoria lasted well into July when the appearance
of the Delta variant of COVID-19 changed the mood, though public
spaces and non-essential businesses and cultural institutions remained
open. The Delta variant was a highly contagious mutation that spread
quickly, at first attacking the unvaccinated, but then infecting vaccinated individuals with milder breakthrough infections thought to be
caused by the decreasing immunity of the initial vaccinations.[82] The
struggle to get everyone vaccinated failed even with New York City
vaccination mandates.

By October 2021, the city remained open but under the threat
of increasing COVID-19 cases with a third peak that, while not as
deadly as the previous two, was elevated enough to renew worry and
anxiety. Hospitals were again full and health-care staff strained, but
the planned reopening of Broadway and movie theaters continued
with proof of vaccination and mask wearing required. Public space
activities, outdoor restaurants, and gatherings in open spaces and
streets continued, but almost everyone wore a mask now, even outside. People were more cautious because of what they had already
been through and hoped that this uptick would not continue through
the upcoming winter.

Conclusion

The three peaks and two valleys in the number of cases of COVID-19
in New York City narrate the course of the pandemic and its impact
on urban public space.[83] The different phases capture the contractions
and expansions of public space use that occurred in response to the

coronavirus and city policies. From March through April 2020 (Phase 1), public spaces were closed, and virtual public space expanded. Beginning May 2020 (Phase 2), the use of some outdoor public spaces was permitted for individuals to stay healthy, and the city closed a few neighborhood streets for pedestrians.

The summer, June through September 2020 (Phase 3), was characterized by Black Lives Matter protests on city streets and squares accompanied by expansion of everyday activities into public spaces including restaurant structures taking over sidewalks and street parking areas. From October 2020 through May 2021 (Phase 4), public spaces and restaurants on sidewalks and streets remained open, but worry and fear of contagion increased, and school and university classes; church, synagogue, and mosque services; and gyms, theaters, and cultural events continued to be closed and held virtually.

With the arrival of vaccinations, NYC residents expanded their use of public spaces from May through October 2021 (Phase 5) with young people flooding popular downtown parks to party and be with others. The city remained open throughout this period even with the increase of Delta variant infections, and by October 14, 2021, the Delta variant began to retreat, raising hopes and new questions about the impending winter of 2021–2022.[84] New variants including Omicron continued to appear through the winter and spring of 2022.

During the COVID-19 pandemic public space mattered, becoming the living room, family room, and in some cases the kitchen of the city. Public space became a medical resource, a distribution hub, an overflow space, a center of protest and resistance, a gym, a senior center, a community center, a daycare center, a schoolyard, a night club, a transportation corridor, an outdoor restaurant, a shopping mall, a children's playground, an outdoor theater, a music venue, a nature center, and a place of belonging and "being at home." There were some positive lessons that emerged including a reassessment of face-to-face relationships, the solace of nature, the psychological costs of social isolation, and the importance of family ties. The exhaustion, brutal symptoms, and uncontrollable ruminations about the trauma of COVID-19 led to personal growth, more deliberate thinking, and a new way of seeing the world. And some people welcomed the long periods of quiet and reflection, and others the reprieve from social events.

Urban planners and city officials wonder whether public spaces will continue to play such an important role once the pandemic has subsided.[85] UN Habitat's document on "Cities and Pandemics" emphasizes land-use planning to preserve and restore blue-green networks and landscape corridors—one positive environmental outcome.[86] But what is most clear is that public space is a critical component of people's resilience, sense of well-being, and ability to keep going in the face of adversity and suffering. The contribution of public space appears even greater in the face of a pandemic, highlighting its multidimensional ability to transform and enhance urban life.

10

How to Study Public Space

The Toolkit for the Ethnographic Study
of Space (TESS) in Tompkins Square Park,
Manhattan, New York City and Other
Strategies

If public space matters for individual and community flourishing and
social justice, it is up to us to support and defend it in our neighborhoods and cities. The ethnographies and case studies illustrate that
there are economic, political, social, and environmental forces that
abandon, restrict, erode, and obstruct open urban spaces and their
degree of publicness. It is only by taking back these spaces—through
augmenting their use, protesting their closure, advocating improvement, encouraging inclusion, and recognizing difference—that public
space can retain its transformative power.

Look around your neighborhood and evaluate the physical and
social conditions of the public spaces. Include the streets and sidewalks,
libraries and museums, and well-used third spaces such as school playgrounds and church lawns that make up the public realm. Hopefully,
you find high-quality green, blue, and paved spaces for everyone to
enjoy. But it is more likely that there are few, and many are exclusionary, deteriorated, or neglected. Is it because of poor maintenance
and reduced funding, limited activities and programs due to a lack
of staff, damaged sidewalks and lack of benches based on municipal

priorities, or the abandonment of all social services including public space? What problems draw your attention? Are people using the space and in what ways? Do they represent the diversity of communities and groups that reside in the neighborhood? What questions arise from your observations? Would you like to know more?

One strategy for addressing public space problems is to undertake your own research with the people residing nearby or using the space. Neighbors, for instance, may be concerned that the local playground is too rundown and dangerous for children. Or it is not inclusive and welcoming for the people who live there. Perhaps an open lot or small garden is culturally significant but may be at risk of being privatized or closed. Park advocates need reliable site information to initiate repairs, renovations, and funding. An ethnographic toolkit helps to assess these situations and effectively communicate the impact of these public spaces on well-being and social cohesion.

The well-known urbanists William H. Whyte and Jane Jacobs had their toolkits—Whyte equipped with an 8 mm movie camera and Jacobs using precise descriptions of her West Village neighborhood—to change the way we plan and design public space.[1] Their writings on the importance of informal interactions to urban vitality resulted in new approaches to city planning. They both argued for mixed-use zoning, urban density, and person-centered design. Whyte is best known for promoting moveable furniture, vest-pocket parks, and privately owned public spaces that transformed parts of New York City so that it became a model for other cities.[2] Jacobs's writings continue to influence the design of neighborhoods by focusing on the complexity of social interactions and the importance of small businesses in creating a lively place.

When working together on the construction of Carnegie Center in Princeton, New Jersey, Whyte was intrigued by my use of ethnographic methods to study walking and recreation patterns in the suburban corporate setting. He thought that employing participant observation and in-depth interviews to elicit meanings and cultural patterns offered an effective way to understand urban landscapes, since filming was limited by the time required and the complexity of frame-by-frame analysis.³ Further, planners and designers needed methods to study human-environment interactions that were rigorous enough to be ecologically valid and reliable enough to predict behavior and actions.

Jane Jacobs's keen observations of street-level life resulted in the publication of *The Death and Life of Great American Cities* in 1961. But it was her organizing of the West Village in opposition to slum clearance and leading a city-wide coalition to defeat the lower Manhattan expressway plan that inspired community-based planning. By formalizing ad hoc opposition into a permanent neighborhood association, "residents not only set their own priorities, but also effectively advocate for them."⁴ Community participation in the design and planning process also required a methodological toolkit for data collection and the translation of the findings.

The development of an ethnographic toolkit to be used by community members and design professionals began in 2016 while attending UN Habitat III in Quito, Ecuador where I met individuals from nonprofit agencies working in Venezuela, India, Vietnam, and Mexico. Struggling to demonstrate that their projects improved the lives of families, they wanted a way to document and evaluate their interventions' efficacy. Collaborations with residents produced what looked like modest results—a cleared vacant lot with a small garden, a low wall built to protect a children's playground from nearby traffic, a zinc and wood bus shelter to protect people from the sun and rain, or a colorfully painted bench placed on a busy sidewalk for older adults to rest and watch people go by—but each increased contact, safety, and community building. These were not small achievements but social transformations that increased well-being and social cohesion in informal settlements with high levels of poverty, underemployment, and inadequate housing.

Traditional fieldwork requires at least a year of participant observation and interviews to produce a reputable ethnography, but design professionals and activists do not have the luxury of spending a year collecting data. Many of the public space ethnographies in this book—the Costa Rican plazas, the ambulatory vendors in Buenos Aires, the study of Prospect Park in Brooklyn, and the gated communities in New York, Texas, and Mexico—took years to complete.

In response to this challenge, I borrowed techniques used by medical anthropologists for assessing health outcomes and malnutrition, and developed the Rapid Ethnographic Assessment Procedure (REAP). This "rapid" methodology still required at least three months for fieldwork and write-up, but was successful at portraying the complex problems, needs, and desires of local communities through an in-depth snapshot of a place at one moment in time. Though REAP lacked the long-term perspective of traditional ethnographies, it used various methods to facilitate a multi-layered description of the social, political, and physical environment.[5]

The methods included historical documentation, behavioral and movement mapping, expert and individual interviewing, participant observation, focus groups, questionnaires and surveys, and user censuses, each resulting in a data set that could compared to the others. This process of "triangulation"—juxtaposing different kinds of data and asking questions of them—produced more reliable findings.

Each method added important details to the overall picture. Behavioral and movement mapping recorded socio-spatial aspects of the research site, while individual interviews and oral histories gathered emotional reactions as well as narratives of spatial use. Participant observation offered an "experience-near" sense of being in a place, and allowed the researcher to be enculturated, that is, taught to behave in a culturally appropriate manner, through interaction with users and nearby residents. Historical documentation provided the longer-term economic and sociopolitical context for understanding contemporary use. Each method was built on the next, adding new information, personal accounts, and local knowledge about the research site.[6]

REAPs, however, are cumbersome for community-based researchers. Most public space colleagues and advocates are collaborating on small-scale neighborhood improvements. In Valencia, Venezuela, for example, a group wanted to evaluate a playground they had created on the corner of a abandoned lot next to the grammar school. With the help of the school children's parents, they put up a low fence, cleaned out the trash, planted drought-resistant grass, and built a long table and benches for children to sit and play. A local group gave them the seed, fencing material, and wood to build the table and chairs, but they wanted to add play equipment. To obtain city contributions they needed to demonstrate that their intervention had a positive impact on the neighborhood. While there was considerable anecdotal evidence—more children used the park, parents joined the children at the table to play games, and people reported that the area felt safer—they did not have a way to collect data to verify these observations.

Using what was learned from the REAP and integrating other behavioral techniques and content analysis produced a method made up of five steps—mapping (Figure 10.1), participant observation (Figure 10.2) including taking fieldnotes (Figure 10.3), interviewing (Figure 10.4), historical documentation (Figure 10.5), and analysis (Figure 10.6). Suzanne Scheld, Erin Lilli, and I piloted it in our ethnography classes and asked students for feedback to identify problems. Troy Simpson drafted the Toolkit for the Ethnographic Study of Space (TESS), incorporating the students' suggestions to produce a ten-page booklet. This version guided the research project at Tompkins Square Park and was tested again at City Park in Nairobi with public space activists. A final version was presented at the 2020 World Urban Forum 10 in a training session for people working in public spaces, especially in the Global South.[7]

The Tompkins Square Park case study illustrates TESS's ability to offer insights into the unresolved and misunderstood communications between the Tompkins Square Park neighbors and the New York City Department of Parks and Recreation. It highlights how a history of social inequality, labor and housing protests, and intense policing produces ongoing class conflicts in the context of rapid gentrification.

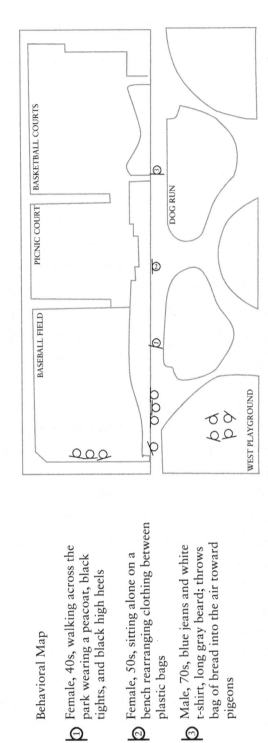

Behavioral Map

① Female, 40s, walking across the park wearing a peacoat, black tights, and black high heels

② Female, 50s, sitting alone on a bench rearranging clothing between plastic bags

③ Male, 70s, blue jeans and white t-shirt, long gray beard; throws bag of bread into the air toward pigeons

Figure 10.1 Mapping (TESS) (Graphic by Troy Simpson)

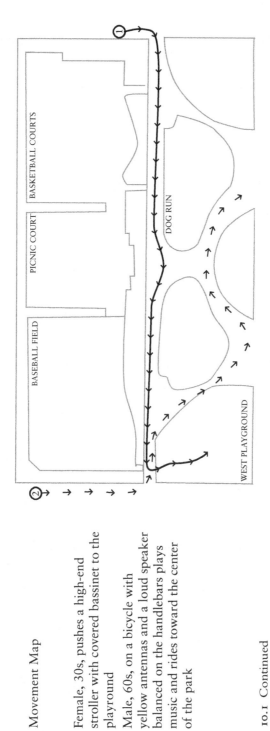

Movement Map

① Female, 30s, pushes a high-end stroller with covered bassinet to the playground

② Male, 60s, on a bicycle with yellow antennas and a loud speaker balanced on the handlebars plays music and rides toward the center of the park

Figure 10.1 Continued

Physical Traces Map

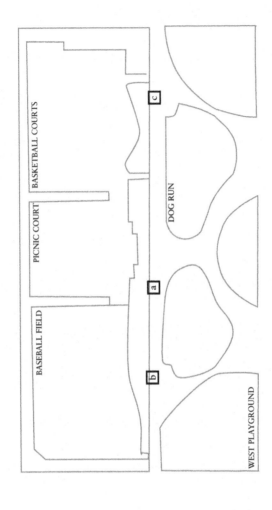

a Cardboard box with various books

b Empty water bottle and a brown
   paper bag underneath a bench

c Dark gray sweatshirt left on bench

Figure 10.1 Continued

Behavioral maps, fieldnotes, excerpts from interviews, and a brief historical overview illustrate the research and recording process.

★ ★ ★

Chain-link fences are a fixture of many New York City parks. They were put in when the city was a more dangerous place. Over time, these same fences act as barriers to park use, restricting access, separating park spaces from neighborhood spaces, and symbolically encoding the message that the park is unwelcoming. Mitchell Silver, a distinguished urban planner and one of the first planning professionals to hold the job of New York City Department of Parks and Recreation commissioner, grew up near Prospect Park in Brooklyn. Returning to his old neighborhood he found the half mile of park border along Flatbush Avenue "marred by fences and crumbling pavers and thick vegetation you can't see through."[8] He found barriers to park entry and high fences caging trees throughout the city, and in response initiated a program of removing or lowering them, rehabilitating park entrances, installing new benches, and adding greenery to blend public spaces into the urban fabric.[9]

New York City residents were asked to nominate parks that needed improvement. That generated a list of 690 parks of which eight were selected. One of these parks, Hugh Grant Circle in the Bronx, had been blocked by a gate that was often locked, while another, Steward Park on the Lower East Side, was rundown with two locked gates and perimeter fencing neighbors described as "very cold and not inviting."[10] Silver pointed out that while parks represent 14 percent of the city, streets and sidewalks contain another 26 percent, and so a total 40 percent of land is in the public domain. His program was to strengthen the relationship between parks and streets and sidewalks and reimagine all public space as accessible parkland.[11]

Parks Without Borders became a city-wide program, expanding with neighborhood consultations to involve residents in the decision-making and design process.[12] In 2018, I contacted Sarah Neilson, chief of policy and long-range planning, and commissioner Silver about the program and its success. He recounted working

Field Notes, Participant Observation

Project	NYC Parks	Researcher	[Researcher Name]
Location	Tompkins Square Park	Date	May 2, 2018
Note Type	Scratch (Field) Interview (circle one)	Weather	Cool / Windy (42°F)
Part ID	N/A	Time	Start: 7:30p.m. Stop: 8:30p.m.
General	Participant observation, sitting with people listening to music		

Observations / Questions	Personal Reflections and Ideas / Responses
I came to the park in the evening to get a better sense of who comes here then, and to listen to the musicians that often play here on summer evenings. When I arrived, there were no seats near the musicians, but a spot eventually opened up on a bench.	My goal for this trip was just to participate in the experience of sitting and enjoying the evening and the music alongside other people doing the same thing. I planned to take fewer notes and just see what it would be like to experience the park in this way.

Record quotations in the original language used by participants. Doing so ensures original expressions are retained and any translations can be returned to, and refined, if necessary.

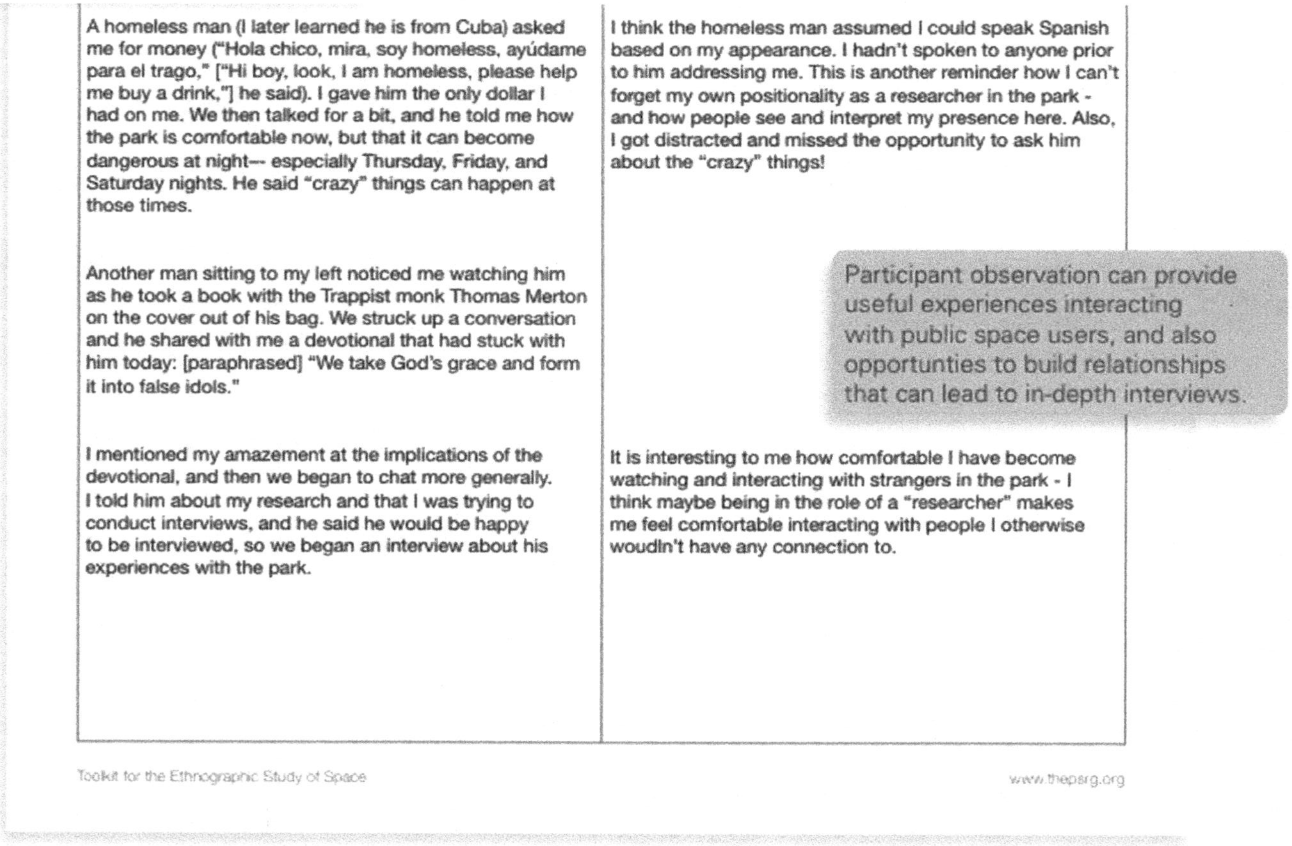

A homeless man (I later learned he is from Cuba) asked me for money ("Hola chico, mira, soy homeless, ayúdame para el trago," ["Hi boy, look. I am homeless, please help me buy a drink,"] he said). I gave him the only dollar I had on me. We then talked for a bit, and he told me how the park is comfortable now, but that it can become dangerous at night— especially Thursday, Friday, and Saturday nights. He said "crazy" things can happen at those times.

I think the homeless man assumed I could speak Spanish based on my appearance. I hadn't spoken to anyone prior to him addressing me. This is another reminder how I can't forget my own positionality as a researcher in the park - and how people see and interpret my presence here. Also, I got distracted and missed the opportunity to ask him about the "crazy" things!

Another man sitting to my left noticed me watching him as he took a book with the Trappist monk Thomas Merton on the cover out of his bag. We struck up a conversation and he shared with me a devotional that had stuck with him today: [paraphrased] "We take God's grace and form it into false idols."

Participant observation can provide useful experiences interacting with public space users, and also opportunities to build relationships that can lead to in-depth interviews.

I mentioned my amazement at the implications of the devotional, and then we began to chat more generally. I told him about my research and that I was trying to conduct interviews, and he said he would be happy to be interviewed, so we began an interview about his experiences with the park.

It is interesting to me how comfortable I have become watching and interacting with strangers in the park - I think maybe being in the role of a "researcher" makes me feel comfortable interacting with people I otherwise woudln't have any connection to.

Figure 10.2 Participant Observation (TESS) (Graphic by Troy Simpson)

Field Notes, General

Project	NYC Parks
Location	Tompkins Square Park
Note Type	Scratch (Field) Interview (circle one)
Part ID	N/A
General	Arrived by subway later than expected

Researcher	[Researcher Name]
Date	March 25, 2018
Weather	Cool / Windy (42°F)
Time	Start: 2:00p.m. Stop: 2:15p.m.

Observations / Questions

Write your observations as carefully as possible, including physical and social details. When taking notes about the actions of others, record what you see and hear and not what you think people are thinking.

I am seated on a green bench in the southwest corner of the park. The bench is the first in a line of approximately ten benches on each side of the sidewalk. I am facing a fenced in grassy green space with my back to the intersection of Avenue A and 8th St. To my left is an entrance to the playground where approximately two dozen very young children are playing and approximately ten adults are standing. There are no other people sitting in my line of benches.

Personal Reflections and Ideas / Responses

On the other half of the sheet you can put down how you feel about your experience.

It is a really nice spring morning, and I feel comfortable sitting outside. I imagine school-age children are in class at this time and I wonder how the park might feel, or who might be here, at different times.

Add any insights or questions you might have about what is going on.

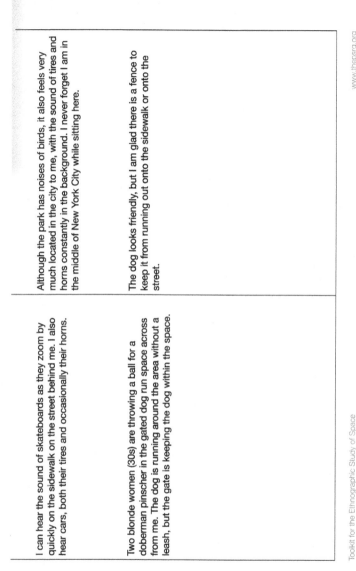

I can hear the sound of skateboards as they zoom by quickly on the sidewalk on the street behind me. I also hear cars, both their tires and occasionally their horns.

Two blonde women (30s) are throwing a ball for a doberman pinscher in the gated dog run space across from me. The dog is running around the area without a leash, but the gate is keeping the dog within the space.

Although the park has noises of birds, it also feels very much located in the city to me, with the sound of tires and horns constantly in the background. I never forget I am in the middle of New York City while sitting here.

The dog looks friendly, but I am glad there is a fence to keep it from running out onto the sidewalk or onto the street.

Figure 10.3 Fieldnotes (TESS) (Graphic by Troy Simpson)

Field Notes, Interview

Project	NYC Parks	Researcher	[Researcher Name]
Location	Tompkins Square Park	Date	Apr. 22, 2018
Note Type	Scratch Field (Interview) (circle one)	Weather	Sunny (64°F)
Part ID	#001	Time	Start: 3:30p.m. Stop: 3:45p.m.
General	Early-20s white female sitting on a bench reading, NYU student		

Observations / Questions	Personal Reflections and Ideas / Responses
List the questions that you are going to use in this column.	Write the answers to the questions in this column. Add any other comments or conversations that you had with the interviewee about the space or the local community.
Why do you come to this space?	"It's within walking distance from where I live, and it's not swarming with NYU students like Washington Square. I need some space sometimes. There's always people here, though, which some people might find annoying, but it's nice to have kids around. It doesn't feel desolate. Some parks in Chicago where I moved here from are often empty, scary. It's nice to have folks around doing things. Parks are good."
	----- I wonder if there are times when this park is empty or feels more "scary"?

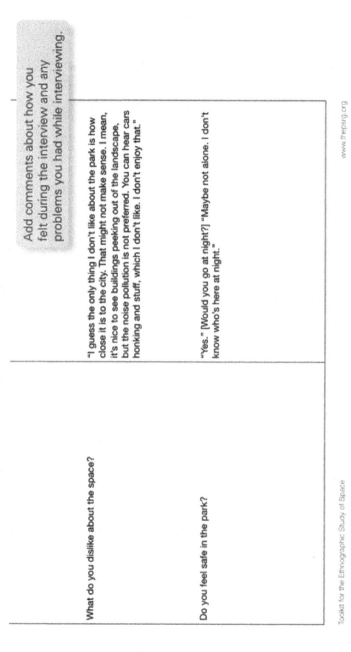

Add comments about how you felt during the interview and any problems you had while interviewing.

What do you dislike about the space?

"I guess the only thing I don't like about the park is how close it is to the city. That might not make sense. I mean, it's nice to see buildings peeking out of the landscape, but the noise pollution is not preferred. You can hear cars honking and stuff, which I don't like. I don't enjoy that."

Do you feel safe in the park?

"Yes." [Would you go at night?] "Maybe not alone. I don't know who's here at night."

Figure 10.4 Interviewing (TESS) (Graphic by Troy Simpson)

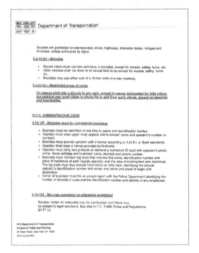

Figure 10.5 Historical Documentation

with the Tompkins Square Park neighborhood that had seven-foot fencing around the children's playgrounds and on the perim-eter. Best practices suggest that four-foot fencing reduces crime by increasing visibility, providing better access, and appearing more welcoming,[13] and initially Tompkins Square Park residents voted to have the park's fences lowered and entrance areas expanded. But in a public meeting park users, particularly parents, spoke out against the plan. Jake Wolff, a father of a four-year-old, argued "that the fence sort of makes us feel safe and protected."[14] In the meantime, $490,000 had already been slated to remove the seven-foot fence around the playground.[15]

This dilemma was an opportunity to try out the TESS. Four graduate students from the Ethnography of Space and Place course agreed to work on Tompkins Square Park,[16] while other students selected nearby parks and playgrounds for comparison. It took four weeks to complete the behavioral, movement, and physical traces mapping; participant observation; user interviews; and archival documentation. Focusing on the children's playground on the west side of the park and the nearby southwest entrance, we collected data to understand why residents did not want to lower the fences.

Tompkins Square Park TESS

History of the Park

We began with the history of Tompkins Square Park since severe winter weather made fieldwork difficult.[17] Materials from local libraries, newspaper archives, personal documents collections, and city maps produced a timeline of events. Illustrations of the kinds of documents collected are presented in Figure 10.5.

Proposed in 1811, but not completed until 1834, Tompkins Square Park is located on the Lower East Side of Manhattan bordered by East 10th Street to the north, Avenue A to the west, East 7th Street to the south, and Avenue B to the east. Designed as an elite space to spur urban development, it was important for immigrants who sought refuge from nearby crowded tenements.[18] A site of worker resistance, in 1857 the American Workers League gathered 4,000 supporters to demand jobs and aid for the unemployed.[19] Tensions between residents over class-based claims to the neighborhood resulted in a clash with the police in 1874 over a public-works program.[20]

Working-class residents fought to retain access to the park, emphasizing its value to low-income families. The central playground

PHYSICAL TRACES MAP

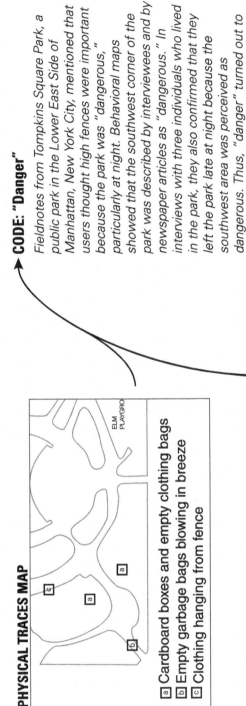

ELM PLAYGRO

ⓐ Cardboard boxes and empty clothing bags
ⓑ Empty garbage bags blowing in breeze
ⓒ Clothing hanging from fence

INTERVIEW

Interviewer: What is your opinion about the fences?

Participant: The fences make me feel safe. They keep my children safe from dangerous locations and people.

CODE: "Danger"

Fieldnotes from Tompkins Square Park, a public park in the Lower East Side of Manhattan, New York City, mentioned that users thought high fences were important because the park was "dangerous," particularly at night. Behavioral maps showed that the southwest corner of the park was described by interviewees and by newspaper articles as "dangerous." In interviews with three individuals who lived in the park, they also confirmed that they left the park late at night because the southwest area was perceived as dangerous. Thus, "danger" turned out to be a useful code that brought together observations, interviews, maps, and even articles from the newspapers. That a section of the park is perceived by users as dangerous is valuable evidence that could be used by park designers, planners, managers, and community members to begin to address this perceived problem.

FIELD NOTES - INTERVIEW

Then we talked for a while. He mentioned that it was dangerous to be at the park during the night. He added that during the night is when the park becomes conflictive. And that the most difficult nights are Thursdays, Fridays, and Saturdays. He said that most people go to party and do crazy things in the park.

FIELD NOTES - INTERVIEW

The primary takeaways are a consciousness about "junkies" or "homeless" in the southwest corner of the park, as well as discourse that connects the built space to relics of drugs and therefore danger (needles, rape).

HISTORICAL DOCUMENTS - NEWSPAPER

"There are hundreds of people who are disheveled and people who you used to call derelicts. I don't know if you're allowed to do that anymore," the Mayor told reporters at City Hall yesterday after making an unannounced visit to the park shortly before 7 P.M. Thursday.

"You see very few, if any, women and children in the park, and I don't blame them because I'd be scared to death," he said.

Figure 10.6 Analysis (TESS) (Graphic by Troy Simpson)

was built in 1894 as one of the first child recreation areas sponsored
by a private donor, who "argued that organized play would get the
children off the dangerous streets, would protect them from crime
and the ill effects of poverty, improve their health, and teach them
to become good citizens."[21] Tompkins hosted multiple protests over
worsening employment and housing conditions into the 1960s and
1970s.[22]

The building of high-rise condominiums and an increasing number
of middle-class renters and owners changed the character of the area
displacing original residents through speculative gentrification.[23] At
the beginning of the 1980s sales prices went from the tens of thousands to the hundreds of thousands, and by the end of the 1990s,
transactions in the millions were commonplace.[24] Newcomers were
uncomfortable with homeless encampments in the park and encouraged police authorities to move them out rather than provide the
social services and support needed.[25] On June 3, 1991, amid concerns
about drug use and a burgeoning tent city, the police forcibly evicted
200 to 300 tent residents.[26] Police squads enforced Mayor David
Dinkins's 1:00 am curfew and by 5:00 am had removed occupants
from their beds, tearing down tents and bulldozing the entire area.
The park was closed and guarded twenty-four hours a day. Neighbors
called it the "occupied territories."[27]

When reopened, fences and other spatial barriers were restored in
the hopes of creating spaces where middle-class residents felt protected from other park users. The iron fences installed in 1860 to
protect planted sections from horses, pigs, and small children, and fencing from the 1930s added under the direction of Robert Moses remained.[28] In 2009 existing fences and gates around the playground
were refurbished as part of a city-funded renovation, and brightly colored play equipment and a sandbox were added to the enclosed area.[29]
The redesign was heralded as successful, but some parents complained
that the low climbing walls obstructed their view of children playing.[30] Another renovation in 2011 replaced mesh garbage baskets with
sealed drums in an attempt to reduce rat infestations.[31] Yet the struggle

between homeless individuals living in tents, protesters defending their right to be there, and city campaigns to clear streets and parks of homeless encampments persists, with sanitation crews removing tents and campers' belongings from the edge of Tompkins Square Park as recently as May 5, 2022.[32]

Mapping

The park contains clearly differentiated sections of grass, playgrounds, dog run, sports fields, skateboard area, and gardens separated by 4-foot, 7-foot, or 8-foot iron fences and integrated by wide circular areas connected to sidewalks. The sections are also separated from the sidewalks by 4-foot fences, further compartmentalizing the space. Benches line both sides of the sidewalk between the pavement and the fencing where adults sit especially in nice weather.[33] The playgrounds and the

Figure 10.7 Tompkins Square Park Gate (Photograph by Merrit Corrigan)

sports fields have tall fences with gates that are unlocked only during daytime hours.[34]

Movement maps emphasized the articulation of the playground to the busy streets including Avenue A that is just a few feet away from

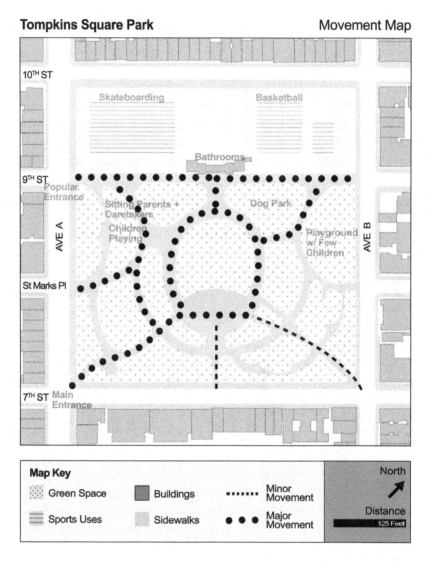

Map 10.1 Movement Map of Tompkins Square Park (Graphic by Abdullah Khawarzad)

the edge of the exterior fences. The playground is also bordered by a thoroughfare that goes directly through the park where cyclists, rollerbladers, dog walkers, and others make their way moving rapidly. There is heavy traffic made up of cars, trucks, bikes, and pedestrians on 10th Street with emergency vehicles and police cars traveling at faster speeds. There is considerably less movement on the walkways in the center section of the park, but within the sports fields and the playground areas, adults and children run and play within the fenced boundaries. The quietest areas are the benches where people are sitting and talking or reading.[35]

A set of sound maps from the northwest section of the park recorded three main sources of noise including car and bus traffic on the streets, banging hockey sticks and yelling in the sports court, and children laughing and screaming in the playground. These noises muffled the sound of birds and leaves rustling. A second set of sound maps from the southwest corner included jackhammers from street repairs, loud conversation by the chess tables, music from speakers on bicycles cruising by, and babies crying in their strollers.[36]

Behavioral maps illustrated who was sharing space and were recorded using the template from Figure 10.1. In the western center section of the park, most adults were standing or sitting outside the playground and not always looking at the children. In fact, some chose benches that directed their eyes in the opposite direction. Conversely, many people did stop and look at the hockey players inside their fenced area. Within the playground children were running and using the play equipment while the sports fields were full of soccer and other pick-up games. The skatepark was heavily used by male youth doing tricks and setting up competitions while the nearby mothers and caretakers watched the activity as their children played in the water fountain during the summer months.[37] Near the playground, next to the bathrooms, and on the southwest corner were many regular users, including the chess players, older men, park enforcement officers, and police officers.

Participant Observation

Participant observation was ongoing throughout the fieldwork period and recorded using the fieldnote template found in Figures

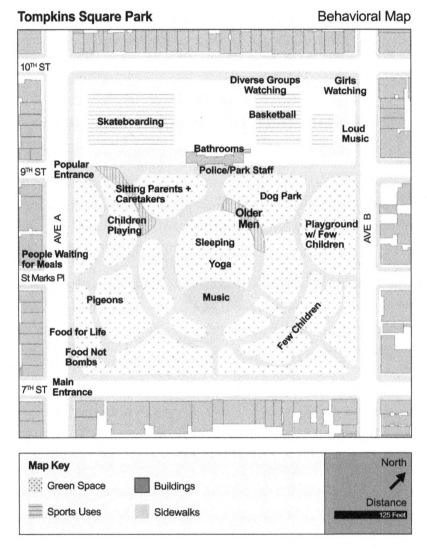

Map 10.2 Behavioral Map of Tompkins Square Park (Graphic by Abdullah Khawarzad)

10.2 and 10.3. From hanging out on the southeast corner, Anthony and Elisandro learned that there was considerable tension when the police close the park. Self-identified homeless individuals sometimes refused to leave and yet had nowhere else to go. Several older Latino men told Elisandro that they cannot stay overnight because it gets too dangerous.[38]

While sitting on the southwest corner, Anthony recorded activities were not allowed according to the list of rules posted at the main entrance. He observed people riding bicycles in undesignated places, playing loud *soca* music on portable speakers, playing radios that "disturbed the peace," leaving dog excrement on the grass, jumping fences, obstructing use of the benches, and ignoring signs to "please do not feed pigeons." He pointed out that these activities were not permitted, but also not policed.[39] Later in the day working next to the western entrance to the playground he saw a line of fourteen people—mostly women—wearing heavy coats bunched together with shopping carts filled with empty shopping bags. They moved back and forth between the line and the southwest corner where a group of about ten men stood around the chess tables.[40]

Bengi, who was also at the southwest corner, noticed that the Parks Enforcement Police car was parked very close to an unconventional artist and his friend keeping them under surveillance. Bengi's fieldnotes give a sense of what she saw and felt during this encounter:

> *I'm across[from] the huge tree in the middle of the circle. Under the tree there is a car of the Parks Enforcement Police. It is warm, partly cloudy; I even took off my sweater and can be in just my shirt for the first time since last fall. I'm sitting on the middle bench in the semi-circle. Two benches to my right, a girl is on her phone with headphones. Three benches to my left, a woman and a man are chatting. To my right, outside the circle, towards the monument there is a film crew. A man is coming into the circle, yelling and chanting. He has green colored hair, very loose clothes; he is big and is smoking. He sits on the bench at the end of the semi-circle. He is whistling. The girl talking on the phone heads off about five minutes after he arrives. I really want to observe him closely, but it*

is difficult as he already seems to know I don't belong, and it would just put me on the spot. Two men nod at him as he yells their names. One more man comes on his bike to chat with him for a while. The green-haired man takes a canvas and paints. The man on the bike leaves yelling he'll be right back, but the man with the dark green hair is too occupied with his canvas, drawing, focused on the work. He drinks from a paper bag.

I get back to observing when the man with the green hair throws his canvas and starts singing very loudly again. I'm unable to hear or understand the lyrics, I wish I could! He throws one more painting to the floor. He yells "hey" to a girl who is passing by, they wave at each other. A man passes by and tells him to be careful.

The man with the bike is in a conversation with the Parks Enforcement Police.

I can hear the kids playing in the green area behind me, there are two very young kids with two women. I look around. One more woman is on the bench to my left. She also has headphones on, coffee in her hands, and is talking on the phone. A lot of people come here to sit while they are on the phone.

The man with the bike comes back. The artist is still throwing his paintings. He has some painted masks and the man on the bike asks, "Who painted the mask?" and takes photos. Behind me (in the green area behind fences) I see more children now, and a man with a dog.

The Parks Enforcement Police car parks in front of me. The man with the bike approaches and exclaims to the person in the car: "he's smoking, he's smoking" (he is referring to the artist). They laugh out loud (the artist and the man with the bike). A police car appears in the exit of the park, but it's gone in a minute. Benches to my left are getting crowded. It's only these two guys (the artist and the man with the bike) to my right though.

The man with the bike starts yelling "Arrest me! Call police! I need help!" "I'm scared officer!" He takes photos of the artist. The Parks Enforcement Police car is leaving, and the man with the bike yells, "Hit the road and don't come back!" The two men are laughing a lot and I'm thinking wow, they are having so much fun![41]

A middle-aged man and woman, approach to check out the paintings.

Merrit watched several interpersonal interactions between visitors at the park who appeared to be strangers including a man approaching another on a bench and handing him a to-go container with food. The two men did not talk but gestured back and forth. She also wrote about more solitary individuals:

An older man with a beanie and a long, gray beard walks slowly into the green area directly across from me. He looks around, throws a bag of breadcrumbs into the air, [and] the pigeons flock to the crumbs. He walks away not looking at the birds.

Another man, about thirty years old wearing a yellow and blue hoodie, stumbles slowly from the street past the playground carrying no belongings or bags. He looks as if he could be physically injured. He returns and again walks past the playground and up the path toward the statue. A middle-aged woman with short black hair sits to my right with several white plastic bags laid out on a bench. She is rearranging the clothes between the bags. A few minutes later she leaves with her bags.

Merrit comments that part of the experience of being in the park is to encounter many types of people each utilizing the shared space for different activities and stretches of time. These disparate uses spark anxiety for some and moments of connection and collaboration for others.[42]

During a field visit in the late afternoon, Anthony and Elisandro encountered a table full of buffet cookware surrounded by many young people and an older man. Behind them was a green tarp that read "*Food Not Bombs*." The organizers told them that they visit the park every week at 5:00 pm and serve anyone who asks for food. They had mixed vegetables, roasted potatoes, a sweetbread, and other dishes. The older man introduced himself as a community crisis chaplain. He explained that his ministry comes to the park on the second and fourth Sunday of each month to offer informal religious and social services but does not come at night because there are "*thugs and dealers*."[43]

Interviews

Interviews offered another perspective for making sense of the observed behavior and socio-spatial relationships of the different groups of visitors. Figure 10.4 presents some of the questions asked, and provides the template used for recording answers.

Parents of Children in the Playground

A young mother of two children said: "*I'm glad [the fence is] there. I can let [my daughter] run around and don't have to be stressed.*" She noted that if the fence was lowered, "*I wouldn't take my daughter here anymore. At least I wouldn't let her run around. There's traffic and strangers, and too many people for that.*"

Another parent found the proximity of the street and large groups of moving people concerning and said: "*I know it's the city, but there are so many people running around it is stressful when she [points to her daughter] isn't in the stroller.*"

Homeless and Older Adult Men

Several interview respondents, particularly homeless men and POC, noted that the police were always watching them, and this made them nervous. An older man noted that the fence itself felt like a policing tactic that assumes they are dangerous, while they fear police violence.

A Spanish-speaking older man on the southwest corner who was collecting cans and waiting for evening meal said that he came to find friends.

> *We care for each other. During the night we recycle and make money for food and beer . . . Many people use this space. People that we know, people that come here to give us food. The people who we already know even come here to help us. You can come here whenever you want . . . but only during the day.*
>
> *The problem is there are people who normally consume drugs. Safety and access influence which places you can use. The bathroom for example is one of the spaces that we can not use because you will find people consuming drugs that do not allow you to go there. The other area is the entrance. They see us and start to talk about us. The best thing for this park would be that the police were close. Not only [here] when they are called.*
>
> *We cannot drink a beer here. We cannot smoke. There are rules. But I don't understand why we can't smoke here if there are people consuming other kinds of drugs. I can sleep here, but what I don't like is there are always many problems. My uncle used to live here, and he lived here the twenty-four hours. Felipe was his name. He died because of alcohol.*"[44]

Young Adults and Gender Perspectives

A young woman in her early thirties described what she does not like about the park: "*the bathrooms are terrifying. In an emergency had to use it once. There are junkies in there. I was afraid I'd be harmed or something.*" She added that "*it's like the scariest park in the city. That corner [the southwest] is to be avoided.*" Another female who did not explicitly say crime was a deterrent to visiting the park, corrected herself when asked if she would visit at night, and replied "*maybe not alone. I don't know who's here at night.*"

A young man in his twenties noted that "*unlike at Central Park or Prospect Park that feels more of an oasis, Tompkins is a city park. But even though the noise is annoying, it's also convenient, because I don't have to go far to get here.*" For him the fence "*doesn't feel foreboding because a wrought iron fence seems decorative to me . . . it's more easily passed through, pretty and more permeable than something behind a chained link or barbed wire.*"

A woman in her thirties lives close to the park.

I like the basketball courts. We play over there sometimes. This park is good to go to on the weekend because there are lots of good restaurants and bars around here, so we can go to brunch and then go to the park. It's fun to walk around and look at the dogs in the dog run. On days like today we can sunbathe or picnic. At night in the summer, they have movie nights, and we bring wine.

But I don't like the rats. There are more rats here than I've seen in my entire life, and I've lived in New York for eight years . . . I also don't like the drug situation. I've seen people shooting heroin multiple times . . . I also really don't like this grassy area (where she is sitting on a blanket in the sun). The grassy area is all rocky and uneven, not well kept. We'll go here but sometimes but can't find a place that doesn't have trash or, like, knives or needles. And that's during the day!![45]

A New York University (NYU) student in her twenties likes the park.

It's within walking distance from where I live, and it's not swarming with NYU students like Washington Square Park. I need some space sometimes. There are always people here, though, which some people might find annoying, but it's nice to have kids around. It doesn't feel desolate. Some parks in Chicago where I moved from are often empty, scary. It's nice to have folks

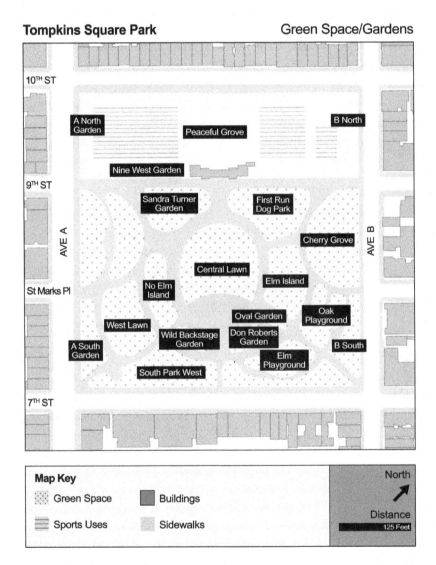

Map 10.3 Green Space and Gardens in Tompkins Square Park (Graphic by Abdullah Khawarzad)

around doing things. Parks are good . . . I guess the only thing I don't like about the park is how close it is to the city. That might not make sense. I mean, its nice to see buildings peeking out of the landscape, but the noise pollution is not preferred. You can hear cars honking and stuff, which I don't like.[46]

Analysis

Interviews were compiled and overlaid with the maps and participant observation fieldnotes then analyzed in relationship to the history of the park and the fence dilemma. Similarities and differences in the data sets emerged providing insights into what was going on.

For example, during initial observations, women were talking to one another while watching the children in the nearby playground. Behavioral maps confirmed that women and caretakers congregate on the benches closest to the children's playground. Physical traces maps, however, indicated that those benches face away from the playground, and the later fieldnotes recorded some women looking in the opposite direction and not necessarily watching the children through the high fencing. Other fieldnotes recorded women drinking coffee and talking on their phones. When asked about the sociality of the area, the women on the benches did not talk about meeting friends there or it being a social center. This contrasts with the older men talking about meeting their friends and enjoying a beer in the park. We wondered whether the multiple layers of fencing and the climbing walls made it difficult to see into the playground to follow the children. At the same time, parents say they rely on the high fences to keep their children safe. These contradictions are important clues to the symbolic meanings and social dynamics of the fences in the park.

Other insights emerged by comparing data on park users. Differences in expectations and enjoyment of the park could be explained by increasing gentrification and subsequent conflicts based on social class. For instance, young adults who recently moved to the neighborhood enjoy brunch nearby and then sunbathe in the park. By contrast, older men, the chess players, and some unhoused individuals consider the park their home, where they spend the day talking to friends and sometimes spend the night. For other people, it is a comforting place to come for a warm meal or social and religious services. There were also glaring contradictions in policing and enforcement of park rules. The differential monitoring of alcohol consumption--penalizing older men for drinking beer while not noticing younger visitors who bring wine to summer concerts— reveals underlying moral assumptions and prejudice based on class, gender, and race.

Almost all Tompkins Square Park users reported some kind of "fear," or felt there was "danger" that influenced the affective atmosphere and their experience of the park. Many people were afraid of being a victim of a crime or being bitten by a rat.[47] Fear of the police, sleeping in the park, and constant surveillance were mentioned by the older Spanish-speaking men, homeless individuals, and some of the youths hanging out at the skatepark.[48] Figure 10.6 illustrates how the various forms of data—fieldnotes, interviews, maps, and historical documents—were used to develop "danger" as a code to integrate these different sources and perspectives.

There were park issues that all groups agreed on. Mothers and caretakers who brought children to the playground wanted to use the bathrooms but could not because they were "dangerous." The artist, his friend, and the older men would use the bathrooms but were reluctant to enter and fearful of the drug users inside "shooting up." Park regulars were just as afraid of the bathrooms as the young women, parents, caretakers, and children.[49]

Local users' and residents' opposition to lowering the fence height around the children's playground was related to these perceived dangers and issues of proximity. The most often mentioned was parents' and caretakers' worry that the playground—at the edge of the park and next to a narrow sidewalk--was too close to a busy street. Another parental concern was the number of older men who spend the day talking and sometimes drinking beer near the entrance to the playground. Even though young women, parents, and caretakers said they were generally comfortable with their presence, a few reported that the men acted in ways that frightened them or their children.

We compared the Tompkins findings with three other TESS projects completed in Washington Square Park, Bleecker Street playground, and Hester Street playground located in nearby. We found that parents in all the playgrounds preferred high fences, and that even in Washington Square Park there were caretakers who avoided the areas where the park was open to the street (the "mounds"). Parents and caretakers in general worried about children running into the street or being "grabbed." The comparative findings found that playgrounds felt safer when: 1) there were adults as well as children within the play area (Hester Street), 2) the playground was below ground level so that the surrounding four-foot fences appeared higher conveying a sense of safety (Bleecker Street), and 3) the park had many users and police surveilling the area (Washington Square Park).

Using triangulation and content analysis we developed a list of findings to present to park users, neighborhood residents, and the Parks Without Borders staff. We found that the competing uses and contradictory meanings resulted in fences being perceived very differently by social groups. They were functional for parents and children, exclusionary for homeless residents, and a symbol of a historic past and part of the gentrification aesthetic for young adults and some residents. Parents and caretakers wanted to retain the high fences around the playground in response to a range of dangers—children running out into traffic, erratic behavior, bathrooms occupied by drug users, and rat infestations. Their fears were materialized in the symbol of the seven-foot wrought-iron fences regardless of whether the height had anything to do with re-establishing safety in the children's playground. The ambivalence about the fences also reflected the tumultuous history of class conflict and police violence that intensified with gentrification. Indeed, class conflict and an inability to work out equitable solutions were at the bottom of the discourse about the fences.

Social Justice Implications

While this study was not specifically undertaken to explore the Social Justice and Public Space Evaluation Framework, it offers insights into how the justice principles might improve residents' and users' experiences and mitigate the perceptions of danger and sense of insecurity.[50]

For example, in terms of **distributive justice**, there was inadequate space for all the users in the park. Indeed, it was the lack of affordable housing, healthy food, mental-health facilities, and medical care that generated the situation in which unhoused individuals waited each day for a meal near the entrance to the children's play area and slept on the grass. Further, in terms of a fair allocation of resources and public goods, the homeless individuals and older men did not have secure spaces with facilities such as a bathroom and showers, and therefore they were perceived as impinging on the children's playground area. Providing the economic resources and housing necessary to remediate the socioeconomic disparities generating these unresolved conflicts would contribute to a more collectively constructed public culture. Distributive justice is not only about spaces in the park but includes an assessment of citywide urban services and resources.

In terms of **procedural justice**, a better relationship of park users could develop through more transparent negotiations of the use of space. A fair procedure for voicing and remediating conflicts that included management, police, park users, and the nonprofit services providers would improve social relations. Based on the procedural justice literature, greater cooperation and tolerance are outcomes when the process of decision-making is collective rather than only in the hands of one group.

A need for greater **interactional justice** was reflected in the inequitable treatment of many of the users who spend the day in the park. The Spanish-speaking older men and homeless residents felt that the city was not keeping them safe from whatever (or whomever) inhabited the park at night. Treatment by the police was perceived as unfair, and we observed multiple cases of differential treatment. Changing the mode of policing—making it more community and grassroots based—and encouraging user interaction through structured forms of contact such as events and targeted programs could enhance the development of a public culture even in this socially diverse situation. Increased social interaction creates familiarity with other groups and individuals and reduces fear and the perception of danger.[51]

Recognition of different cultural patterns and practices was not apparent during our study. Nearby Hester Street Playground accommodated many different cultural groups, and we observed that everyone conversed while their children played together and celebrated holidays. In Tompkins Park there seemed to be less social interaction among the diverse social and cultural groups. There were exceptions such as the young woman who sunbathed in the grassy areas shared with a homeless man who slept there. But in general, there was less recognition of cultural and behavioral differences except for the vociferous complaints about the perceived transgressions of "others."

On the other hand, an **ethic of care** was evident in the many volunteer groups that provided social services and meals to anyone in need. Also, the children's caretakers—both parents and nannies—said that they watch out for one another, and the chess players and other regulars "keep an eye out for danger." We did not get a clear view of the role of the police in relation to care, but they were present and recognized many of the park regulars including the artist, the chess players, and some homeless individuals. The empowerment of park users to offer care and care-based social services contributed to a sense of social justice overall.

★ ★ ★

There are many other methods—questionnaires and surveys, behavioral checklists, digital participatory mapping, digital applications such as Minecraft,[52] and design-based evaluation models—that can be used to understand public space. Organizations such as UN Habitat, university centers such as the Luskin Center at UCLA, private consulting firms such as the Gehl Institute and the Project for Public Space, and municipal agencies in many cities have generated a plethora of guidelines, handbooks, assessment tools, and policy manuals. Some of the best toolkits can be found on the PSRG website and are briefly reviewed here.

UN Habitat Programs

The UN Habitat Global Public Space Program began in 2012 to encourage cities to take actions that would lead to creating safe, inclusive, and accessible public space for all. Ten years later the program has completed 137 upgrading projects in ninety cities impacting the lives of over 2.3 million people.[53] Working through partnerships with communities, engaging in co-design and participatory workshops, and conducting site-specific and city-wide assessments, they have produced several toolkits, policy papers, and reports on their methods and procedures. Although often targeting city officials, NGOs, and design and planning professionals, many of their ideas, strategies, and case studies are helpful models for undertaking local public space projects.

The *Global Public Space Toolkit* published in 2016 is a user-friendly guide to help cities and residents improve the availability, quality, and distribution of good public spaces. The toolkit is a practical reference for local governments who want to develop projects by implementing the recommended public space principles and policies. While mostly focusing on policy tools, the toolkit outlines survey and mapping methods to assess the quantity, quality, and distribution of public space and utilizes previously tested assessment tools to evaluate walkability, access, and recreation.

City-wide Public Space Strategies: A Guidebook for City Leaders[54] that helps communities to map and analyze their public space network and the *City-wide Public Space Assessment Toolkit: A Guide to Community-led Digital Inventory and Assessment of Public Spaces*[55] that provides a step-by-step methodology to evaluate the quality of specific public spaces were added in 2020. The site-specific methodology draws on methods from the TESS and the REAP such as transect and walking interviews, behavioral mapping, observational schedules, and other ethnographic strategies, but also includes digital methodologies that expand the program's ability to connect with communities building capacity and greater awareness.

Digital toolkits such as *Block-by-Block Playbook* encourage greater participation in the planning and design process. The Playbook provides guidelines on how to use Minecraft, a videogame described as a kind of digital "Lego," to co-design public space, especially involving children and youth. "Her City Toolbox," a project that targets girls and women who feel excluded in public space, supports digital interactive activities and an online database to help rethink and co-design the city.[56] The launch of the digital platform in 2021 expanded their reach to over 950 users in 350 cities worldwide. Digital methods are increasingly available with expanded internet service and Wi-Fi connectivity and the ubiquity of mobile phones. Digital technologies and methodologies—while still relying on careful observations, interviews, and mapping—add valuable data resources, websites, and virtual ways of reaching more people and getting them involved in participatory design processes.

Life Between Buildings

The Dutch architect Jan Gehl began a series of architectural studios in Copenhagen recording standing, sitting, waiting, and talking as part of the design process. In 1971 he published *Life Between Buildings*, a critique of new modernist suburbs that demonstrated how a lack of life between the buildings had public space consequences.[57] His interest in documenting urban life and using behavioral data to create more people-centered urban design resulted in the establishment of Gehl Architects, a privately held urban design practice in 2007, followed by the satellite Gehl Studio in San Francisco, and the Gehl Institute, an independent nonprofit research and advocacy group in New York City.

While Gehl Architects focused on human-scale design practice, the studio and the institute produced a series of significant reports including the *Public Life Diversity Toolkit* to measure social mixing and economic integration in public space, *A Mayor's Guide to Public Life* with simple steps for improving urban spaces, and a *Public Life Data Protocol* creating a common language for collecting people-based data.[58] Their approach focused on behaviors, demographics, and activities that could be observed and quantified, compared to other sites, and related to patterns of use and disuse. They employed several methods including intercept surveys, observational analyzes, and census techniques with sampling strategies and pretesting to increase the reliability of the measurement instruments. City officials, planners, and designers who need hard data (i.e., quantification) to argue for design interventions that increase social engagement and participation in public life might find these toolkits particularly useful.

The Gehl Institute's most ambitious undertaking, *Inclusive Healthy Places. A Guide to Inclusion and Health in Public Space: Learning Globally to Transform Locally*, utilized Gehl's Public Space, Public Life methodology to understand how place is integral to health.[59] Arguing that everyday environments play a fundamental role in health and well-being, they brought together global expert advisors to develop the Inclusive Healthy Places Framework. The framework considers the context and processes that produce healthy places, but also identifies designs and programs to implement and sustain these relationships. Measurable indicators are organized into a typology of predictors of exclusion, community assets, indicators of civic trust, participation, and social capital, as well as an assessment of the quality of public space across multiple scales. It is a conceptual toolkit intended to integrate public space research findings that impact community health.

Project for Public Spaces

Project for Public Spaces (PPS) was started by Fred Kent and Kathy Madden in 1975 as a private consulting firm dedicated to enhancing public space design. They developed a "placemaking" approach to inspire people to collectively reimagine and reinvent public spaces as the center of their community. PPS defines placemaking as a collaborative process that promotes better urban design, but also facilitates "creative patterns of use, paying particular attention to the physical, cultural, and social identities that define a place and support its ongoing evolution."[60]

Working with over 3,500 communities over forty years, PPS maintains an active website, a newsletter, and blog as well as seminars and workshops that offer up-to-date materials and direct collaborative projects to improve public space. They have an extensive library of specialized toolkits and guidelines, case studies of collaborative community projects, and effective marketing tools focused on placemaking as a process and a philosophy. While their methodology is centered around observing, listening, and asking questions about a particular space, they are more concerned with implementation strategies, beginning with small-scale *Lighter, Quicker, Cheaper*" improvements that bring immediate benefits both to the spaces themselves and to the people who use them.[61] PPS is now two distinct organizations: PPS that continues to examine the impact of public space on cities and remains the main research and consulting business,[62] and Placemaking X that focuses on developing placemaking organizations around the world.

Active Design Guidelines

Public-sector programs have contributed to the development of guidelines and public space assessments at the city level. The relationship of public space to health has been the New York City centerpiece with the publication the Active Design Guidelines Promoting Physical Activity and Health in Design in 2010. David Burney, an architect and commissioner of design and construction at the time, analyzed and rated the growing body of evidence that architectural and urban design strategies can increase physical activity and healthy behaviors. He utilized this research to develop guidelines that included recommendations for the design of healthy public space by expanding and utilizing streetscapes and traffic circles more effectively.[63]

Based on the success of these guidelines the Center for Active Design emerged, a nonprofit organization promoting evidence-based design to foster healthy and engaged communities. Their initiative on public space and civic life produced a civic engagement survey and toolkit for assessing the relationship of local public space with social and political participation.[64] The research, survey, and toolkit are available on their website.

Observing Play and Recreation in Communities

Observational methodologies of physical activity are popular with researchers and communities who need a way to assess the impact of parks on health. The System for Observing Play and Recreation in Communities (SOPARC) was developed by the RAND Corporation to address childhood obesity in low-income and high-risk communities and to examine how environments and policies influence active living for children and their families. SOPARC gathers direct information on community park use by assessing users' physical-activity levels, gender, activity modes/types, estimated age, and race/ethnicity groupings. It also collects information on the accessibility, usability, supervision, and organization of distinct park areas.[65]

Quantifying physical activities and user characteristics in natural settings where the number of participants and activities change frequently, SOPARC uses "momentary assessments" counting the number and type of park users and cataloging their activities at a single point in time. With multiple assessments, observations provide an estimate of weekly park use. Organized as a series of "scans," peoples' activities are coded as "sedentary" (i.e., lying down, sitting, or standing), "walking," or "vigorous." Separate scans approximate the gender, age, and race/ethnicity groupings of participants. Summary counts permit activity comparisons among different environments or within the same setting over different time periods and different groups of people.[66]

The Bronx Community Health Network and New Yorkers for Parks (NY4P) used SOPARC for their *Measuring Neighborhood Park Use: A Citizen's Guide* that puts the tools in the "hands of local experts." It offers a method for residents to observe how people use a neighborhood park, to determine what works and what does not work, and to make a case to local decision makers.[67]

Educational Institutions

There are numerous research groups that focus on public space in educational institutions such as the Luskin Center at UCLA, the Public Space Observatory Research Centre (PSORC) at Cardiff University, the Barcelona Lab for Urban Environmental Justice and Sustainability at the Universitat Autònoma de Barcelona, and the Interdisciplinary Center for Urban Culture and Public Space at TU Wein. These centers, labs, and research units produce research reports on public space as well as guidelines for special populations such as older people[68] or toolkits for creating new kinds of public space such as parklets.[69] Global organizations such as Women in Informal Employment Globalizing and Organizing (WIEGO) also produce toolkits for their members such as the Supporting Informal Livelihoods in Public Space publication for improving and supporting street vending.[70] There are available resources, guidelines, toolkits, and organizations for developing your own strategy for understanding, evaluating, advocating, renovating, and designing public spaces that will enhance your life and those of your neighborhood and community.

Conclusion

Bringing together the multiple answers to why public space matters is a never-ending challenge because the impact of public space on people, neighborhoods, and cities is constantly growing and changing. The effects of socially just public space are infinite when you consider how each positive contact or social interaction can be transformed into a sense of belonging and inclusion. Each additional garden, tree, or green space improves the quality of the air and water. Protests, social movements, and political activism lead to better communication and understanding of underlying conflicts while playgrounds and unstructured open fields provide nourishment for free play and creativity. Every beautiful walkway, sidewalk, and strolling park encourages walking and engaging with nature in ways that increase well-being and wonder. Cultural continuity, identity, and expression depend on symbolic and ritual practices and collective participation. Public spaces enact and embody democratic practices when designed and managed for equitable and equal access. Even during periods of economic contraction, public spaces offer workplaces and job improvisation.

Each domain of flourishing—social justice and democracy, health and well-being, play and creativity, informal work and social capital, cultural identity and place attachment, and ecological sustainability—is promoted and enhanced by access to and use of public space. Of course, there are many other domains that were not touched upon including public space as an infrastructure of circulation and mobility and its role in the provision of temporary shelter. Public space development, for instance, can be a strategy for neighborhood revitalization and community empowerment when gentrification is controlled and managed. But public space renovations and design improvements often result in economic gain for some—often developers and newcomers—at the expense of the loss of homes, community space, and place attachment for current residents.

How public space contributes such benefits—and accomplishes so much—is based on the ability to promote publicness, inclusive sociality, and being together with difference. The three necessary ingredients of social contact, public culture, and affective atmosphere encourage people to come together in ways that can be transformative. The everyday sociality and joyous cacophony of the Latin American plaza encompass informal work, play, and meaningful conversations intertwined with cultural practices and religious routines. The diversity of users and acceptance of difference in Prospect Park and Jones Beach are facilitated by the circular drive or boardwalk where people meet, and yet there is plenty of space and privacy for separate activities. The hum of conversations, shopping for specialty foods, and various kinds of music in public markets provide a lively context for social interaction and cultural integration. The basic elements of a "good" public space, one that enhances life and social relations, requires social encounters, a set of tacit rules and ways of being that are comfortable for most people, and an affective atmosphere of openness, exploration, or any structure of feeling that encourages people to be together with respect and dignity.

Whether a public space is socially just can be answered through the application of the Social Justice and Public Space Evaluation Framework. This framework enables practitioners, researchers, activists, and community members to ascertain whether a public space enhances inclusion and equity or redirects energy and funds in ways that are deleterious for some groups and individuals. Of course, public space alone cannot solve all social justice issues. Social injustice and inequality extend beyond any park, plaza, sidewalk, beach, or street.

Public spaces, though, provide a place to start, where ongoing conflicts and forms of injustice are visible and exposed by exploring spatial relations and group behavior. Social injustice is more likely to permeate the entire neighborhood, city, or region, instead of a single site; but sometimes, as with a highly privatized space like Hudson Yards, changing the governance, design, and accessibility of a public space can make a difference. An evaluation or assessment framework is useful as you move from understanding a space to diagnosing its problems and determining what solutions are available.

Undertaking the research to determine what is occurring in a particular public space is the final contribution of this book. The example of Tompkins Square Park is a larger space than you might take on, and certainly a contentiously diverse place; however, it offers some perspective on how the methods work and what they can provide in a short time. TESS is one strategy that can help to uncover and understand the public space(s) you want to improve or create. It is not a design toolkit but an ethnographic one developed to enable you to become your own social scientist and get directly involved in public space activism to improve cities for the future. With a toolkit, a desire for improving your local space, and a set of social justice and equality principles it is possible to transform your own neighborhood and city. The impact of public space is overwhelmingly positive when it is open, accessible, green, and socially just. Public space matters in so many ways. It is time to get started on making it what it has the potential to be.

Appendix

Contact, Public Culture, and Affective Atmospheres: A Theoretical Framework

Contact Theory and Social Interaction

Public space provides settings and opportunities to see and encounter diverse kinds of people in unmediated situations where new connections, ideas, activities, and practices can emerge. These interactions are the basis of transformations that occur through cooperation, conflict, and negotiation, such that without this platform for unplanned contact and social relations, understanding and social cohesion deteriorate.[1] Poorly executed or maintained spaces are avoided and underutilized such that the location, organization, and design of public spaces are crucial to their success.

Urban sociologists observe that social interaction with strangers sustains urban life. Erving Goffman writes about behavior in public documenting the many ways that individuals both avoid and interact with others.[2] While Goffman dissects how people form social acquaintances and causal engagements, Richard Sennett champions the contention that contact and cooperation—as well as thoughtful design and ethical architecture—are fundamental to social interaction and urban life.[3] Lyn Lofland proposes that social-psychological spaces—such as parks, plazas, streets, bars and buses—where strangers meet actually create the "public realm,"[4] while Sophie Watson offers a feminist critique of this unfettered sociality by identifying the borders and boundary conditions necessary for such social encounters.[5] Eric Klinenberg echoes these same sentiments arguing that public institutions provide the social infrastructure for people to gather and linger, strengthening a sense of community.[6]

As early as 1896, however, DuBois' study of African Americans living Philadelphia emphasized the constraints of structural racism on any "stranger encounter" and revealed internal class hierarchies and exclusionary behavioral norms.[7] Elijah Anderson, drawing upon DuBois and Goffman, describes the racial and class ruptures that impact contiguous white and Black neighborhoods to emphasize the complexities that shape public engagement such as knowing the "code" and being "streetwise."[8] Anderson argues that some places—such as the Reading Terminal in downtown Philadelphia—encourage the relaxation of these racial and class tensions and enable the emergence of new social relations under "the cosmopolitan canopy" of particular urban environments.[9]

Anthropologist John L. Jackson's portrayal of public space interactions interrogates how class and race are enacted with surprising personal and social consequences.[10] He delves into the class histories of Harlem and emerges with a deeper analysis of how African American residents "do" class and race within a particular place and time. Enoch Page contends that there is no Black public sphere in white public space, because of white control of communication technology.[11] And in his most recent book, Anderson argues that the stigma and discomfort of being Black in white space is due to the symbolism of the iconic ghetto associated with Black male identity.[12]

Marxist and feminist geographers who focus on conflict, protest, and resistance[13] and activist planners and landscape architects who reclaim public space[14] emphasize gender, race, and class histories and hierarchies in their work. They argue that collaborative and co-production processes create a recognition of difference sufficient to imagine public spaces as locations for open political encounters. Julian Agyeman, an urban planner, draws upon Eli Anderson's cosmopolitan canopy to imagine socially just and inclusive public spaces even within settler-colonial and racial capitalist societies.[15]

★ ★ ★

Social psychologists question whether intergroup contact reduces prejudice and improves social harmony utilizing the well-established "contact hypothesis."[16] Intergroup contact is defined as "the actual or symbolic interaction between representatives of different social groups" with the underlying premise that contact with a member of another group has the potential to reduce prejudice toward all members of the other group and to the group as a whole.[17] A review of studies from 1946 to 2017 finds that direct face-to-face contact, cross-group friendship, indirect contact, and even simulated contact contribute to various positive outcomes. Contact is a liberalizing agent that shapes human cognition and makes respondents less inward-looking and more open to experiences.[18] Social interaction with other groups broadens respondents' worldview, deprovincializes their perspective, and encourages more flexible thinking, creativity, and problem solving.

Not only does contact improve attitudes toward other groups, but there are transfer effects toward other noncontacted groups and to cognitive processes in general.[19] Some studies suggest that contact offers a practical means of improving group relations and even affects perceptions of trust as well as improving the accuracy of trust decisions.[20] While researchers caution that implicit racial bias is relatively stable because it is dependent on structural qualities in the environment, interpersonal contact accompanied by transforming social conditions offers the greatest possibility for change.[21] Overall social psychologists conclude that contact is good for much more than is commonly recognized and a central tenet of human psychology.[22]

These findings have implications for intergroup tolerance—as different from prejudice—in culturally diverse societies. To encourage intergroup tolerance, contact may not be enough and instead requires policies to set norms about the willingness to disagree and put up with group differences. Perspective taking and intercultural inter-actions around concrete cases or situations provide the best outcomes accompanied by the building of inclusive institutions and egalitarian settings.[23]

While skeptical that social interaction in and of itself can transform public space, the social psychological data are provocative. Fieldwork in the United States and Latin America provides evidence that pro-test, contestation, and resistance facilitate socially just change, while enclosure, surveillance, and policing reinforce unequal class relations, gender bias, and racism.[24] The most compelling arguments, however, come from observing, interviewing, and working with people who recount the positive role that public space plays in their lives and neighborhoods. Ethnographic research in parks, beaches, plazas, and walkways offers rich stories of how public space encourages social justice, ethnic and racial integration, and tolerance, while at the same time reveals that public space can not reach its promise through social interaction and contact alone.

Public Culture

The missing ingredient that transforms everyday contact into something more socially substantial is public culture. While social interaction and contact theories emphasize the importance of neigh-borhood connections, public culture refers to social formations, meanings, beliefs, practices, and modes of communication expressed in civic public spaces such as central squares, plazas, parks, and city streets. These centers of civil society, forums for discussion and dis-sent, and locations for the circulation of news and information are capacious enough to include multiple publics and counter-publics. Legally, they are considered a "commons," and restricted only through ownership rights and health and safety restrictions.[25] They represent peoples, societies, governments, and nations collectively and have the capacity to broaden the public sphere.

I first came across the term "public culture" as the title of a new journal.[26] The editors, Arjun Appadurai and Carol Breckenridge, were interested in the emergence of a global economy in which cosmopolitan cultural forms are increasingly recruited to form new and emergent group identities. These processes of cultural circulation and consumption produce what they identify as public culture, that is, the interaction and interrelationships of public phenomena that exist locally and globally. Public culture is not a coherent domain, but constituted as flows of cultural information, materials, and peoples transnationally and trans-locally as part of a new kind of modernity.[27] Public culture in this sense is not linked to any spatial configuration and is a characteristic of contemporary cultural globalization. But it suggests an important role for public space as the location where the circulation of ideas, peoples, materials, and other cultural forms becomes visible.

Public culture also refers to the dynamic negotiation of beliefs, values, and attitudes regarding collective association, through media and social practices. It is responsive to norms of open access and voluntary response creating an umbrella under which public opinion is formed. "Public" when used in this context means unrestricted communication across civil society, while "culture" emphasizes the creation of public opinion that is dependent on contextual factors.[28]

Ash Amin includes the "total dynamic—human and non-human—of a public setting" in what he calls "situated multiplicity" or the "thrown togetherness of bodies, mass of matter, and of many uses and needs in a shared physical space"[29] to characterize its emergent potential. Public culture is more than social interaction and not sufficient without the inclusion of material and non-human actants of a place; it relates to everything that is collective and shared.

Public culture then is an emergent set of visible behaviors and symbols, flows of information, and communication norms that are constantly challenged, changed, and replaced, but over time form a collective understanding—a relatively stable social construction—of how to be together. Any dense collection of diverse people and objects cannot function without shared infrastructure, such as collective institutions and spaces.[30] But infrastructural hardware requires a software of shared symbols, interpretations, intentions, meanings, and ways of being informed by embodied experience. Public culture generates the human patterns and collectivities that spring up, some to endure for years and others for just a moment like a flash mob in Philadelphia or subway dance in New York City.

Public culture like public space is socially produced by the history, political economy, and materiality of a specific time and place. It mediates the relationship of public space and the public sphere by communicating ideas and feelings that shape structures of social relations and interactions. Public culture is fluid and ever-changing, produced and reproduced by people's thoughts and actions within complex social, physical, and affective environments. When observed ethnographically it appears to have a stabilizing and socially cohesive role in public spaces that are successful in being a place for all.

Affective Atmosphere

Ben Anderson, who first used the concept affective atmosphere was intrigued by the way the term is used in everyday speech as in the atmosphere of a room, a city, an epoch, a street, a painting, a scene, or a time of day—anything that surrounds, envelops, or presses upon the person. He suggests that affective atmospheres are "a class of experience that occur *before* and *alongside* the formation of subjectivity, *across* human and non-human materialities, and *in-between* subject/object distinctions…atmospheres are the shared ground from which subjective states and their attendant feelings and emotions emerge."[31] Affective atmospheres are inherently spatially, properties of objects and subjects, and of bodies affecting other bodies, but at the same time exceed the boundaries of a collection of bodies.

Programming public space through lighting, design, images, and signs with integrated mobile technologies, social media, and internet websites is pervasive and potentially harmful. Affective responses can be designed into urban spaces as a "form of landscape engineering that is gradually pulling itself into existence, producing new forms of power as it goes."[32] Nigel Thrift is apprehensive that corporate and state institutions employ this knowledge to influence and in some cases constitute political and social practice.[33] The ability of the state to manipulate the affective dimension of the city has dangerous consequences and must be understood to withstand the seductive lure of state-programmed regimes of feeling and retain spaces for alternative affective forms and experiences.

★ ★ ★

Contact and social interaction, public culture, and affective atmosphere are mediators that can transform the social production of public space—its history, politics, territory, economics, governance, and planning—into meaningful and inclusive places. The context of any public space always includes multiple variables including the area's demographics, such as the socioeconomic and racial diversity of the neighborhood, and reflects the composition of users and potential visitors. The geographical location, microclimate, and vegetation or lack of it, and other aspects of the landscape are also critical to any analysis, as are spatial relations and design form. The discursive practices of social media, newspaper images, and circulating urban myths shape the way that the public space is encountered even before entering the space. These contextual factors are discussed in the history and background of the ethnographic cases and research examples. The theoretical focus of this book, however, is on the way that these three processes can generate more socially just public space outcomes.

Notes

CHAPTER 1

1. Eric Klinenberg, *Palaces for the People: How Social Infrastructure Can Help Fight Inequality, Polarization, and the Decline of Civic Life* (New York: Crown, 2018).

   John Parkinson, *Democracy and Public Space: The Physical Sites of Democratic Performance* (Oxford: Oxford University Press, 2012).
2. Setha Low, *Behind the Gates: Life, Security and the Pursuit of Happiness in Fortress America* (New York and London: Routledge, 2004).
3. An unarmed Black American brutally suffocated while being arrested by white policemen in Minneapolis.
4. Kyle Chayka, "The Mimetic Power of D.C.'s Black Lives Matter Mural: The Pavement Itself Has Become Part of the Protest," *New Yorker*, June 9, 2020. https://www.newyorker.com/culture/dept-of-design/the-mimetic-power-of-dcs-black-lives-matter-mural.
5. Mark Leibovitch, "Forbidding Obstacle Turns Symbol of Hope: Changing Views on a Chain-Link Fence, *New York Times*, June 11, 2020, A22.
6. Michael J. Sandel, *What Money Can't Buy* (New York: Farrar, Straus and Giroux, 2012), 203.
7. Frank Bruni, "Dogs Will Fix Our Broken Democracy," *New York Times*, August 31, 2019, https://www.nytimes.com/2019/08/31/opinion/dogs-democracy.html.
8. Kimberly J. Shinew, Troy D. Glover, and Diana C. Parry, "Leisure Spaces as Potential Sites for Interracial Interaction: Community Gardens in Urban Areas," *Journal for Leisure Research* 36, no. 3 (2004): 336–55, https://doi.org/10.1080/00222216.2004.11950027.
9. Richard Sennett, *Together: The Rituals, Pleasures and Politics of Cooperation* (New Haven and London: Yale University Press, 2012).
10. Andy Merrifield, *The Politics of the Encounter: Urban Theory and Protest Under Planetary Urbanization* (Athens: University of Georgia Press, 2013).

11. Anna Barker, Adam Crawford, Nathan Booth, and David Churchill, "Everyday Encounters with Difference in Urban Parks: Forging 'Openness to Otherness' in Segmenting Cities," *International Journal of Law in Context* 15, no. 4 (2019): 495–514, https://doi.org/10.1017/S1744552319000387.

12. Setha Low, *On the Plaza: The Politics of Public Space and Culture* (Austin: University of Texas Press, 2000).

13. Zygmunt Bauman, *City of Fears, City of Hopes.* (Goldsmiths' College: Centre for Urban and Community Research, 2003)

14. Gilles Deleuze and Félix Guattari, *A Thousand Plateaus: Capitalism and Schizophrenia* (Minneapolis: University of Minnesota Press, 1987).

15. Barker et al., "Everyday Encounters," 495–514.

16. Barker et al., "Everyday Encounters," 495–514.

17. Setha Low, *Spatializing Culture: The Ethnography of Space and Place* (New York and London: Routledge, 2017).

18. Jason Kosnoski, "Democratic Vistas: Frederick Law Olmsted's Parks as Spatial Mediation of Urban Diversity," *Space and Culture* 14, no. 1 (2011): 51–66,

19. Martin E. P. Seligman, *Flourish: A Visionary New Understanding of Happiness and Well-Being* (New York: Free Press, 2011).

20. Martin E. P. Seligman and Mihaly Csikszentmihalyi, "Positive Psychology: An Introduction," *American Psychologist* 55, no. 1 (2000): 5.

21. John Kinyon, Ike Lasater, and Julie Stiles, *From Conflict to Connection: Transforming Difficult Conversations into Peaceful Resolutions* (El Sobrante: Global Reach Books, 2015).

22. Tyler J. VanderWeele, "On the Promotion of Human Flourishing," *Proceedings of the National Academy of Sciences* 114, no. 31 (2017): 8148–56, .

23. Such as class, race, sexual orientation, age, physical ability, cultural background, and language preference.

CHAPTER 2

1. Setha Low, Dana Taplin, and Suzanne Scheld, *Rethinking Urban Parks: Public Space and Cultural Diversity* (Austin: University of Texas Press, 2005).

2. Elizabeth Dias, John Eligon, and Richard A. Oppel, Jr., "Outrage for Some, for Others It's Just Everyday Life," *New York Times,* April 2018, A11.

3. Faculty members who taught in the Department of Landscape Architecture and Regional Planning at the University of Pennsylvania at that time.

4. Setha Low, *Behind the Gates: Life, Security and the Pursuit of Happiness in Fortress America* (New York: Routledge, 2003).

5. Devon Johnson, Amy Farrell, and Patricia Y. Warren, eds., *Deadly Injustice: Trayvon Martin, Race, and the Criminal Justice System* (New York: New York University Press, 2015).

6. Sverre Bjerkeset and Jonny Aspen, "Public Space Use: A Classification," in *Companion to Public Space*, eds. Vikas Mehta and Danilo Palazzo (New York: Routledge, 2020), 221–33.

7. Stephen Carr, Mark Francis, Leanne G. Rivlin, and Andrew M. Stone, *Public Space* (Cambridge and New York: Cambridge University Press, 1992).

8. Benjamin Shepard and Greg Smithsimon, "Fences and Piers: An Investigation of a Disappearing Queer Public Space," in *The Beach Beneath the Streets: Contesting New York City's Public Spaces*, eds. Benjamin Shepard and Greg Smithsimon (Albany: State University of New York Press, 2011), 99–126.

9. Matthew Carmona, "Principles for Public Space Design, Planning to Do Better," *Urban Design International* 24 (2019): 47, https://doi.org/10.1057/s41289-018-0070-3.

   Hadi Zamanifard, Tooran Alizadeh, Caryl Bosman, and Eddo Coiacetto, "Measuring Experiential Qualities of Urban Public Spaces: Users' Perspective," *Journal of Urban Design* 24, no. 3 (2018): 340–64, https://doi.org/10.1080/13574809.2018.1484664.

10. One example was the May 2020 incident of a white woman calling the police on a Black bird-watcher who she said was "threatening her life," when he only asked her to leash her dog. Her 911 call and subsequent false claims reflect the intersectional complexity of perceived threat in a "white public space." See the Appendix for a discussion of white public space theory.

    Sebastian Murdock, "White Woman Who Called Cops on Central Park Bird-Watcher Made 2nd Bogus 911 Claim," *Huffington Post*, October 14, 2020, https://huffpost.com/entry/manhattan-district.

11. Benjamin Shepard and Gregory Smithsimon, *The Beach Beneath the Streets: Contesting New York City's Public Spaces* (Albany: State University of New York, 2011)

12. https://www.mobotix.com/en/solutions/tourism/hudson-river-park on surveillance company that installed the cameras.

    Clara Irazabal and Claudia Herta, "Intersectionality and Planning at the Margins: LGBTQ Youth of Color in New York," *Gender, Place and Culture* (2015), http://dx.doi.org/10.1080/0966369X.2015.1058755.

13. Jen Jack Gieseking, *A Queer New York: Geographies of Lesbians, Dykes, and Queers* (New York: New York University Press, 2020).

14. William H. White, *Social Life of Small Urban Spaces* (Washington D.C.: Conservation Foundation, 1980).

15. Jerold S. Kayden, *Privately Owned Public Spaces: The New York City Experience* (New York: Wiley and Sons, 2000).

16. Jeremy Nemeth, "Defining a Public: The Management of Privately Owned Public Space," *Urban Studies* 46, no. 11 (2009/10): 2463–90, https://doi.org/10.1177%2F0042098009342903.

17. Troy Simpson, fieldnotes 2020.

18. Delia Paunescu, "Despite Controversial Vessel Photo Policy, Visitors Kept Instagramming," *Curbed*, March 21, 2019, https://ny.curbed.com/2019/3/21/18275790/hudson-yards-vessel-photo-policy-social-media.

19. "Related's Hudson Yards: Smart City or Surveillance City?," Global Property and Asset Management, Inc., last modified March 17, 2019, https://globalpropertyinc.com/2019/03/17/hudson-yards-smart-city-or-surveillance-city.

20. Jeffrey Fleisher, "The Multiple Histories of Public Space" (unpublished manuscript), typescript.

21. Monica L. Smith, "Urban Empty Spaces: Contentious Places for Consensus-Building," *Archaeological Dialogues* 15, no. 2 (2008): 216–31, https://doi.org/10.1017/S1380203808002687.

22. Smith, "Urban Empty Spaces," 228.

23. Andrew Curry, "Seeking the Roots of Ritual," *Science* 319, no. 5861 (2008): 278–80, https://www.science.org/doi/10.1126/science.319.5861.278.

24. Curry, "Seeking the Roots of Ritual," 278–80.

25. Other accounts set the date at 2,800 years ago, while general texts at 4,000–5000 years ago. This is the 2010 carbon dating from Oxford.

26. Fleisher, "Multiple Histories."

27. Barbara Bender, ed., *Landscape: Politics and Perspectives* (Providence and Oxford: Berg, 1993).

28. Takeshi Inomata and Lawrence S. Coben, eds., *Archaeology of Performance: Theaters of Power, Community and Politics* (Lanham: Altamira Press, 2006). Cynthia Robin, "Outside of Houses: The Practices of Everyday Life at Chan Nòohol, Belize," *Journal of Social Archaeology* 2, no. 2 (2002): 245–68, https://doi.org/10.1177/1469605302002002397.

29. Jeffrey Fleisher and Federica Sulas, "Deciphering Public Spaces in Urban Contexts: Geophysical Survey, Multi-element Soil Analysis, and Artifact Distributions at the 15th-16th-century AD Swahili Settlement

of Songo Mnara, Tanzania," *Journal of Archaeological Science* 55 (2015): 55–70, https://doi.org/10.1016/j.jas.2014.12.020.

30. Jeffrey Fleisher, "Performance, Monumentality and the 'Built Exterior' on the Eastern African Swahili Coast," *Azania: Archaeological Research in Africa* 48, no. 2 (2013): 263–81, https://doi.org/10.1080/0067270X.2013.788872.

31. Jeffrey Fleisher, "The Complexity of Public Space at the Swahili Town of Songo Mnara, Tanzania," *Journal of Anthropological Archaeology* 35 (2014): 1–22, https://doi.org/10.1016/j.jaa.2014.04.002.

32. Arthur A. Joyce, "The Main Plaza of Monte Albán: A Life History of Place," in *The Archaeology of Meaningful Places*, eds. Brenda J. Bowser and María Nieves Zedeõ (Salt Lake City: University of Utah Press, 2009), 32–51.

33. Javier Urcid and Arthur A. Joyce, "Early Transformations of Monte Albán's Main Plaza and Their Political Implications, 500 BC–AD 200," in *Mesoamerican Plazas: Arenas of Community and Power*, eds. Kenichiro Tsukamoto and Takeshi Inomata (Tucson: University of Arizona Press, 2014), 149–228.

34. The Aztec city that is now Mexico City.

35. A. R. Pagden, *Hernán Cortés: Letters from Mexico*, introduction by J. H. Elliott (New York: Grossman Publishers, 1971).

36. Setha Low, *On the Plaza: The Politics of Public Space and Culture* (Austin: University of Texas Press, 2000).

37. Michael J. Heckenberger, J. Christian Russell, Carlos Fausto, Joshua R. Toney, Morgan J. Schmidt, Edithe Pereira, Bruna Franchetto, and Afukaka Kuikuro, "Pre-Columbian Urbanism, Anthropogenic Landscapes, and the Future of the Amazon," *Science* 321, no. 5893 (2017): 1214–17, https://www.science.org/doi/10.1126/science.1159769.

38. Low, *On the Plaza*.

CHAPTER 3

1. Marcel Henaff and Tracy B. Strong, eds., *Public Space and Democracy* (Minneapolis: University of Minnesota Press, 2001).

2. Galen Cranz, *The Politics of Park Design: A History of Urban Parks in America* (Cambridge: MIT Press, 1982).

3. Benjamin Heim Shepard and Gregory Smithsimon, *The Beach Beneath the Streets: Contesting New York City's Public Spaces* (Albany: Excelsior Editions/State University of New York Press, 2011).

4. Thomas J. Campanella, "Robert Moses and His Racist Parkway, Explained," *CityLab*, July 9, 2017, https://www.bloomberg.com/news/articles/2017-07-09/robert-moses-and-his-racist-parkway-explained.

   Robert Caro is citing Sidney Shapiro, an engineer and close associate of Moses, and discusses this relationship's future in his recent book *Working* (New York: Alfred A. Knopf/Penguin Random House, 2019).

5. Christopher Robbins, "Robert Caro Wonders What New York Is Going to Become," *Gothamist*, February 17, 2016, https://gothamist.com/news/robert-caro-wonders-what-new-york-is-going-to-become.

6. Campanella, "Robert Moses."

7. We devised a project in two stages: first, a brief survey of visitor characteristics, park destination, and visiting patterns, and second, a series of small-scale ethnographic studies of the most popular areas. To complete the survey, we interviewed every sixth person as they entered from the parking lots carrying their beach and picnic paraphernalia. It was difficult to convince people to participate even though we offered park mugs, beach toys, and other small gifts for their assistance. Claire Panetta, Martin Cobian, Bryce Dubois, Maria Heyaca, and Kevin Zemlicka, graduate students in our respective academic programs, worked long, hot, and sometimes frustrating days during the peak summer weeks to administer the short questionnaire to 639 randomly selected visitors. The results from the survey enabled us to describe visitors and determine their activities and interests.

   The second stage took much longer and included participant observation—hanging out at various locations talking and interacting with visitors—and "behavioral mapping" of activities and where they took place. We completed 164 in-depth interviews and produced over a hundred pages of fieldnotes. Suzanne Scheld, Dana Taplin, and I returned over the ensuing years, noting changes as well as tracking ongoing conflicts such as beach sand replenishment after Hurricane Sandy. What we learned is based on the survey and ethnographies collected from 2012 to 2013 as well as from field visits in 2018 and 2019.

8. I joined the Jones Beach Club on November 25, 2019, and began to read the posted commentaries. Many are contributed by local Long Island users, but visitors also add their perspectives. Newcomers are introduced and then can post to other members.

9. Claire Panetta records this sense of diversity in her observations on a hot July afternoon. Fieldnotes July 22, 2012.

10. Of the 639 people in the general user survey, 42 percent self-identify as white, 30 percent as Latino/Hispanic, 9 percent as African American,

3 percent as Middle Eastern, 2 percent as Asian, and 4 percent as "biracial" or other such as Native American. In our survey the majority are adults aged thirty-one to sixty, a quarter are young adults aged eighteen to thirty-one, and only 11 percent are seniors. We did not interview anyone younger than eighteen.

11. A community on the eastern end of Long Island next to Southampton, about a 1.5-hour drive to Jones Beach.

12. Dr. Suzanne Scheld and Dr. Dana Taplin completed this interview.

13. Excerpt from Kevin Lemlicka, "The Gay Beach at Jones Beach," presented at the American Anthropological Association, November 2014.

14. Mark Davidson and Deborah Martin, eds., *Urban Politics: Critical Approaches* (London: Sage Publications, 2014).

15. Don Mitchell, "People's Park Again: On the End and Ends of Public Space," *Environment and Planning A: Economy and Space* 49, no. 3 (2017): 503–18.

16. Cédric Terzi and Stéphane Tonnelat, "The Publicization of Public Space," *Environment and Planning A: Economy and Space* 49, no. 3 (2017): 519–36.

17. John R. Parkinson, *Democracy and Public Space: The Physical Sites of Democratic Performance* (Oxford: Oxford University Press, 2012).

18. Wendy Brown, *In the Ruins of Neoliberalism: The Rise of Antidemocratic Politics in the West* (New York: Columbia University Press, 2019).

19. Cecilia Andersson was the director of the Public Space Public Space Programme at UN Habitat in Nairobi, Kenya at that time.

20. George Varna and Steve Tiesdell, "Assessing the Publicness of Public Space: The Star Model of Publicness," *Journal of Urban Design* 15, no. 4 (2010): 575–98. .

Vikas Mehta, "The Continued Quest to Assess Public Space," *Journal of Urban Design* 24, no. 3 (2019): 365–67.

Jeremy Németh and Stephen Schmidt, "The Privatization of Public Space: Modeling and Measuring Publicness," *Environment and Planning B: Planning and Design* 38, no. 1 (2011): 5–23.

21. Stephen Gibson, Anastasia Loukaitou-Sideris, and Vinit Mukhija, "Ensuring Park Equity: A California Case Study," *Journal of Urban Design* 24, no. 3 (2018): 385–405, https://doi.org/10.1080/13574 809.2018.1497927.

22. Susan S. Fainstein, *The Just City* (Ithaca: Cornell University Press, 2010). "Cities and Diversity: Should We Want It? Can We Plan for It?" *Urban Affairs Review* 41, no. 1 (2005): 3–19.

23. Ruth Fincher and Kurt Iveson, *Planning and Diversity in the City: Redistribution, Recognition and Encounter* (Basingstoke: Palgrave Macmillan, 2008).

24. Edward W. Soja, *Seeking Spatial Justice* (Minneapolis: University of Minnesota Press, 2010).

25. Joel Lefkowitz, *Ethics and Values in Industrial-Organizational Psychology*, 2nd ed. (New York and London: Routledge, Taylor & Francis Group, 2017).

26. J. A. Colquitt, B. A. Scott, J. B. Rodell, D. M. Long, C. P. Zapata, D. E. Conlon, and M. J. Wesson, "Justice at the Millennium, a Decade Later: A Meta-Analytic Test of Social Exchange and Affect-Based Perspectives," *Journal of Applied Psychology* 98, no. 2 (2013): 199–236, https://doi.org/10.1037/a0031757.

27. https://justspacesproject.org.

28. Alessandro Rigolon, Mariela Fernandez, Brandon Harris, and William Stewart, "An Ecological Model of Environmental Justice for Recreation," *Leisure Sciences: An Interdisciplinary Journal* (March 2019): 1–22, https://doi.org/10.1080/01490400.2019.1655686.

29. Setha Low, "How Public Interests Take Over Public Space," in *The Politics of Public Space*, eds. S. Low and N. Smith (New York and London: Routledge, 2006): 81–104.

CHAPTER 4

1. Erik Kulleseid was the director at the time and instrumental in pushing through the funding for this research project. We thank him for his vision of the importance of public space research.

2. This chapter is partly based on the project report written for the Open Space Institute.

    Suzanne Scheld, Dana Taplin, and Setha Low, "Proposed Model for Park User Assessment Based on Jones Beach, Lake Welch, and Walkway Over the Hudson" (Albany: Open Space Institute, 2013).

3. Harvey K. Flad and Clyde C. Griffen, *Main Street to Mainframes: Landscape and Social Change in Poughkeepsie* (Albany: SUNY Press, 2009).

4. Jackie Corley, "Three Hudson Valley Cities Named Most Dangerous in New York," *92.7/96.9 WRRV, Townsquare Media, Inc.*, September 21, 2016, https://wrrv.com/three-hudson-valley-cities-named-most-dangerous-in-new-york/?utm_source=tsmclip&utm_medium=referral.

5. As of the 2010 Census, Poughkeepsie was 52.8 percent white, 35.7 percent African American or Black, 10.6 percent Hispanic or Latino, 1.6

percent Asian, 0.4 percent Native American, 5.3 percent other "races," and 4.1 percent two or more "races."

6. Our findings are based on these two methods plus participant observation and fieldnotes of interactions with residents, tourists, local visitors, and daily users and what we learn by hanging out in town and on Walkway.

   Scheld, Taplin, and Low, "Proposed Model for Park User Assessment."

7. Christine Negroni, "A 21st-Century Makeover for a 19th-Century Wonder," *New York Times*, April 24, 2009, https://www.nytimes.com/2009/04/25/nyregion/25metjournal.html?_r=0.

8. Karen Angel, "This Hamlet Is Now More Than a Pass-Through," *New York Times*, April 3, 2022, LI Real Estate Section 9.

9. C. J. Hughes, "Poughkeepsie, N.Y.: A Postindustrial City Ready for Its Revival," *New York Times*, June 12, 2019, https://www.nytimes.com/2019/06/12/realestate/poughkeepsie-ny.

10. Angel, "This Hamlet." LI Real Estate Section 9.

11. There are three studies that contribute to understanding of the relationship of public space to health and well-being: 1) the World Health Organization (WHO) Report of 2016 and associated quantitative studies; 2) the Place-Value-Wiki created by Matthew Carmona that covers research of interest to planners and designers of public spaces; and 3) the Public Space Database, TerraPublica, produced by the Center for the Future of Places and the Ax:son Johnson Foundation in Stockholm, Sweden. Each emphasizes a different perspective on why public space contributes to health and well-being and suggests alternative ways to think about applying this knowledge to a neighborhood or city. We are grateful to these researchers for sharing their work and bibliographies.

12. Here I am referring to "modern" health concepts. Hippocrates was an early observer of the relationship between the environment, disease, and health.

   J.S. Gordon, "Holistic Medicine and Mental Health Practice: Toward a New Synthesis," *American Journal of Orthopsychiatry* 60, no. 3 (July 1990): 357–70, https://doi.org/10.1037/h0079185.

13. Peter Vinten-Johansen, Howard Brody, Nigel Paneth, Stephen Rachman, and Michael Rip, *Cholera, Chloroform, and the Science of Medicine: a Life of John Snow* (New York and Oxford: Oxford University Press, 2003).

14. Nicholas Freudenberg, Sandro Galea, and David Vlahov, eds., *Cities and the Health of the Public* (Nashville: Vanderbilt University Press, 2006).

15. Lisa M. Powell, Sandy Slater, Frank J. Chaloupka, and Deborah Harper, "Availability of Physical Activity–Related Facilities and Neighborhood

Demographic and Socioeconomic Characteristics: A National Study," *American Journal of Public Health* 96, no. 9 (2006): 1676–80, https://dx.doi.org/10.2105%2FAJPH.2005.065573.

16. *Urban Green Spaces and Health* (Copenhagen: WHO Regional Office for Europe, 2016), https://www.euro.who.int/__data/assets/pdf_file/0005/321971/Urban-green-spaces-and-health-review-evidence.pdf.

17. Rachel Kaplan and Stephen Kaplan, "Well-Being, Reasonableness, and the Natural Environment," *Applied Psychology: Health and Well-Being* 3, no. 3 (2011): 304–21, https://doi.org/10.1111/j.1758-0854.2011.01055.x.

18. Edward O. Wilson, *Biophilia* (Cambridge: Harvard University Press, 1984).

19. Charis Lengen and Thomas Kistemann, "Sense of Place and Place Identity: Review of Neuroscientific Evidence," *Health & Place* 18, no. 5 (2012): 1162–71, https://doi.org/10.1016/j.healthplace.2012.01.012.

20. Anne Caroline Krefis, Matthias Augustin, Katharina Heinke Schlünzen, Jürgen Oßenbrügge, and Jobst Augustin, "How Does the Urban Environment Affect Health and Well-Being? A Systematic Review," *Urban Science* 2, no. 1 (2018): 1–21, https://www.mdpi.com/2413-8851/2/1/21.

   Jolanda Maas, Robert A. Verheij, Peter P. Groenewegen, Sjerp deVries, and Peter Spreeuwenberg, "Green Space, Urbanity, and Health: How Strong Is the Relation?," *Journal of Epidemiology and Community Health* 60, no. 7 (2006): 587–92, https://doi.org/10.1136/jech.2005.043125.

   Mireia Gascon, Wilma Zijlema, Cristina Vert, Mathew P. White, and Mark J. Nieuwenhuijsen, "Outdoor Blue Spaces, Human Health and Well-Being: A Systematic Review of Quantitative Studies," *International Journal of Hygiene and Environmental Health* 220, no. 8 (November 2017): 1207–21, https://doi.org/10.1016/j.ijheh.2017.08.004.

21. Tytti P. Pasanena, Mathew P. White, Benedict W. Wheeler, Joanne K. Garrett, and Lewis R. Elliott, "Neighbourhood Blue Space, Health and Wellbeing: The Mediating Role of Different Types of Physical Activity," *Environment International* 131 (2019): 105–16, https://doi.org/10.1016/j.envint.2019.105016.

22. Sebastian Völker and Thomas Kistemann, "Developing the Urban Blue: Comparative Health Responses to Blue and Green Urban Open Spaces in Germany," *Health Place* 35 (September 2015): 196–205, https://pubmed.ncbi.nlm.nih.gov/25475835/#:~:text=doi%3A%2010.1016/j.healthplace.2014.10.015.

   Sebastian Völker and Thomas Kistemann, "'I'm Always Entirely Happy When I'm Here!' Urban Blue Enhancing Human Health and

Well-Being in Cologne and Düsseldorf, Germany," *Social Science and Medicine* 78 (February 2013): 113–24, https://doi.org/10.1016/j.socsci med.2012.09.047.

23. Erin Hayward, Chidinma Ibe, Jeffery Hunter Young, Karthya Potti, Paul Jones III, Craig Evan Pollack, and Kimberly A. Gudzune, "Linking Social and Built Environmental Factors to the Health of Public Housing Residents: A Focus Group Study," *BMC Public Health* 15 (2015): 351, https://doi.org/10.1186/s12889-015-1710-9.

24. https://matthew-carmona.com/place-value-wiki/

25. Maas et al., "Green Space," 587–92.

26. Chanuki Illushka Seresinhe, Tobias Preis, and Helen Susannah Moat, "Quantifying the Impact of Scenic Environments on Health," *Scientific Reports* 5, no. 16899 (2015): 1–9, https://doi.org/10.1038/srep16899.

27. Anne Ellaway, G. Morris, John Curtice, C. Robertson, G. Allardice, and R. Robertson, "Associations between Health and Different Types of Environmental Incivility: A Scotland-Wide Study," *Public Health* 123, no. 11 (2009): 708–13, https://doi.org/10.1016/j.puhe.2009.09.019.

28. Vicky Cattell, Nick Dines, Wil Gesler, and Sarah Curtis, "Mingling, Observing, and Lingering: Everyday Public Spaces and Their Implications for Well-Being and Social Relations," *Health & Place* 14, no. 3 (2008): 544, https://doi.org/10.1016/j.healthplace.2007.10.007.

29. The final set of studies that are relevant to understanding Walkway are from the Public Space Database, TerraPublica. The PSRG participates in this ongoing effort to curate a multi-disciplinary database of public space field studies. The database includes a range of topics and concepts from the physical design of public space to its cultural, psychological, and economic outcomes. Searching its contents, a number of qualitative studies on the relationship of public space to health, emphasizing the importance of social interaction and psychological needs, underscore the findings of the Walkway study.

30. Lorna Haughton McNeill, Matthew W. Kreuter, S. V. Subramanian, "Social Environment and Physical Activity: A Review of Concepts and Evidence," *Social Science and Medicine* 63, no. 4 (2006): 1011–22, https://doi.org/10.1016/j.socscimed.2006.03.012.

31. Stephen C. Gibson, "'Let's Go to the Park': An Investigation of Older Adults in Australia and Their Motivations for Park Visitation," *Landscape and Urban Planning* 180 (2018): 234–46, http://dx.doi.org/10.1016/j.landurbplan.2018.08.019.

32. Anastasia Loukaitou-Sideris, "Is it Safe to Walk? Neighborhood Safety and Security Considerations and their Effects on Walking," *Journal of*

Planning Literature 20, no. 3 (2006): 219–32, https://doi.org/10.1177%2F0 885412205282770.

33. Ruth Butler and Sophia Bowlby, "Bodies and Spaces: An Exploration of Disabled People's Experiences of Public Space," *Environment and Planning D: Society and Space* 15, no. 4 (1997): 411–33, https://doi.org/ 10.1068%2Fd150411.

34. WHO, *Urban Green Spaces and Health.*

CHAPTER 5

1. David Whitebread, Dave Neale, Hanne Jensen, Jennifer M. Zosh, Claire Liu, Lynneth Solis, Emily J. Hopkins, and Kathy Hirsh-Pasek, "The Role of Play in Children's Development: A Review of the Evidence," *The LEGO Foundation, DK* (November 2017): 4–33, http://dx.doi.org/ 10.13140/RG.2.2.18500.73606.

2. Michael Yogman, Andrew Garner, Jeffrey Hutchinson, Kathy Hirsh-Pasek, and Roberta Michnick Golinkoff, "The Power of Play: A Pediatric Role in Enhancing Development in Young Children," *Pediatrics* 142, no. 3 (September 2018): 2058, https://doi.org/10.1542/peds.2018-2058.

3. Stuart Lester and Wendy Russell, "Children's Right to Play: An Examination of the Importance of Play in the Lives of Children Worldwide," *Working Papers in Early Childhood Development* no. 57 (January 2010): ix–xi, https://eric.ed.gov/?id=ED522537.

4. Pamela J. Wridt, "An Historical Analysis of Young People's Use of Public Space, Parks and Playgrounds in New York City," *Children, Youth and Environments* 14, no. 1 (2004): 86–106, http://www.jstor.org/stable/ 10.7721/chilyoutenvi.14.1.0086.

5. Roger Hart, professor of environmental psychology, the Graduate Center, CUNY, personal communication. For more popular accounts of this trend, see https://www.theatlantic.com/magazine/archive/ 2014/04/hey-parents-leave-those-kids-alone/358631.

6. Kenneth R. Ginsburg, "The Importance of Play in Promoting Healthy Child Development and Maintaining Strong Parent-Child Bonds," *Pediatrics* 119, no. 1 (January 2007): 182–91, https://doi.org/10.1542/ peds.2006-2697.

7. Andrea Faber Taylor, Angela Wiley, Frances E. Kuo, and William C. Sullivan, "Growing Up in the Inner City: Green Spaces as Places to Grow," *Environment and Behavior* 30, no. 1 (1998): 3–27, https://doi.org/ 10.1177%2F0013916598301001.

8. Place attachment is the result of these affective and social bonds established over time in association with a particular piece of land or locale.

9. Construction of roads, visitor facilities, and other amenities at Bear Mountain and Harriman State Parks was placed in the capable hands of Major William A. Welch in 1912. Over his nearly thirty-year tenure, Welch directed the construction of Hessian Lake, Sebago, and thirty other lakes; Seven Lakes Drive and other roads; and the visitor amenities at Bear Mountain. There were major advances in the construction of trails, roads, and other visitor facilities during the 1930s as the Civilian Conservation Corps set hundreds of crews to work. Welch supervised the establishment of 103 woodland camps for city children, designed Bear Mountain Bridge and Storm King Highway, and proposed a parkway to New York City. Upon his death in 1941, he was celebrated as the father of the state-park movement.

10. Because so many visitors originally were from the Caribbean, I am using the term "Hispanic" to indicate Spanish-speaking since many Americans from Puerto Rico and the Dominican Republic do not self-identify as "Latino," saying that they are not from Latin America. Latino is used as a form of political solidarity, as being from Latin America interpreted broadly, and I will employ it when used in this way.

11. Javier E. Otero Peña, Hanish Kodali, Emily Ferris, Katarzyna Wyka, Setha Low, Kelly R. Evenson, Joan M. Dorn, Lorna E. Thorpe, and Terry T. K. Huang, "The Role of the Physical and Social Environment in Observed and Self-Reported Park Use in Low-Income Neighborhoods in New York City," *Frontiers in Public Health* 9, no. 656988 (2021), https://doi.org/10.3389/fpubh.2021.656988.

12. Dana Taplin, fieldnotes.

13. Kevin Zemlicka, fieldnotes.

14. Orchard Beach is a well-known constructed beach that is part of Pelham Bay Park in the northern Bronx. It has a long history of Hispanic use, particularly by people from Puerto Rico and the Dominican Republic who made it their own through instituting "salsa" bands and dancing on summer nights. See Setha Low, Dana Taplin, and Suzanne Scheld, *Rethinking Urban Parks: Public Space and Cultural Diversity* (Austin: University of Texas Press, 2005).

15. Zemlicka, fieldnotes.

16. Paul Rouse, personal communication. Allen Guttman, *Sports: The First Five Millennia* (Amherst and Boston: University of Massachusetts Press, 2004). Richard O. Davies, *Sports in American Life: A History*, 3rd ed.

(Hoboken: John Wiley & Sons, 2017). Roberte Hamayon, *Why We Play: An Anthropological Study* (Translated by Damien Simon. Chicago: Hau Books, 2016).

17. Taplin, fieldnotes.

18. Alessandro Rigolon and Jeremy Németh, "A QUality INdex of Parks for Youth (QUINPY): Evaluating Urban Parks through Geographic Information Systems," *Environment and Planning B: Urban Analytics and City Science* 45, no. 2 (2018): 275–94, https://doi.org/10.1177%2F02658 13516672212.

19. Loretta Lees, "The Ambivalence of Diversity and the Politics of Urban Renaissance: The Case of Youth in Downtown Portland, Maine," *International Journal of Urban and Regional Research* 27, no. 3 (2003): 613–34, https://doi.org/10.1111/1468-2427.00469.

20. Anastasia Loukaitou-Sideris, "Children's Common Grounds: A Study of Intergroup Relations Among Children in Public Settings," *Journal of the American Planning Association* 69, no. 2 (2010): 130–34, https://doi.org/10.1080/01944360308976302.

21. Rebecca Madgin, Lisa Bradley, and Annette Hastings, "Connecting Physical and Social Dimensions of Place Attachment: What Can We Learn from Attachment to Urban Recreational Spaces?," *Journal of Housing and the Built Environment* 31 (2016): 677–93, https://doi.org/10.1007/s10901-016-9495-4.

22. Olivia Saracho, "Young Children's Creativity and Pretend Play," *Early Child Development and Care* 172, no. 5 (2002): 431–38, https://doi.org/10.1080/03004430214553.

23. Irwin W. Silverman, "In Defense of the Play-Creativity Hypothesis," *Creativity Research Journal* 28, no. 2 (2016): 136–43, https://doi.org/10.1080/10400419.2016.1162560.

24. Shallu Sansanwal, "Pretend Play Enhances Creativity and Imagination," *Journal of Arts and Humanities* 3, no. 1 (2014): 70–83, https://doi.org/10.18533/journal.v3i1.340.

25. Sandra W. Russ, "Play and Creativity: Developmental Issues," *Scandinavian Journal of Educational Research* 47, no. 3 (2003): 291–303, https://doi.org/10.1080/00313830308594.

26. Olivia Saracho, "Preschool Children's Cognitive Style and Play and Implications for Creativity," *Creativity Research Journal* 5, no. 1 (1992): 35–47, https://doi.org/10.1080/10400419209534421.

27. Russ, "Play and Creativity," 291–303.

28. Sandra W. Russ and C. E. Wallace, "Pretend Play and Creative Processes," *American Journal of Play* 6, no. 1 (2013): 136–48.

29. UN Habitat Best Practices Database, *Courtyard System for Management of Public Space* (Nairobi, Kenya: UN Habitat Practice Details, 2017), https://mirror.unhabitat.org/bp/bp.list.details.aspx?bp_id=5101.

30. Michael Mehaffy and Celicia Andersson, colleagues from the workshop with the Global Public Space Programme, were part of the Dandora tour that day.

31. "Nairobi's Dandora Neighborhood Shines Again—Thanks to UN-Habitat's Waste Management Led Public Space Planning," UN Habitat, October 7, 2019, https://unhabitat.org/nairobis-dandora-neighborh ood-shines-again-thanks-to-un-habitats-waste-management-led-pub lic-space.

32. *Declaration of the Rights of the Child*, G.A. res. 1386 (XIV), 14 U.N. GAOR Supp. (No. 16) at 19, U.N. Doc. A/4354 (1959)

33. Office of the United Nations High Commissioner for Human Rights, *Convention on the Rights of the Child*, General Assembly Resolution 44/25 of November 20, 1989.

34. UN Committee on the Rights of the Child (CRC), *General Comment No. 17 (2013) on the Right of the Child to Rest, Leisure, Play, Recreational Activities, Cultural Life and the Arts (art. 31)*, April 17, 2013, CRC/C/GC/17, https://www.refworld.org/docid/51ef9bcc4.html, accessed April 18, 2022.

35. Nir Hasson, "With Belgian Funding and Without Building Permits: The First Playground in Sur Baher," *Israel News, Haaretz, last modified* April 10, 2018, https://www.haaretz.com/israel-news/.premium-sur-baher-gets-its-first-playground-1.5402756 .

CHAPTER 6

1. International Labor Organization, *Women and Men in the Informal Economy: A Statistical Picture*, 3rd ed. (Geneva: ILO, April 2018), https://www.ilo.org/global/publications/books/WCMS_626831/lang--en/index.htm.

2. Juan Sebastián Benítez Bustamante, "Informal Work in the Public Space: Adaptation and Social Resilience in Colombia," *Oxford Urbanists*, accessed April 13, 2021, https://www.oxfordurbanists.com/oxford-urbani sts-monthly/2019/6/20/informal-work-in-the-public-space-adaptat ion-and-social-resilience-in-colombia.

Also see Michael G. Donovan, "Informal Cities and the Contestation of Public Space: The Case of Bogota's Street Vendors, 1988–2003," *Urban Studies* 45, no. 1 (2008): 29–51, http://www.jstor.org/stable/43198368.

3. Bustamante, "Informal Work."

4. Hesam Kamalipour and Nastaran Peimani, "Negotiating Space and Visibility: Forms of Informality in Public Space," *Sustainability* 11, no. 17: 4807 (2019): 1–19, https://www.mdpi.com/2071-1050/11/17/4807#.

5. Sandra C. Mendiola García, *Street Democracy: Vendors, Violence, and Public Space in Late Twentieth-Century Mexico* (Lincoln: University of Nebraska Press, 2017), 17.

   "Informal Economy," WEIGO, accessed May 9, 2021, https://www.wiego.org/informal-economy.

6. Thomas F. Alexander, "The Global Informal Economy: Large but on the Decline," *Chart of the Week, International Monetary Fund*, accessed May 3, 2021, https:/blogs.imf.org/2019/10/30/the-global-informal-economy.

7. "Informal Economy," WEIGO.

8. International Labor Organization, *Women and Men.*

9. Martha Alter Chen, Jenna Harvey, Caroline Wanjiku Kihato, and Caroline Skinner, "Inclusive Public Spaces for Informal Livelihoods: A Discussion Paper for Urban Planners and Policy Makers," *Manchester and Brussels: WIEGO and Cities Alliance*, https://www.wiego.org/publications/inclusive-public-spaces-informal-livelihoods-discussion-paper-urban-planners-and-policy.

10. Anat Bracha and Mary A. Burke, "Informal Work Activity in the United States: Evidence from Survey Responses," *Current Policy Perspectives*, 2014 Series, no. 2014–2013, Federal Reserve Bank of Boston, accessed April 28, 2022, https://www.bostonfed.org/publications/current-policy-perspectives/2014/informal-work-in-the-united-states-evidence-from-survey-responses.aspx#:~:text=The%20authors%20calculate%20the%20following,about%2044%20percent%20of%20the.

11. Judith Butler writes that precariousness and precarity are intersecting concepts. Lives are precarious: they can be expunged at will or by accident; their persistence is in no sense guaranteed. Precarity, on the other hand, is a state of existential and physical vulnerability accompanied by invisibility from the social and political institutions that are supposed to mitigate these risks. It is a "politically induced condition in which certain populations suffer from failing social and economic networks and support and become differentially exposed to injury, violence, and death." See "Rethinking Vulnerability and Resistance," in *Vulnerability in Resistance*, eds. Judith Butler, Zeynep Gambetti, and Leticia Sabsay (Durham: Duke University Press, 2016), 12–27.

12. Lorena Rodríguez, "UN: Argentina Could Lose 850,000 Jobs in 2020 amid Virus Crisis," *Buenos Aires Times*, June 27, 2020, https://www.bati mes.com.ar/news/economy/un-argentina-could-lose-850000-jobs-in-2020-amid-virus-crisis.phtml.

13. Vinay Gidwani and Anant Maringanti, "The Waste-Value Dialectic: Lumpen Urbanization in Contemporary India," *Comparative Studies of South Asia, Africa and the Middle East* 36, no. 1 (May 2016): 112–33, https://muse.jhu.edu/article/615055.

14. Carlos A. Forment, "Trashing Violence/Recycling Civility: Buenos Aires' Scavengers and Everyday Forms of Democracy in the Wake of Neoliberalism," *Anthropological Theory* 18, nos. 2–3 (2018): 409–31, https://doi.org/10.1177%2F1463499618761298.

15. Forment, "Trashing Violence/Recycling," 414.

16. Kate Parizeau, "Re-Representing the City: Waste and Public Space in Buenos Aires, Argentina in the Late 2000s," *Environment and Planning A* 47, no. 2 (February 2015): 284–99, http://dx.doi.org/10.1068/a130094p.

17. Parizeau, "Re-Representing," 289.

18. Parizeau, "Re-Representing," 289.

19. Mariano Perelman, "Precarious Labor, Inequality, and Public Space: Trash Pickers and Ambulant Vendors in Buenos Aires, Argentina," in *The Routledge Handbook of Anthropology and the City*, ed. Setha Low (London: Routledge, 2019), 41–54.

    Natalia Cosacov and Mariano Perelman, "Struggles over the Use of Public Space: Exploring Moralities and Narratives of Inequality: *Cartoneros* and *Vecinos* in Buenos Aires," *Journal of Latin American Studies* 47, no. 3 (August 2015): 521–42, https://www.jstor.org/stable/24544372.

20. Perelman, "Precarious Labor," 45.

21. Amelia Nierenberg and Rachel Wharton, "New York Police Will Stop Enforcing Street-Vendor Laws, but Questions Linger," *New York Times*, June 12, 2021, https://www.nytimes.com/2020/06/12/dining/nypd-str eet-vendors.html.

22. Anne Babette Audant, "From Public Market to La Marqueta: Shaping Spaces and Subjects of Food Distribution in New York City, 1930–2012" (PhD diss., The Graduate Center, CUNY, 2013

23. Margaret Chin, Corey Johnson, and Carlos Menchaca, "More Street Vendors, Better Regulated: City Council Supporters Defend a Reform Bill," *New York Daily News*, January 26, 2021, https://www.nydailynews. com/opinion/ny-oped-more-street-vendors-better-regulated-20210 126-k7mx4tx6mfae7htcwvm2s22q6y-story.html.

24. David Gonzalez, "Bill to Increase Permits in New York City Offers Relief for Street Vendors," *New York Times*, January 20, 2019, A19.

25. Audant, "From Public Market."

26. Audant, "From Public Market."

27. Moore Street Market vendor interview conducted by Dr. Rodolfo Hernandez Corchado, July 2008.

28. Moore Street Market vendor interview conducted by Dr. Rodolfo Hernandez Corchado, June 2008.

29. Rodolfo Hernandex Corchado added this note about the unregulated migration process based on his research on indigenous Mexican migration to the U.S.

30. Moore Street Market vendor interview conducted by Dr. Rodolfo Hernandez Corchado, July 2008.

31. Puerto Rican, Mexican, Hasidic Jews, hipsters, recent Chinese immigrants, and African Americans

32. Individual interviews employed a semi-structured, open-ended format covering the use of the market, its cultural and community importance, and its role in neighborhood identity and politics. Life histories of the vendors were recorded and used for a deeper understanding of their migration experience and sense of the market as a workplace. Expert interviews with political, religious, and community representatives were conducted in addition to archival research—in the New York City Department of Markets' archives and the New York Public Library—on how the market was created and functioned during different historical periods.

33. Moore Street Market vendor interview conducted by Dr. Rodolfo Hernandez Corchado, August 2008.

34. "NYC EDC and Elected Officials Announce $2.7 Million Renovation of Moore Street Market," *Cityland: New York City Land Use News and Legal Research* (September 18, 2019), https://www.citylandnyc.org/nyc-edc-and-elected-officials-announce.

35. Jeffrey Hou, ed., *Insurgent Public Space: Guerrilla Urbanism and the Remaking of Contemporary Cities* (London and New York: Routledge, 2010).

36. B. Lynne Milgram, "Unsettling Urban Marketplace Redevelopment in Baguio City, Philippines," *Economic Anthropology* 2, no. 1 (2015): 22–41, https://doi.org/10.1002/sea2.12016.

37. B. Lynne Milgram, "Remapping the Edge: Informality and Legality in the Harrison Road Night Market, Baguio City, Philippines," *City & Society* 26, no. 2 (2014): 153–74, https://doi.org/10.1111/ciso.12038.

38. Tamara Mose Brown, *Raising Brooklyn: Nannies, Childcare, and Caribbeans Creating Community* (New York: NYU Press, 2011), 4.

39. John Krinsky and Maud Simonet, *Who Cleans the Park? Public Work and Urban Governance in New York City* (Chicago: University of Chicago Press, 2017), 2.

40. Krinsky and Simonet, *Who Cleans the Park?*, 4.

41. Lisa Law, "Defying Disappearance: Cosmopolitan Public Space in Hong Kong," *Urban Studies* 39, no. 9 (2002): 1625–45, https://doi.org/ 10.1080%2F00420980220151691.

42. Jeffrey Hou, "Rupturing, Accreting and Bridging: Everyday Insurgencies and Emancipatory City-Making in East Asia," in *Public Space Unbound: Urban Emancipation and the Post-Political Condition*, eds. Sabine Knierbein and Tihomir Viderman (New York: Routledge, 2018), 85–98.

43. AbdouMaliq Simone, "People as Infrastructure: Intersecting Fragments in Johannesburg," *Public Culture* 16, no. 3 (2004): 407–29, https://muse. jhu.edu/article/173743.

44. Simone, "People as Infrastructure."

45. Simone goes on to redefine urban public spaces as a "thickening of fields" made up of assemblages of objects, people, places, and practices of unregulated encounters utilized to produce a marginal living ("People as Infrastructure," 410).

46. Suzanne Hall, Julia King, and Robin Finlay, "Migrant Infrastructure: Transaction Economies in Birmingham and Leicester, UK," *Urban Studies* 54, no. 6 (May 2017): 1311–27, https://doi.org/10.1177/00420 98016634586.

47. Ryanne Flock and Werner Breitung, "Migrant Street Vendors in Urban China and the Social Production of Public Space," *Population, Space and Place* 22, no. 2 (2015): 158–69, https://doi.org/10.1002/psp.1892.

48. Chihsin Chiu, "Informal Management, Interactive Performance: Street Vendors and Police in a Taipei Night Market," *International Development Planning Review* 35, no. 4 (2013): 335–52, https://doi.org/10.3828/ idpr.2013.24.

49. Julie Kleinman, "Adventures in Infrastructure: Making an African Hub in Paris," *City & Society* 26, no. 3 (2014): 286, https://doi.org/10.1111/ ciso.12044.

   For example, the Gard du Nord train station is a hub of social and economic relationships for many West Africans who transform this public space into a transnational community where they find temporary work, a place to sleep, and a network of friends and acquaintances. They meet every day during their commute or spend the day passing on information about jobs, greeting others, and flirting with women while still being on the move. These informal workers and migrants employ what they call "the Gard du Nord method" to refer to their use of knowledge and practices to create opportunities and construct alternative pathways to happiness and success. The combination of social networks and a central public space replaces the nearby temporary work agencies and becomes a socio-spatial node in their career trajectory.

50. Albert Acedo, M. Painho, and Sven Casteleyn, "Place and City: Operationalizing Sense of Place and Social Capital in the Urban Context," *Transactions in GIS* 21, no. 10 (2017): 503–20, http://dx.doi.org/10.1111/tgis.12282.

51. Acedo et al., "Place and City."

52. Ali Madanipour, "Rethinking Public Space: Between Rhetoric and Reality," *Urban Design International* 24, no. 1 (2019): 38–46, https://doi.org/10.1057/s41289-019-00087-5.

53. Antoaneta Tileva, "A Seat at the Table: Immigrant Businesses and Placemaking" (PhD diss., American University, 2019).

54. David Trouille, *Fútbol in the Park: Immigrants, Soccer, and the Creation of Social Ties* (Chicago: University of Chicago Press, 2021).

55. Francesca Piazzoni, "Visibility as Justice: Immigrant Street Vendors and the Right to Difference in Rome," *Journal of Planning Education and Research* (September 2020), https://doi.org/10.1177/0739456X20956387.

CHAPTER 7

1. G. Brundtland, *Report of the World Commission on Environment and Development: Our Common Future* (Oxford: United Nations General Assembly Document A/42/427, 1987), available at http://www.un-documents.net/our-common-future.pdf, accessed April 18, 2022.

2. Will Steffen, Katherine Richardson, Johan Rockström, Sarah E. Cornell, Ingo Fetzer, Elena M. Bennett, Reinette Biggs, Stephen R. Carpenter, Wim De Vries, Cynthia A. De Wit, Carl Folke, Dieter Gerten, Jens Heinke, Georgina M. Mace, Linn M. Persson, Veerabhadran Ramanathan, Belinda Reyers, and Sverker Sörlin, "Planetary Boundaries: Guiding Human Development on a Changing Planet," *Science* 347, no. 6223 (January 2015), https://doi.org/10.1126/science.1259855.

3. Steffen et al., "Planetary Boundaries," 736.

4. This list is derived from research at the Stockholm Resilience Center, located at KTH, which was one of the centers at KTH during my tenure as a visiting scholar at the Center for the Future of Places.

5. Mark Davidson, "Sustainability as ideological praxis: The acting out of planning's master-signifier," *City* 14, no. 4 (2010): 390-405, https://doi.org/10.1080/13604813.2010.492603.

   Earl Harper, "Ecological Gentrification in Response to Apocalyptic Narratives of Climate Change: The Production of an Immuno-Political Fantasy," *International Journal of Urban and Regional Research* 44, no. 1 (2019): 55–71, https://doi.org/10.1111/1468-2427.12842.

6. "The period of time during which human activities have had an environmental impact on the Earth regarded as constituting a distinct geological age. Most scientists agree that humans have had a hand in warming Earth's climate since the industrial revolution—some even argue that we are living in a new geological epoch, dubbed the Anthropocene." *Nature* 427, no. 6975 (February 12, 2004).

7. Melissa Checker, Gary McDonogh, and Cindy Isenhour, "Urban Sustainability as Myth and Practice," in *Sustainability in the Global City: Myth and Practice*, eds. Cindy Isenhour, Gary McDonogh, and Melissa Checker (Cambridge: Cambridge University Press, 2015), 1-26.

   Melissa Checker, *The Sustainability Myth: Environmental Gentrification and the Politics of Justice* (New York: New York University, 2020).

8. Alesia Montgomery, *Greening the Black Urban Regime: The Culture and Commerce of Sustainability in Detroit* (Detroit: Wayne State University, 2020).

9. Montgomery, *Greening the Black*.

10. Checker et al., "Urban Sustainability as Myth."

11. Montgomery, *Greening the Black*.

12. Kenneth A. Gould and Tammy L. Lewis, *Green Gentrification: Urban Sustainability and the Struggle for Environmental Justice* (New York: Routledge, 2017).

13. Sharon Zukin, *Naked City: The Death and Life of Authentic Urban Places* (New York and London: Oxford University Press, 2010).

14. Julian Brash, *Bloomberg's New York: Class and Governance in the Luxury City* (Athens: University of Georgia Press, 2011).

    Benjamin Shepard and Greg Smithsimon, *The Beach Beneath the Streets: Contesting New York City's Public Spaces* (Albany: SUNY Press, 2011).

15. Nada Petrovic, Troy Simpson, Ben Orlove, and Brian Dowd-Uribe, "Environmental and Social Dimensions of Community Gardens in

East Harlem," *Landscape and Urban Planning* 183 (March 2019): 36–49, https://doi.org/10.1016/j.landurbplan.2018.10.009.

16. Petrovic et al., "Environmental and Social Dimensions," 36–49.

17. Zukin, *Naked City*, 196.

18. "The Sankofa Community Farm at Bartram's Garden," *Bartram's Garden*, accessed June 29, 2021, https://www.bartramsgarden.org/explore-bartrams/the-farm.

19. Antoinette M. G. A. WinklerPrins, ed., *Global Urban Agriculture* (Oxfordshire: CAB International, 2017).

20. Martin Cobian, "Breaking the Colonial Food Chain: The Import Food Fix, the Criollo Comprador Block and the Struggle for Food Sovereignty in Puerto Rico" (PhD diss., The Graduate Center, CUNY, 2022).

21. Francis Johnston and Setha M. Low, *Children of the Urban Poor: The Sociocultural Environment of Growth, Development and Malnutrition in Guatemala City* (Boulder: Westview Press, 1995).

22. Johnston and Low, *Children of the Urban Poor*.

23. Tony Frangie Mawad, "How an Argentine City Turned its Urban Spaces into Farms and Markets," *CityLab Environment, Bloomberg*, June 29, 2021, https://www.bloomberg.com/news/articles/2021-06-29/argentine-city-s-urban-farms-win-sustainability-prize.

24. Mawad, "How an Argentine."

25. Mawad, "How an Argentine."

26. "United Nations Sustainable Development Goals," Department of Economic and Social Affairs: Sustainable Development, United Nations, accessed April 18, 2022, https://sdgs.un.org/.

27. WinklerPrins, ed., *Global Urban*.

28. Silvio Caputo, Victoria Schoen, Kathrin Specht, Baptiste Gerard, Chris Blythe, Nevin Cohen, Runrid Fox-Kämper, Jason Hawes, Joshua Newell, and Lidia Poniży, "Applying the Food-Energy-Water Nexus approach to urban agriculture: from FEW to FEWP (Food-Energy-Water-People)," *Urban Forestry and Urban Greening* no.126934 (2020): 1–12, https://doi.org/10.1016/j.ufug.2020.126934.

29. Galen Cranz, *The Politics of Park Design: A History of Urban Parks in America* (Cambridge: MIT Press, 1982).

30. Cranz, *The Politics of Park Design*.

31. Galen Cranz and Michael Boland, "Defining the Sustainable Park: A Fifth Model for Urban Parks," *Landscape Journal* 23, no. 2 (2004): 104, http://dx.doi.org/10.3368/lj.23.2.102.

32. Cranz and Boland, "Defining the Sustainable Park," 104.

33. Cranz and Boland, "Defining the Sustainable Park,' 104.

34. Andrew Newman, *Landscape of Discontent: Urban Sustainability in Immigrant Paris* (Minneapolis: University of Minnesota Press, 2015).

35. Newman, *Landscape of Discontent*.

36. Andrew Newman, "Contested Ecologies: Environmental Activism and Urban Space in Immigrant Paris," *City and Society* 23, no. 2 (2011): 192–209, https://doi.org/10.1111/j.1548-744X.2011.01062.x.

37. This case study draws upon the publications Andrew Newman cited as well as personal communications that occurred during the writing of his PhD dissertation. As a thesis committee member, I read fieldnotes and worked closely with him as he collected and analyzed his data. The conclusions described here are based mostly on his publication "Contested Ecologies: Environmental Activism and Urban Space in Immigrant Paris," *City and Society* 23, no. 2 (2011): 192–209 as well as his book on this project, *Landscape of Discontent: Urban Sustainability in Immigrant Paris* (Minneapolis: University of Minnesota Press, 2015).

38. Newman, "Contested Ecologies," 198.

39. Newman, "Contested Ecologies," 201.

40. Newman, "Contested Ecologies," 201.

41. Newman, "Contested Ecologies," 201.

42. Newman, *Landscape of Discontent*, 128.

43. William J. Cohen, *Ecohumanism and the Ecological Culture: The Educational Legacy of Lewis Mumford and Ian McHarg* (Philadelphia: Temple University Press, 2019).

44. Cohen, *Ecohumanism and the Ecological Culture*, xxii.

45. Ian L. McHarg, "Human Ecological Planning at Pennsylvania," in *To Heal the Earth: Selected Writings of Ian L. McHarg*, eds. Ian L. McHarg and Frederick R. Steiner (Washington D.C.: Island Press, 1998), 144.

46. McHarg, "Human Ecological Planning."

47. Ian L. McHarg, *Design with Nature* (Garden City, NY: Published for the American Museum of Natural History [by] the Natural History Press, 1969).

48. Adapted from the work of the geographer Carl Sauer.

49. Ann S. Spirn, "Urban Nature and Human Design: Renewing the Great Tradition," *Journal of Planning Education and Research* 5, no. 1 (Autumn 1985): 39–51, https://annewhistonspirn.com/sharefiles/Spirn-UrbanNatureDesign-JPER-1985.pdf.

50. Spirn, "Urban Nature and Human Design," 39–51.

51. Kate Orff, a landscape architect at Columbia University, is taking on these challenges by focusing on regional ecosystems and the political ecologies that create them. Her work on restoring decaying and fragile

coastlines and identifying the oil and gas industries as the perpetuators of this destruction echo earlier concerns. Orff's attention to the biophysical and biodiversity consequences of climate change and global warming relies on a commitment to designing with nature to regenerate green wetlands, dunes, mangroves, and reefs to reduce flooding and erosion.

52. Mark A. Benedict and Edward T. McMahon, *Green Infrastructure: Linking Landscapes and Communities* (Washington D.C.: Island Press, 2006), 2.

53. Suzanne Simard, *Finding the Mother Tree: Discovering the Wisdom of the Forest* (New York: Knopf, 2021).

54. Millennium Ecosystem Assessment, *Ecosystems and Human Well-Being: Wetlands and Water Synthesis* (Washington D.C.: World Resources Institute, 2005).

55. https://www.millenniumassessment.org/en/About.html.

56. Viniece Jennings, Myron F. Floyd, Danielle Shanahan, Christopher Coutts, and Alex Sinykin, "Emerging Issues in Urban Ecology: Implications for Research, Social Justice, Human Health, and Well-Being," *Population and Environment* 39 (2017): 69–86, https://doi.org/10.1007/s11111-017-0276-0.

57. Jennings et al., "Emerging Issues in Urban Ecology," 69–86.

58. Millennium Ecosystem Assessment, *Ecosystems*.

59. Henrik Ernstson, "The Social Production of Ecosystem Services: A Framework for Studying Environmental Justice and Ecological Complexity in Urbanized Landscapes," *Landscape and Urban Planning* 109, no. 1 (2013): 7–17, https://doi.org/10.1016/j.landurbplan.2012.10.005.

60. Ernstson, "The Social Production of Ecosystem Services," 7.

61. Navjot S. Sodhi, Greg Acciaioli, Maribeth Erb, and Alan Khee-Jin Tan, eds., *Biodiversity and Human Livelihoods in Protected Areas: Case Studies from the Malay Archipelago* (Cambridge: Cambridge University Press, 2007).

62. C. Scott Shafer, David Scott, John Baker, and Kirk Winemiller, "Recreation and Amenity Values of Urban Stream Corridors: Implications for Green Infrastructure," *Journal of Urban Design* 18, no. 4 (2013): 478–93, https://doi.org/10.1080/13574809.2013.800450.

63. Cassandra Johnson Gaither, "Socioecological Production of Parks in Atlanta, Georgia's Proctor Creek Watershed: Creating Ecosystem Services or Negative Externalities?" *Environmental Justice* 12, no. 6 (2019): 231–41, https://doi.org/10.1089/env.2019.0008.

64. Adina Solomon, "Pop-up Parks Lead to More Biodiversity in Cities, Study Finds, *Next City*, July 3, 2019, https://nextcity.org/urbanist-news/pop-up-parks-lead-to-more-biodiversity-in-cities-study-finds#:~:text=

%E2%80%9CIf%20you%20think%20about%20all,in%20an%20ecosys tem%2C%20Mata%20says.

65. Jennings et al., "Emerging Issues," 69–86.

66. Brentin Mock, "Why Detroit Residents Pushed Back Against Tree-Planning," *CityLab Environment, Bloomberg*, January 5, 2019, ttps://www. bloomberg.com/news/articles/2019-01-11/why-detroiters-didn-t-trust-city-tree-planting-efforts#:~:text=But%20the%20reasons%20 Detroit%20folks,didn't%20trhust%20the%20city.

67. Feargus O'Sullivan and Linda Poon, "The Darker Side of Tree-Planting Pledges," *CityLab Environment, Bloomberg*, July 30, 2021, https://www. bloomberg.com/news/features/2021-07-30/what-happens-after-pled ges-to-plant-millions-of-trees.

68. O'Sullivan and Poon, "The Darker Side of Tree-Planting Pledges."

69. "The 2015 Tree Census," NYC Parks, accessed April 18, 2022, http:// media.nycgovparks.org/images/web/TreesCount/Index.html.

70. Chen Ly, "Trees Cool the Land Surface Temperature of Cities by up to 12°C," *Environment, New Scientist*, November 23, 2021, https://www. newscientist.com/article/2298675-trees-cool-the-land-surface-temp erature-of-cities-by-up-to-12c/#ixzz7QrbWnO7K.

Jonas Schwaab, Ronny Meier, Gianluca Mussetti, Sonia Seneviratne, Christine Bürgi, and Edouard L. Davin, "The Role of Urban Trees in Reducing Land Surface Temperatures in European Cities," *Nature Communication* 12, no. 6763 (2021), https://doi.org/10.1038/s41 467-021-26768-w.

71. Louise McKenzie and Susan Thompson, "Resilience in a Warming Climate: Public Place-Making for Health and Well-Being in Hot Cities," in *The Routledge Handbook of People and Place in the 21st-Century City*, eds. Kate Bishop and Nancy Marshall (New York: Routledge, 2019), 282–93.

72. Simard, *Finding the Mother*.

73. Deborah Martin, "Place as Human–Environment Network: Tree Planting and Place-Making in Massachusetts, USA," in *The Routledge Handbook of Place*, eds. Tim Edensor, Ares Kalandides, and Uma Kothari (London: Routledge, 2020), 109–17.

74. Ian Leahy and Yaryna Serkez, "Since When Have Trees Existed Only for Rich Americans?," *New York Times*, July 4, 2021, https://www.nytimes. com/interactive/2021/06/30/opinion/environmental-inequity-trees-critical-infrastructure.html.

75. Mock, "Why Detroit Residents."

76. Hamil Pearsall and Isabelle Anguelovski, "Contesting and Resisting Environmental Gentrification: Responses to New Paradoxes and Challenges for Urban Environmental Justice," *Sociological Research Online* 21, no. 3 (August 2016): 121–27, https://doi.org/10.5153/sro.3979.

77. Checker, *The Sustainability Myth*, 7.

78. Checker, *The Sustainability Myth*, 50.

79. Julian Agyeman, Robert D. Bullard, and Bob Evans, "Exploring the Nexus: Bringing Together Sustainability, Environmental Justice and Equity," *Space and Polity* 6, no. 1 (2002): 77–90, https://doi.org/10.1080/13562570220137907.

80. Julian Agyeman and Bob Evans, "'Just Sustainability': The Emerging Discourse of Environmental Justice in Britain?," *The Geographical Journal* 170, no. 2 (2004): 155–64, http://www.jstor.org/stable/3451592.

81. Agyeman and Evans, "Just Sustainability," 157.

82. Julian Agyeman, *Introducing Just Sustainabilities: Policy, Planning and Practice* (New York and London: Zed Books, 2013).

83. Juliana Maantay, "Environmental Justice and Fairness," in *The Routledge Companion to Environmental Planning*, eds. Simin Davoudi, Richard Cowell, Iain White, and Hilda Blanco (Oxford: Routledge, 2020), 109–19.

84. John Leland, "To Measure Inequality, Just Count the Trees," *New York Times*, LI Metropolitan Section, August 22, 2021, 1 and 6.

85. Isabelle Anguelovski and James J. T. Connolly, *The Green City and Social Injustice: 21 Tales from North America and Europe* (New York and London: Routledge, 2021).

CHAPTER 8

1. Irwin Altman and Setha M. Low, *Place Attachment* (New York and London: Plenum Press, 1992).

2. H. M. Proshansky, A. K. Fabian, and R. Kaminoff, "Place-Identity: Physical World Socialization of the Self," *Journal of Environmental Psychology* 3, no. 1 (1983): 57–83, https://doi.org/10.1016/S0272-4944(83)80021-8.

3. Altman and Low, *Place Attachment*, 166.

4. "Liberty Island Chronology," Statue of Liberty National Monument, New York, National Park Service, last modified February 4, 2018, https://www.nps.gov/stli/learn/historyculture/liberty-island-a-chronology.htm.

5. "Liberty Island Chronology."

6. "Liberty Island Chronology."

7. Setha Low, Gabrielle Bendiner-Viani, and Yvonne Hung, *Attachments to Liberty: A Special Ethnographic Study of the Statue of Liberty National Monument* (New York: Department of the Interior, National Park Service, 2005).

8. Altman and Low, *Place Attachment*, 165.

9. "Liberty Island Chronology."

10. Gabrielle Bendiner-Viani and Yvonne Hung were instrumental both in gathering and analyzing the data from the Liberty Island project. We wrote the research report for the National Park Service together. Many of the ideas presented emerged during our collective discussions.

11. The World Trade Center is an example of a place to which people have a symbolic connection.

12. I want to thank Anna Harwin for her help with this passage.

13. In this chapter, I employ the concept of culture from a broader point of view that includes these shared symbols, interpretations, intentions, affects, and meanings as well as the actively negotiated rules of everyday life—but also draws upon the underlying structures of people's beliefs, knowledge, and practices. Culture is made up of a myriad of artifacts, behaviors, languages, customs, arts, memories, values, and ideas that people learn, contest, and share. These ways of living and being produce—and are produced by—social institutions such as family, kinship, religion, arts, economics, politics, education, media and communication, and many others. Power dynamics permeate and organize this system generating socially constructed group and individual hierarchies based on history, race, class, gender, sexual orientation, ability, ethnic identity, location, age and generation, or other characteristics.

14. Cedric J. Robinson, *Black Marxism: The Making of the Black Radical Tradition* (Chapel Hill: University of North Carolina Press, 2000).

15. Edward W. Said, "Invention, Memory, and Place," *Critical Inquiry* 26, no. 2 (Winter 2000): 175–92, https://www.jstor.org/stable/1344120.

16. Small, local parks and sidewalks are no less significant in strengthening local cultural identity or demarcating a turf. Small public spaces with symbols, such as painted murals, or remaking a playground can be extremely meaningful to community members as well.

17. Joe Heim, "Recounting a Day of Rage, Hate, Violence and Death," *Washington Post*, August 14, 2017, https://www.washingtonpost.com/graphics/2017/local/charlottesville-timeline/.

18. Heim, "Recounting a Day."

19. Julianne Pepitone, "NYC Has Only 5 Statues of Women—But Not for Much Longer," *MSNBC*, January 24, 2019, https://www.nbcnews.

com/know-your-value/feature/nyc-has-only-5-statues-women-not-much-longer-ncna962171.

20. "CHART Santa Fe: Culture, History, Art, Reconciliation and Truth," *Artful Life*, accessed May 3, 2022, https://www.chartsantafe.com/.

21. Don Mitchell and Lynn A. Staeheli, "Clean and Safe? Property Redevelopment, Public Space, and Homelessness in Downtown San Diego," in *The Politics of Public Space*, eds. Setha Low and Neil Smith (New York and London: Routledge, 2006), 143–75.

22. Setha Low, *On the Plaza: The Politics of Public Space and Culture* (Austin: University of Texas Press, 2000).

23. Low, *On the Plaza*.

24. Querine Kommandeur, "Post-Urbanism in San José: Social Exclusion through Transitions in Public Space" (PhD diss., Utrecht University, 2020).

25. Low, *On the Plaza*.

26. For more information about life on the Plaza de la Cultura before its redesign, see Low, *On the Plaza*.

27. Kommandeur, "Post-Urbanism in San José." 48.

28. Kommandeur, "Post-Urbanism in San José," 48.

29. Charles Price, fieldnotes 1996.

30. Setha Low, Dana Taplin, and Suzanne Scheld, *Rethinking Urban Parks: Public Space and Cultural Diversity* (Austin: University of Texas Press, 2005).

31. Shira Gabriel, Esha Naidu, Elaine Paravati, C. D. Morrison, and Kristin Gainey, "Creating the Sacred from the Profane: Collective Effervescence and Everyday Activities," *The Journal of Positive Psychology* 15, no. 1 (2020): 129–54, https://doi.org/10.1080/17439760.2019.1689412.

32. Émile Durkheim, *The Elementary Forms of Religious Life* (New York: Free Press, 1995).

33. For some time, homeless individuals could camp in the park and were able to use the facilities; however, policies change from administration to administration. There is a large shelter for homeless people and a house for trans people near the park—both housing individuals who are marginalized in society. The park offers a relatively safe place for these individuals as well as for the LGBTQ community. There have been infrequent episodes of assault, especially in the past, but in the contemporary moment, conflicts more often occur outside the park.

34. Portions of this discussion of Battery Park City are drawn from Setha M. Low, Dana H. Taplin, and Mike Lamb, "Battery Park City: An Ethnographic Field Study of the Community Impact of 9/11," *Urban*

Affairs Review 40, no. 5 (May 2005): 655–82, https://doi.org/10.1177/1078087404272304.

35. Interview with Roland Baer, December 12, 2021.

36. Interview with Roland Baer, December 12, 2021.

37. Low et al., "Battery Park City."

38. Gregory Smithsimon, *September 12: Community and Neighborhood Recovery at Ground Zero* (New York: NYU Press, 2011).

39. Elizabeth Greenspan, *Battle for Ground Zero: Inside the Political Struggle to Rebuild the World Trade Center* (New York: Palgrave Macmillan, 2013).

40. Low et al., "Battery Park City."

41. Smithsimon, *September 12*. Greenspan, *Battle for Ground Zero*.

42. Low et al., "Battery Park City."

43. Greenspan, *Battle for Ground Zero*. Smithsimon, *September 12*.

44. Low et al., "Battery Park City."

45. Low et al., "Battery Park City."

46. Low et al., "Battery Park City," and fieldnotes.

47. Smithsimon, *September 12*.

48. Smithsimon, *September 12*, 171–72.

49. Fieldnotes 2003.

50. Patricia Simões Aelbrecht, Quentin Stevens, and Sanjeev Kumar, "European Public Space Projects with Social Cohesion in Mind: Symbolic, Programmatic and Minimalist Approaches," *European Planning Studies* (2021), https://doi.org/10.1080/09654313.2021.1959902.

51. "Aga Khan Award for Architecture," AKDN, accessed April 7, 2021, https://www.akdn.org/architecture/project/superkilen.

52. Jonathan Daly, "Architectures of Encounter: Shaping Social Interaction in the Intercultural City" (PhD diss., University of Melbourne, 2020).

53. Daly, "Architectures of Encounter," 313.

54. Daly, "Architectures of Encounter," 316.

55. Ruth Fincher, Kurt Iveson, Helga Leitner, and Valerie Preston, *Everyday Equalities: Making Multicultures in Settler Colonial Cities* (Minneapolis: University of Minnesota Press, 2019).

56. Fincher et al., *Everyday Equalities*.

CHAPTER 9

1. Daniel Defoe, *A Journal of the Plague Year, 1722* (Coppell: Public Edition, 2021), 13.

2. Ares Kalandides, "The Epidemics Behind Urban Planning: The Foundations," *Institute of Place Management Blog*, March 25, 2020, http://

blog.placemanagement.org/2020/03/25/the-epidemics-behind-urban-planning.

3. Lee Flannery, "Design in the Time of Cholera: How Pandemics Reshaped the Built Environment," *Planetizen*, May 8, 2020, https://www.planetizen.com/news/2020/05/109286-design-time-cholera-how-pandemics-reshaped-built-environment.

4. Vanessa Chang, "The Post-pandemic Style," *Metropolis, Slate*, April 19, 2020, https://slate.com/business/2020/04/coronavirus-architecture-1918-flu-cholera-modernism.html.

5. Chelsey Cox, "Fact Check: COVID-19 Is Deadlier Than the 1918 Spanish Flu and Seasonal Influenza," *USA Today*, August 25, 2020, https://www.usatoday.com/story/news/factcheck/2020/08/20/fact-check-covid-19-deadlier-than-1918-spanish-flu-seasonal-flu/3378208001/.

6. Lawrence Wright, *The Plague Year: America in the Time of COVID* (New York: Alfred A. Knopf, 2021).

7. Data are as of May 9, 2022, when 996,612 deaths had been reported in the United States including Puerto Rico and the US territories of American Samoa, Guam and the Northern Mariana Islands, and the Virgin Islands.

    Amy Harmon, Danielle Ivory, Lauren Leatherby, Albert Sun, Jeremy White, and Sarah Almukhtar, "How Covid Claimed the Lives of So Many in the U.S.," *New York Times*, May 15, 2022, National Section, 19–20.

8. One major exception is the four-volume series edited by Brian Doucet, Pierre Filion, and Rianne van Melik, *Global Reflections on COVID-19 and Urban Inequalities* (Bristol: Bristol University Press, 2021).

9. NYC Health, "Trends and Totals," COVID-19: Data, accessed May 7, 2022, https://www1.nyc.gov/site/doh/covid/covid-19-data-totals.page.

10. By January 2022 Omicron had taken the place of Delta as the fastest-spreading variant; however, my analysis did not continue into 2022.

11. Gabriel J. X. Dance and Lazaro Gamio, "As Coronavirus Restrictions Lift, Millions in U.S. Are Leaving Home Again," *New York Times*, May 13, 2020, http://www.nytimes.com/interactive/2020/05/12/us/coronavirus-reopening-shutdown.html.

    I had just returned from the World Urban Forum in Abu Dhabi, where I had spoken about the global importance of public space, and was back teaching at the Graduate Center of the City University of New York (CUNY) located in midtown Manhattan. Because of my recent trip, I was more aware than most about the threat of COVID-19 and switched to virtual classes starting March 7. By March 14 I stopped going out of the house, except for groceries, and cancelled my previously planned birthday party. Friends who did attend a party on March 15 and had taken the subway and train that day came down with COVID-19. They were older adults and one ended up in the hospital.

12. Ronda Chapman, Lisa Foderaro, Linda Hwang, Bill Lee, Sadiya Muqueeth, Jessica Sargent, and Brendan Shane, "Parks and an Equitable Recovery: A Trust for Public Land Special Report," *Trust for Public Land*, May 27, 2021, https://www.tpl.org/parks-and-an-equitable-recovery-parkscore-report.

13. Chapman et al., "Parks and an equitable recovery."

14. Setha Low, "Lessons from Imagining the World Trade Center Site: An Examination of Public Space and Culture," *Anthropology & Education Quarterly* 33, no. 3 (September 2002): 395–405, https://www.jstor.org/stable/3211099.

15. Kevin Quealy, "The Richest Neighborhoods Emptied Out Most as Coronavirus Hit New York City," *New York Times*, May 15, 2020, https://www.nytimes.com/interactive/2020/05/15/upshot/who-left-new-york-coronavirus.html.

16. Highly educated people also reported an increase in depressive symptoms based on a 1,143-person national survey comparing responses in April 2019 with April 2020.

17. Setha Low, *Behind the Gates: Life, Security and the Pursuit of Happiness in Fortress America* (New York and London: Routledge, 2004).

18. Shannon Bond, "A Pandemic Winner: How Zoom Beat Tech Giants to Dominate Video Chat," *Morning Edition, NPR WNYC Radio*, March 19, 2021, https://www.npr.org/2021/03/19/978393310/a-pandemic-winner-how-zoom-beat-tech-giants-to-dominate-video-chat.

19. Daria Radchenko, "Easter Online: Constructing Sacred Space During Quarantine," paper presented at "Museum in the City – City in the Museum" conference, Moscow, December 12, 2020.

20. Dance and Gamio, "As Coronavirus Restrictions Lift."

21. Caroline Spivack, "NYC Opens 7 Miles of Streets in and Near Parks," *Curbed*, May 1, 2020, https://ny.curbed.com/2020/5/1/21244055/new-york-open-streets-parks-social-distancing-coroanvirus.

22. Kimiko de Freytas-Tamura, "How Neighborhood Groups Are Stepping In Where the Government Didn't," *New York Times*, last modified March 6, 2021, https://www.nytimes.com/2021/03/03/nyregion/covid-19-mutual-aid-nyc-html.

23. Zeynep Tufekci, "Keep the Parks Open," *The Atlantic*, April 7, 2020, https://www.theatlantic.com/health/archive/2020/04/closing-parks-ineffective-pandemic-theater/609580/.

24. Ron Lee, "Social Distancing Practiced by Some, Ignored by Others Over Warm Weekend," *Spectrum News NY 1*, last modified May 4, 2020, https://www.ny1.com/nyc/all-boroughs/news/2020/05/04/social-distancing-practiced-by-some--ignored-by-others-over-warm-weekend-.

25. Shannan Ferry, "Brooklyn Zip Code Has City's Highest Coronavirus Death Rate," *Spectrum News NY 1*, last modified May 19, 2020, https://www.ny1.com/nyc/all-boroughs/news/2020/05/18/we-may-finally-know-which-parts-of-nyc-have-been-hit-hardest-by-coronavirus.

26. Ferry, "Brooklyn Zip Code."

27. Amy Harmon, Danielle Ivory, Lauren Leatherby, Albert Sun, Jeremy White, and Sarah Almukhtar, "How Covid Claimed the Lives of So Many in the U.S.," *New York Times*, May 15, 2022, National Section, 19–20.

28. Yaryna Serkez, "Who Is Most Likely to Die from the Coronavirus?" *Sunday Review, Opinion Section, New York Times*, June 4, 2020, 2.

29. Gerard Goggin and Katie Ellis, "Disability, Communication, and Life Itself in the COVID-19 Pandemic," *Health Sociology Review* 29, no. 2 (2020): 168–76, https://doi.org/10.1080/14461242.2020.1784020.

30. Didier Fassin, "Hazardous Confinement During the COVID-19 Pandemic: The Fate of Migrants Detained yet Nondeportable," *Journal of Human Rights* 19, no. 5 (2020): 613–23, https://doi.org/10.1080/14754835.2020.1822155.

31. Stephen F. Sullivan, "Sound Politics in COVID-19 Brooklyn," *Anthropology News*, October 19, 2020, https://www.anthropology-news.org/articles/sound-politics-in-covid-19-brooklyn/.

32. "New Yorkers Say: Don't Re-open the Economy Before June," CUNY New York City COVID-19 Survey Week 6, CUNY SPH, accessed May 7, 2022, https://sph.cuny.edu/research/covid-19-tracking-survey/week-6/.

33. Jonathan Daly, Kim Dovey, and Quentin Stevens, "We Can't Let Coronavirus Kill Our Cities: Here's How We Can Save Urban Life," *The Conversation*, May 4, 2020, https://theconversation.com/we-cant-let-coronavirus-kill-our-cities-heres-how-we-can-save-urban-life-137063.

34. Jason Hanna, Dakin Andone, and Amir Vera, "Memorial Day Weekend: Americans Visit Beaches and Attractions with Pandemic Warnings in Mind," *CNN*, May 24, 2020, https://www.cnnphilippines.com/

world/2020/5/24/us-memorial-weekend-beaches-attractions-pande
mic.html.

35. Richard Oppel and Audra D. S. Burch, "With Masks at Beaches, Nation Marks Muted Holiday," *New York Times*, March 26, 2020, A14.

36. Lisa Prevost, "Sorry, That Surf and Sand Are for Local Toes Only," LI Real Estate, *New York Times,* August 9, 2020, 11.

37. Derrick Bryson Taylor, "George Floyd Protests: A Timeline," *New York Times*, November 5, 2021, https://www.nytimes.com/article/george-floyd-protests-timeline.html.

38. "George Floyd: Huge Protests against Racism Held across US," BBC News, June 7, 2020, https://www.bbc.com/news/world-us-canada-52951093.

39. Hanna et al., "Memorial Day Weekend."

40. Julie Mazziotta, "The Risk of Getting Coronavirus Outdoors Is Low—If Precautions Are Taken," *People*, May 18, 2020, https://people.com/health/risk-getting-coronavirus-outdoors-low-with-precautions/.

41. Steve Almasy, Holly Yan, and Christina Maxouris, "As Covid-19 Cases Rise in 17 States, Americans Still Divided on Whether Masks Should Be Mandated," *CNN Health*, May 26, 2020, https://www.cnn.com/2020/05/26/health/us-coronavirus-tuesday/index.html.

42. Michael Wilson, "New York: Much More Social, Much Less Distant," *New York Times*, June 19, 2020, A1.

43. Elizabeth Joseph, Mallika Kallingal, and Elizabeth Hartfield, "35 of the 40 People Arrested for Social Distancing Violations in Brooklyn Were Black," *CNN*, May 8, 2020. https://www.cnn.com/2020/05/08/us/nypd-social-distancing-35-of-40-people-arrested-black-trnd/index.html.

44. Elie Mystal, "Covid Is About to Become the Newest Excuse for Police Brutality," *The Nation*, May 5, 2020. https://www.thenation.com/article/society/coronavirus-police-brutality/.

45. For years NYC restaurants and cafes wanted to expand their footprint onto the sidewalk with awnings, tables, chairs, and food service. Resistance to these proposed incursions were based on urban planning principles that urban space in the public domain should not be used for commercial purposes. Advocates for outside seating argued that occupied sidewalks improve the quality of urban life by attracting more people thus making the area safer and more vibrant. In fact, a revitalization project transformed the streets and sidewalks along Broadway, near Times Square, by closing the street, widening the sidewalks, and

adding tables and chairs that allowed visitors to bring their own food. But many neighborhoods resisted adding restaurant seating and sidewalk cafes, arguing locals would be excluded by the high price of a cup of coffee—like what happened after the renovation of Bryant Park and the installation of an expensive and trendy coffee kiosk.

46. "Recovery Agenda: Mayor de Blasio Extends Outdoor Dining Season Year-Round," Office of the Mayor, NYC, September 25, 2020, https://www1.nyc.gov/office-of-the-mayor/news/680-20/recovery-agenda-mayor-de-blasio-extends-outdoor-dining-season-year-round.

47. Vikas Mehta, "The New Proxemics: COVID-19, Social Distancing, and Sociable Space," *Journal of Urban Design* 25, no. 6 (2020): 669–74, https://doi.org/10.1080/13574809.2020.1785283.

48. D. Angelo, K. Britt, M. L. Brown, and S. L. Camp, "Private Struggles in Public Spaces: Documenting COVID-19 Material Culture and Landscapes," *Journal of Contemporary Archaeology* 8, no. 1 (2021): 154–84, https://doi.org/10.1558/jca.43379.

49. Jennifer Medina and Robert Gebeloff, "Virus Packs Its Deadliest Punch in the Places Where Democrats Live," *New York Times*, May 25, 2020, A1 and A11.

50. Maria Cramer, "Sobering Reality: Many Are Drinking to Excess," *New York Times*, May 27, 2020, A4.

51. Roni Caryn Rabin and Tim Arango, "Gun Deaths Surged During the Pandemic's First Year, the C.D.C. Reports," *New York Times*, May 13, 2022, https://www.nytimes.com/live/2022/05/10/world/covid-19-mandates-vaccine-cases.

52. Edgar Sandoval, "After Battling Gangs and Guns, A Neighborhood Faces a New Killer," New York City Region, *New York Times*, May 24, 2020, 15.

53. Tim Gill, "Child in the City: Making Connections in Times of Corona," *Webinar from Child in the City*, September 22, 2020, https://www.childinthecity.org/webinar/.

54. Jennifer M. Pipitone and Svetlana Jović, "Urban Green Equity and COVID-19: Effects on Park Use and Sense of Belonging in New York City," *Urban Forestry & Urban Greening* 65, no. 127338 (2021), https://doi.org/10.1016/j.ufug.2021.127338.

55. J. E. Otero Peña, H. Kodali, E. Ferris, K. Wyka, S. Low, K. R. Evenson, J. M. Dorn, L. E. Thorpe, and T. T. K. Huang, "The Role of the Physical and Social Environment in Observed and Self-Reported Park Use in Low-Income Neighborhoods in New York City," *Frontiers in Public Health* 9, no. 656988 (2021), https://doi.org/10.3389/fpubh.2021.65698

8 As the summer wore on, social and political divisions became evident in the uneven pattern of mask use and virus impact. Possibly in reaction to the BLM demonstrations and calls to "defund the police," police officers were photographed not wearing masks even when on duty, suggesting a disregard for COVID-19 public health and safety guidelines. Mask wearing both indoors and in public space became a politicized and ideological act in the coming months.

56. Gerhard Reese, Karen R. S. Hamann, Lea M. Heidbreder, Laura S. Loy, Claudia Menzel, Sebastian Neubert, Josephine Tröger, and Marlis C. Wullenkord, "SARS-Cov-2 and Environmental Protection: A Collective Psychology Agenda for Environmental Psychology Research," *Journal of Environmental Psychology* 70, no. 101444 (2020), https://doi.org/10.1016/j.jenvp.2020.101444.

57. NYC Health, "Trends and Totals."

58. Benjamin Mueller, "Depression and Anxiety Declined in the First Half of 2021 but Remained High, the C.D.C. Reports," *New York Times*, October 5, 2021, https://www.nytimes.com/2021/10/05/health/covid-depression-anxiety.html.

59. Amr Alfiky, "New Yorkers Cope with a Lonely Holiday Season," *New York Times*, December 23, 2020, A15.

60. Matt Simon, "Who Will We Be When This Is All Over?," *Wired*, December 7, 2020, https://www.wired.com/story/who-will-we-be-when-the-pandemic-is-over/.

61. Hamilton Nolan, "A Year in the Life of Safeway 1048," *In These Times*, March 26, 2021, https://inthesetimes.com/article/safeway-frontline-workers-coronavirus-safety-measures.

62. Danny Pearlstein and Giselle Routhier, "Governor Cuomo Owes Subway Riders and Homeless New Yorkers a Housing Plan," *Gotham Gazette*, May 13, 2020, https://www.gothamgazette.com/columnists/other/130-opinion/9384-governor-cuomo-subway-riders-homeless-new-yorkers-housing-plan.

63. Conor Dougherty, "One Way to Get People Off the Streets: Buy Hotels," *Sunday Business, New York Times*, April 17, 2020, 1.

64. With travel curtailed because of the pandemic, NYC residents appreciated the absence of tourist crowds and enjoyed having their public spaces for themselves. The changes in the streetscape prompted the city to experiment with closing even more streets and allowing more restaurants to extend onto sidewalks and streets. The "Open Streets, Open Restaurants" program enabled people to rethink the design of the city with more public space for pedestrians, bicycles, and entertainment.

65. Michiko Kakutani, "Finding Refuge, and a Snowy Owl, in Central Park," Long Island Region, *New York Times*, March 7, 2021, 6.

66. Adam Gopnik, "A Brief Anatomy of Outdoor Dining," *New Yorker*, March 20, 2021, https://www.newyorker.com/culture/cultural-comm ent/a-brief-anatomy-of-outdoor-dining.

67. Winnie Hu, "'Outdoor Living Rooms' Serve as Escape from Grim Winter," *New York Times*, January 5, 2021, A5.

68. Luis Ferré-Sadurní and Joseph Goldstein, "1st Vaccination in U.S. Is Given in New York, Hard Hit in Outbreak's First Days," *New York Times*, last modified June 22, 2021, https://www.nytimes.com/2020/12/14/ nyregion/coronavirus-vaccine-new-york.html.

69. David Goodhue and Mary Ellen Klas, "Wealthy Keys Enclave Received COVID Vaccines in January Before Much of the State," *Miami Herald*, March 3, 2021, https://www.miamiherald.com › news › local › commu- nity › florida-keys › article249666463.html.

70. Steven Kurutz, "The Young and the Restless," Sunday Styles, *New York Times*, June 13, 2021, 1.

71. Ben Sisario and Emma G. Fitzsimmons, "Turning the Page with a Central Park Concert," Arts/Cultural Desk, *New York Times*, June 8, 2021, C1.

72. Jonathan Mahler, "The City Awakens," *New York Times Magazine*, June 13, 2021, 4–20.

73. Mahler, "The City Awakens."

74. Pete Wells, "What People Missed Most About Restaurants (It Wasn't the Food)," National, *New York Times*, May 22, 2021, A12.

75. John Leland, "Over a Long Weekend, a City Rediscovers Itself," *New York Times*, July 6, 2021, 1.

76. Chapman et al., "Parks and an Equitable Recovery."

77. Troy Closson, "The Disparities in Access to New York's Parks," *New York Times*, last modified May 28, 2021, https://www.nytimes.com/ 2021/05/27/nyregion/parks-access-nyc.html.

78. Hsiu-Lan Cheng, Helen Youngju Kim, J. D. Reynolds Taewon Choi, Yuying Tsong, and Y. Joel Wong, "COVID-19 Anti-Asian Racism: A Tripartite Model of Collective Psychosocial Resilience," *American Psychologist* 76, no. 4 (2021): 627–42, https://doi.org/10.1037/amp 0000808.

79. Kimiko de Freytas-Tamura, "Whose Park Is It? Residents and Revelers Clash over Washington Square," *New York Times*, June 18, 2021, https:// www.nytimes.com/2021/06/18/nyregion/washington-square-park- police.html.

80. Winnie Hu, "The Pandemic Gave New York City 'Open Streets': Will They Survive?," *New York Times*, last modified August 19, 2021, https://www.nytimes.com/2021/08/09/nyregion/open-streets-jackson-heights.html.

81. Winnie Hu, "The Pandemic Gave New York City 'Open Streets': Will They Survive?," *New York Times*, last modified August 19, 2021, https://www.nytimes.com/2021/08/09/nyregion/open-streets-jackson-heights.html.

82. Julia Carmel, "Seven Weeks of Jubilation," Metropolitan, *New York Times*, August 8, 2021, 4.

83. The *New York Times*' October 24, 2021, edition released an interactive set of maps that depicted the rise and fall of the total cases in the United States that was determined to be made up of five rather than three peaks. I struggled to reconcile my analysis with theirs, but the trajectory of the disease was different in New York City because it peaked early, and the rate of vaccination acceptance was high.

84. Emily Anthes, "'Lurching Between Crisis and Complacency': Was This Our Last Covid Surge?," *New York Times*, October 14, 2021, https://www.nytimes.com/2021/10/14/health/coronavirus-delta-surge.html.

85. Edward Glaeser and David Cutler, *Survival of the City: Living and Thriving in an Age of Isolation* (New York: Penguin Press, 2021).

86. "Cities and Pandemics: Towards a More Just, Green and Healthy Future," UN Habitat, Nairobi, March 30, 2021, https://unhabitat.org/cities-and-pandemics-towards-a-more-just-green-and-healthy-future-1.

CHAPTER 10

1. William H. Whyte, *Analysis of Bryant Park* (New York: Rockefeller Brothers Fund, 1977).

   Sonia Hirt, "Jane Jacobs, Modernity and Knowledge," in *The Urban Wisdom of Jane Jacobs*, eds. Sonia Hirt and Diane Zahm (New York: Routledge, 2012).

2. Richard K. Rein, *American Urbanist: How William H. Whyte's Unconventional Wisdom Reshaped Public Life* (Washington: Island Press, 2022).

3. William H. Whyte, *City: Rediscovering the Center* (New York: Anchor Books, 1988), 303.

4. Christopher Klemek, "The Rise and Fall of New Left Urbanism," *Daedalus* 138, no. 2 (Spring 2009): 73–82, https://go.gale.com/ps/

i.do?p=AONE&u=googlescholar&id=GALE | A200387169&v=
2.1&it=r&sid=bookmark-AONE&asid=7dba7de6.

5. Setha Low, Dana Taplin, and Suzanne Scheld, *Rethinking Urban Parks: Public Space and Cultural Diversity* (Austin: University of Texas Press, 2005).

6. Walkway Over the Hudson, Jones Beach, Lake Welch, Central Park, Jacob Riis Park, the Statue of Liberty, and Liberty Island State Park were REAPs though the details of each varied depending on research objectives. Park managers who wanted to develop a culturally sensitive five-year plan or understand the cultural dynamics of park users preferred using a REAP rather than quantitative surveys to elicit park meanings, memories, and attachments. Often the REAP uncovered emerging problems not previously identified—much to the surprise of project collaborators. The Jacob Riis Park and Jones Beach studies were undertaken to reduce miscommunication between park administrators and the increasing diversity of users whose needs were not addressed by park facilities built with others in mind. Most often, the park managers and nonprofit groups wanted to improve user satisfaction and thought the REAP would be an expedient way to gather this information.

7. With Erin Lilli, graduate student in environmental psychology.

8. Mitchell Silver, "Parks Without Borders: A Free Vision for Urban Space," *MDP SmartGrowth Manager, Smart Growth Online,* June 29, 2016, https://smartgrowth.org/parks-without-borders-free-vision-urban-space/.

9. Rick Rojas and Noah Remnick, "Overhauling 8 Parks, New York Seeks to Create More Inviting Spaces," *New York Times,* May 24, 2016, https://www.nytimes.com/2016/05/25/nyregion/overhauling-8-parks-new-york-seeks-to-create-more-inviting-spaces.html.

10. Rojas and Remnick, "Overhauling 8 Parks."

11. Silver, "Parks Without Borders."

12. "Parks Without Borders: Making our parks more open and welcoming," New York City Department of Parks and Recreation, accessed May 12, 2022, https://www.nycgovparks.org/planning-and-building/plann ing/parks-without-borders#:~:text=With%20the%20Parks%20With out%20Borders,to%20make%20our%20parks%20safer.

13. William Castro, the Manhattan borough commissioner for parks, defended the lowering of fences in that it allows police and PEP (Parks Enforcement Patrol) officers and parents to look into the parks.

14. Allegra Hobbs, "Don't Lower Tompkins Sq. Park Playground Fences, Parents Beg City," *Parks and Recreation, DNAinfo,* February 28, 2017, https://www.dnainfo.com/new-york/20170228/east-village/parents-ask-parks-department-not-to-lower-playground-fences/.

15. Hobbs, "Don't Lower Tompkins."

16. Merrit Corrigan (Cultural Anthropology), Bengi Sullu (Environmental Psychology), Elisandro Garza Roldan (Archaeology), and Anthony Ramos (Cultural Anthropology) agreed to work on Tompkins Square Park and have generously allowed me to use their fieldnotes cited with attribution in this chapter. Their hard work and interest made this research possible.

    Where is endnote 19? Will this be fixed?

17. The research team decided who would observe what part of the park, selected days and times of the various observations, and coordinated schedules to obtain the most complete coverage. Anthony and Elisandro spent more time in the late afternoon and evening, while Bengi and Merrit did more observations during the day. Their previous experience, language abilities, gender, and age influenced their fieldwork choices. Researcher subjectivity is an important part of any ethnographic methodology, and we were fortunate to have a diverse group of individuals and learned from their different perspectives, expectations, and positionalities.

18. Deborah S. Gardner, "Tompkins Square: Past and Present," *The Journal of American History* 77, no. 1 (1990): 233.

19. Andy Newman and Sean Piccoli, "Face-Offs at Tent City Test Policy on Homeless," National, *New York Times*, May 5, 2022, A22.

20. Newman and Piccoli, "Face-Offs at Tent City."

21. Marci Reaven and Jeanne Houck, "A History of Tompkins Square Park," in *From Urban Village to East Village: The Battle for New York's Lower East Side*, ed. Janet L. Abu-Lughod (Oxford: Blackwell, 1994), 89.

22. Reaven and Houck, "A History of Tompkins Square."

23. Andrew O. Mattson and Stephen R. Duncombe, "Public Space, Private Place: The Contested Terrain of Tompkins Square Park," *Berkeley Journal of Sociology* 37, (1992): 129–61, http://www.jstor.org/stable/41035458.

24. Elisandro Garza Roldan, fieldnotes 2018.

    Also drawn from William Sites, *Remaking New York: Primitive Globalization and the Politics of Urban Community* (Minneapolis: University of Minnesota Press, 2003), 69–100.

25. Neil Smith, *The New Urban Frontier: Gentrification and the Revanchist City* (New York: Routledge, 1996).

26. Depending on which news account, the number of evictees ranges from 50 to 300. I use the account of 200–300 individuals evicted from Smith's *The New Urban Frontier* (1996), 6.

27. Elizabeth Hess, "No Place Like Home," *Artforum*, October 1991, https://www.artforum.com/print/199108/no-place-like-home-33737.

28. Merrit Corrigan, fieldnotes 2018. I want to especially thank Merrit for many of the references and observational insights in this section.

29. "Tompkins Square Park: Parks Cuts The Ribbon On Improvements To Tompkins Square Park Playground," New York City Department of Parks and Recreation, August 19, 2009, https://www.nycgovparks.org/parks/tompkins-square-park/pressrelease/20861.

30. Harry Bartle, "New Tompkins Square Playground Is an Overdue Hit," *The Villager* 79, no. 12 (August–September 2009).

31. Ellyn Marks, "Brief: Even in the Daytime, Rats Overrun Tompkins Square Park," State and Regional News PIX11, *New York, WPIX-TV*, July 28, 2011.

32. Newman and Piccoli, "Face-Offs at Tent City."

33. Corrigan, fieldnotes 2018.

34. Corrigan, fieldnotes 2018.

35. Corrigan, fieldnotes 2018.

36. Compilation of all the fieldnotes.

37. Setha Low and Project for Public Spaces, fieldnotes 2019.

38. Combined Anthony Ramos and Elisandro Garza Roldan, fieldnotes 2018.

39. Ramos, fieldnotes 2018.

40. Ramos, fieldnotes 2018.

41. Bengi Sullu, fieldnotes 2018.

42. Corrigan, fieldnotes 2018.

43. Ramos, fieldnotes 2018.

44. Elisandro Garza Roldan, interview 2018.

45. Merrit Corrigan, interview 2018.

46. Corrigan, fieldnotes 2018.

47. We observed physical traces, confirmed by interviews, that there was a rat population located near the playground that remained active. Interviewees complained about the rats, and we overheard parents talking about the precautions they take to keep their children away from rat-infested bushes.

48. The self-identified homeless and older individuals interviewed expressed their concerns about the danger of being in the park late at night. Even though they wanted to stay, they were fearful of the central grassy area after midnight, but we were unable to learn the nature of the perceived danger.

49. Yet there was no indication that park enforcement officers policed the bathrooms. Instead, they monitored the older men and homeless individuals.

50. The Social Justice and Public Space Evaluation Framework is also discussed in Chapter 3.

51. Sally Engle Merry, *Urban Danger: Life In A Neighborhood Of Strangers* (Philadelphia: Temple University Press, 1981).

52. Minecraft is a videogame and technology that can be used to simulate the built environment, from individual homes and gardens to larger-scale design and plans. It has been successful in encouraging communities to engage directly in imagining and renovating their own environments.

53. "Global Public Space Programme Annual Report 2021," United Nations Human Settlements Programme, 2022, https://unhabitat.org/sites/default/files/2022/02/20220207_annual_report_gpsp_2021.pdf.

54. "City-Wide Public Space Strategies: A Guidebook for City Leaders," United Nations Habitat, 2020, https://unhabitat.org/city-wide-public-space-strategies-a-guidebook-for-city-leaders

55. "City-wide Public Space Assessment Toolkits: A Guide to Community-led Digital Inventory and Assessment of Public Spaces. UN Habitat, 2020, https://unhabitat.org/city-wide-public-space-assessment-toolkit-a-guide-to-community-led-digital-inventory-and-assessment-of-public spaces.

56. hercity.unhabitat.org

57. Jan Gehl, *Life Between Buildings: Using Public Space* (New York: Van Nostrand Reinhold, 1986).

58. "Public Life Diversity Toolkit: A Prototype for Measuring Social Mixing and Economic Integration in Public Space," Gehl Studio San Francisco and the Knight Foundation, April, 2015, https://gehlinstitute.org/wp-content/uploads/2017/02/Gehl_PublicLifeDiversityToolkit_Pages-1.pdf.

    A Mayor's Guide to Public Life, eds. Shin-pei Tsay and Riley Gold (New York: Gehl Institute, 2017), https://mayorsguide.gehlinstitute.org/MAYORS_GUIDE_Complete.pdf.

    The Open Public Life Data Protocol (New York: Gehl Institute, City of San Francisco Planning Department, Copenhagen Municipality's City Data Department, Seattle Department of Transportation, Gehl, 2017), https://gehlinstitute.org/wp-content/uploads/2017/09/PLDP_BETA-20170927-Final.pdf.

59. "Inclusive Healthy Places: A Guide to Inclusion & Health in Public Space: Learning Globally to Transform Locally," *Gehl Institute*, June

2018, https://gehlinstitute.org/wp-content/uploads/2018/07/Inclus ive-Healthy-Places_Gehl-Institute.pdf.

60. "What is Placemaking?," Project for Public Spaces, accessed May 12, 2022, https://www.pps.org/category/placemaking.

61. "The Lighter, Quicker, Cheaper Transformation of Public Spaces," Project for Public Spaces, accessed May 12, 2022, https://www.pps.org/ article/lighter-quicker-cheaper.

62. Hanna Love and Cailean Kok, "Beyond Traditional Measures: Examining the Holistic Impacts of Public Space Investments in Three Cities," *Brookings*, July 27, 2021, https://www.brookings.edu/essay/bey ond-traditional-measures-examining-the-holistic-impacts-of-public-space-investments-in-three-cities/.

63. "Active Design Guidelines: Promoting Physical Activity and Health in Design," City of New York, 2010, https://www1.nyc.gov/assets/doh/ downloads/pdf/environmental/active-design-guidelines.pdf.

64. *Assembly: Shaping Space for Civic Life* (New York: Center for Active Design, June 2017).
    Assembly: Civic Design Guidelines: Promoting Civic Life Through Public Space Design (New York: Center for Active Design, 2018).

65. Thomas L. McKenzie, Deborah A. Cohen, Amber Sehgal, Stephanie Williamson, and Daniela Golinelli, "System for Observing Play and Recreation in Communities (SOPARC): Reliability and Feasibility Measures," *Journal of Physical Activity & Health* 3, suppl. 1 (2006): S208–S222.

66. Energy expenditure estimates (i.e., Kcal/kg/min and METs) for a target area of a park can be calculated based on previously validated constants for each level of activity. McKenzie et al., "System for Observing Play." O. Marquet, J. A. Hipp, C. Alberico, J. H. Huang, D. Fry, E. Mazak, G. S. Lovasi, and M. F. Floyd, "Use of SOPARC to Assess Physical Activity in Parks: Do Race/Ethnicity, Contextual Conditions, and Settings of the Target Area, Affect Reliability?," *BMC Public Health* 19, no. 1 (2019): 1730, https://doi.org/10.1186/s12889-019-8107-0.

67. "Measuring Neighborhood Park Use: A Citizen's Guide," New Yorkers for Parks (NY4P), accessed May 12, 2022, http://www.ny4p.org/client-uploads/pdf/Other-reports/NY4P_Measuring-Neighborhood-Park-Use.pdf.

68. Anastasia Loukaitou-Sideris, Madeline Brozen, and Lené Levy-Storms, "Placemaking for an Aging Population: Guidelines for Senior-Friendly Parks," *UCLA Luskin School of Public Affairs, The Ralph and Goldy Lewis*

Center for Regional Policy Studies, 2014, https://escholarship.org/uc/item/45087ihz.

69. Anastasia Loukaitou-Sideris, Madeline Brozen, and Colleen Callahan, "Reclaiming the Right of Way: A Toolkit for Creating and Implementing Parklets," *Lewis Center for Regional Policy Studies, the Luskin Center for Innovation, and the Institute of Transportation Studies in the UCLA Luskin School of Public Affairs*, September 2012, accessed May 12, 2022, https://nacto.org/docs/usdg/reclaiming_the_right_of_way_brozen.pdf.

70. Caroline Skinner, Sarah Orleans Reed, and Jenna Harvey, "Supporting Informal Livelihoods in Public Space: A Toolkit for Local Authorities," *WIEGO*, 2018, https://www.wiego.org/sites/default/files/publications/files/Public%20Space%20Toolkit.pdf.

APPENDIX

1. Patrician Aelbrecht and Quentin Stevens, *Public Space Design and Social Cohesion* (New York and London: Routledge, 2019).

2. Erving Goffman, *Behavior in Public Places: Notes on the Social Organization of Gatherings (by) Erving Goffman* (New York: Free Press, 1966).

3. Richard Sennett, *The Fall of Public Man* (New York and London: W.W. Norton & Company, 1974).

    Richard Sennett, *The Conscience of the Eye: The Design and Social Life of Cities* (London: Faber, 1990).

    Richard Sennett, *Building and Dwelling: Ethics for the City* (New York: Farrar, Straus and Giroux, 2018).

4. Lyn H. Lofland, *A World of Strangers: Order and Action in Urban Public Space* (Prospect Heights: Waveland, 1973).

    Lyn H. Lofland, *The Public Realm: Exploring the City's Quintessential Social Territory* (Hawthorne: Aldine de Gruyter, 1998).

5. Sophie Watson, ed., *Playing the State: Australian Feminist Interventions* (London: Verso, 1989).

    Sophie Watson, *City Publics: The (Dis)enchantments of Urban Encounters* (London: Routledge, 2006).

6. Eric Klinenberg, *Palaces for the People: How Social Infrastructure Can Help Fight Inequality, Polarization, and the Decline of Civic Life* (New York: Crown, 2018).

7. W. E. B DuBois, *The Philadelphia Negro* (Philadelphia: University of Pennsylvania Press, 1899).

8. Elijah Anderson, *StreetWise: Race, Class, and Change in an Urban Community* (Chicago: University of Chicago Press, 1990).

9. Elijah Anderson, "The Cosmopolitan Canopy," *The Annals of the American Academy of Political and Social Science* 595, no. 1 (2004): 14–31.

10. John L. Jackson, *Harlemworld: Doing Race and Class in Contemporary Black America* (Chicago: University of Chicago Press, 2001).

11. Helán Enoch Page, "No Black Public Sphere in White Public Space: Racialized Information and Hi-Tech Diffusion in the Global African Diaspora," *Transforming Anthropology* 8, nos. 1–2 (1999): 111–28, https://doi.org/10.1525/tran.1999.8.1-2.111.

12. Elijah Anderson, *Black in White Space [The Enduring Impact of Color in Everyday Life]* (Chicago: University of Chicago Press, 2022)

13. Don Mitchell, *The Right to the City: Social Justice and the Fight for Public Space* (New York: Guilford Press, 2003).

    Kurt Iveson, *Publics and the City* (Malden and Oxford: Blackwell, 2007).

14. Jeffrey Hou, ed., *Insurgent Public Space: Guerrilla Urbanism and the Remaking of Contemporary Cities* (New York and London: Routledge, 2010).

    Ron Shiffman, Rick Bell, Lance Jay Brown, and Lynne Elizabeth, eds., *Beyond Zuccotti Park: Freedom of Assembly and the Occupation of Public Space* (Oakland: New Village Press, 2012).

15. Julian Agyeman, *Introducing Just Sustainabilities: Policy, Planning and Practice* (London: Zed Books, 2013).

16. Thomas F. Pettigrew and Linda R. Tropp, "A Meta-analytic Test of Intergroup Contact Theory," *Journal of Personality and Social Psychology* 90, no. 5 (2006): 751–83, https://doi.org/10.1037/0022-3514.90.5.751.

17. Gordon Hodson, Richard J. Crisp, Rose Meleady, and Megan Earle, "Intergroup Contact as an Agent of Cognitive Liberalization," *Perspectives on Psychological Science* 13, no. 5 (2018): 526, https://doi.org/10.1177/1745691617752324.

18. Hodson et al., "Intergroup Contact," 523–48.

19. Rose Meleady, Richard J. Crisp, Gordon Hodson, and Megan Earle, "On the Generalization of Intergroup Contact: A Taxonomy of Transfer Effects," *Current Directions in Psychological Science* 28, no. 5 (2019): 430–35, https://doi.org/10.1177/0963721419848682.

20. Pettigrew and Tropp, "A Meta-analytic Test," 751–83.

    Oliver Schilke and Laura Huang, "Worthy of Swift Trust? How Brief Interpersonal Contact Affects Trust Accuracy," *Journal of Applied Psychology* 103, no. 11 (2018): 1181–97, https://doi.org/10.1037/apl0000321.

21. Heidi A. Vuletich and B. Keith Payne, "Stability and Change in Implicit Bias," *Psychological Science* 30, no. 6 (2019): 854–62, https://doi.org/10.1177/0956797619844270.

John Dixon, Kevin Durrheim, and Colin Tredoux, "Beyond the Optimal Contact Strategy: A Reality Check for the Contact Hypothesis," *American Psychologist* 60, no. 7 (2005): 697–711, http://dx.doi.org/10.1037/0003-066X.60.7.697.

Elizabeth Levy Paluck, Seth A. Green, and Donald P. Green, "The Contact Hypothesis Re-evaluated," *Behavioural Public Policy* 3, no. 2 (2019): 129–58, https://doi.org/10.1017/bpp.2018.25.

22. The current rise in loneliness and personal suffering from physical distancing as well as the increasing number of hate crimes and social division over wearing masks during COVID-19 reiterate this conclusion.

23. Maykel Verkuyten, Kumar Yogeeswaran, and Levi Adelman, "Intergroup Toleration and its Implications for Culturally Diverse Societies," *Social Issues and Policy Review* 13, no. 1 (2019): 5–35, https://dx.doi.org/10.1111%2Fsipr.12051.

24. Setha Low, *Behind the Gates: Life, Liberty and the Pursuit of Happiness in Fortress American* (New York: Routledge, 2004).

25. Zygmunt Bauman, *City of Fears, City of Hopes* (London: Goldsmiths College, Centre for Urban and Community Research, 2003).

26. Arjun Appadurai and Carol A. Breckenridge, "Why Public Culture?," *Public Culture* 1, no. 1 (1988): 5–9, https://doi.org/10.1215/08992363-1-1-5.

27. Arjun Appadurai, *Modernity at Large: Cultural Dimensions of Globalization* (Minneapolis: University of Minnesota Press, 1996).

28. Robert Donald Hariman, "Public Culture," in *Oxford Research Encyclopedia of Communication*, ed. J. Nussbaum (Oxford University Press, 2017), https://doi.org/10.1093/acrefore/9780190228613.013.32.

29. Ash Amin, "Lively Infrastructure," *Theory Culture & Society* 31, no. 7/8 (2014):137–61, https://doi.org/10.1177%2F0263276414548490.

30. Ali Madanipour, "Rethinking Public Space: Between Rhetoric and Reality," *URBAN DESIGN International* 24, no. 1 (2019): 38–46, https://doi.org/10.1057/s41289-019-00087-5.

31. Ben Anderson, "Affective atmospheres," *Emotion, Space and Society* 2, no. 2 (2009): 77–81, https://doi.org/10.1016/j.emospa.2009.08.005.

32. Nigel Thrift, *Non-representational Theory: Space, Politics, Affect* (London: Routledge, 2008), 187.

33. Thrift, *Non-representational Theory*, 188.

Index

For the benefit of digital users, indexed terms that span two pages (e.g., 52–53) may, on occasion, appear on only one of those pages.

Page numbers followed by *t* and *f* indicate tables and figures, respectively.